***

In our society we don't talk a whole lot about the edges that are lived between the norms and maps of our everyday world and the mysteries we might sense within. We don't talk about our True Nature or the processes that might plunge us into depth. We don't speak of the extraordinary potentials inherent in our human existence.

And if we do mention that our desperation might also be our turning point, if we declare that our crumbling life is a godsend, if we suggest that risking ourselves into the unknown might turn out to be our savior, well then ... then people will think we're crazy. Mad.

And so I'm writing this chapter (and to some extent this book), because it is hard to be out there on your own, standing on an edge. It's hard to live in a world in which there is so little understanding or vocabulary for processes that are spiritually profound or spiritually meant.

And it's even harder to trust that when you let go of the edge, you will have wings that will spread you into flight.

The true measure and expanse of Life is forever calling us Home.

from the chapter, *Edges*

***

Spirituality is about as 'real life' as it can possibly get. Spirituality is a very deep inquiry into the nature of Truth, into what is real, and into who or what I actually am. It is a movement deeper and deeper into my humanity, into my body, into my suffering, into my life. It is utterly grounded, utterly down-to-earth, and utterly present.

from the preface

***

There will always be people along the way who tell you it can't be done, that it isn't possible. They will tell you that it's too difficult and too arduous, that there will be too much pain and muddiness to work through, too much torment held in the darkest recesses of your body and soul. There will be those who think you are quite strange or mad to pursue 'all that spiritual stuff' or even 'all that therapy stuff'. There will even be those who say that awakening and spiritual realization are not the stuff of very ordinary lives lived in ordinary suburbia.

But I am writing this book to say that it is possible. It is possible to move from desperate suffering to peace. And to contentment, sanity, freedom, wholeness and joy.

This book is the story of my journey into Life. Into Truth. It is the story of my journey Home. And truly it is everything, everything, I could ever have wanted.

from the preface

***

SUFFERING, SPIRITUALITY
AND THE
INNER JOURNEY HOME

walking the path from desperation and
fear to the peace of lived awakening

MARIANNE BROUG

Suffering, Spirituality and the Inner Journey Home

First published in Australia by True Home Books 2017
www.truehomebooks.com

National Library of Australia Cataloguing-in-Publication entry (pbk):

Creator: Broug, Marianne, author
Title: Suffering, Spirituality and the Inner Journey Home : walking the path
              from desperation and fear to the peace of lived awakening

ISBN: 978-0-6480787-0-8 (paperback)

Subjects: BODY, MIND & SPIRIT / Inspiration & Personal Growth
             BIOGRAPHY & AUTOBIOGRAPHY / Personal Memoirs
             RELIGION / Spirituality
             SELF-HELP / Spiritual

Also available as an ebook: 978-0-6480787-1-5 (ebk)

Artwork and photography by Marianne Broug © 2017

Typesetting and design by Publicious Book Publishing
Published in collaboration with Publicious Book Publishing
www.publicious.com.au

This book is a work of non-fiction.

for all those who suffer,
for all those who long for their true Home

Marianne Broug

Marianne Broug was a professional musician and music teacher, and is now a writer. She has performed extensively throughout Australia in all arenas of music including opera, chamber music and symphony orchestra.

She has also worked as a concert organizer, an artist, a mental health advocate, and a care worker for people living with both a 'mental illness' and a terminal illness. She lives in the beautiful Adelaide Hills with her partner and two dogs.

In 2003 her music book for children, *Flute with a Twist,* was published by Bushfire Press. In 2008, her book *Seventeen Voices: Life and Wisdom from inside 'mental illness'* was published by Wakefield Press.

For over twenty years Marianne suffered from depression and anxiety, and for over twenty years she sought out healing, wholeness and Truth. She underwent two rigorous and lengthy therapies as well as pursued intensive spiritual practices, meditation, dialectic and inquiry.

Early in 2008 Marianne had a deep awakening into her true identity as Emptiness or Consciousness. However, rather than an ending, this awakening was just a beginning. Much integration, unravelling and clearing has since taken place and the deepening continues to this day. However, in knowing this Truth, rather than the suffered turmoil and suicidality of the past, there is peace, contentment and the sense that all is deeply well ...

Also see websites:
www.truehomebooks.com
www.meaningofdepression.com

***

contents

gratitude

Gratitude always to the magnificent thrust of Life.

Gratitude to my beautiful partner, Sharon. I love you so very much. Thank you for believing in this book. Thank you for standing with me through so many years.

Gratitude to my therapists, most particularly Mollie and Colette. Even though I have not used your real names in this book, you know who you are. Thank you for your patience, your understanding, your insight, your time, your integrity and your love. Thank you for bearing with me through some of the most difficult times in my life.

Gratitude to my teachers, both past and present, who with grace, knowing, love and wisdom, have gone before, and shown me the way. Special thanks to Lesley Skylar.

Gratitude to the teachers I will never meet, whose quiet and wise words so often guided me through difficult times. Particular thanks to the work of AH Almaas and Adyashanti.

Gratitude to those who have offered their time, experience, editing advice, suggestions and encouragement for this book. Thanks to Eugene, Jacqui, Deb, Mollie, Colette and Mike. Thanks also to Sharon and Lesley.

Gratitude to my dogs Elliot and Lucy, who remind me in every moment of simple joy, unconditional love and the riotous delight of unabashed mischief-making.

***

preface

In 2008 my book *Seventeen Voices: Life and Wisdom from Inside 'Mental Illness'* was published.

In it I wanted the voices and humanity of the real experts on 'mental illness', the people themselves, to be heard. All too often in the clamor of stereotypes, diagnostic labels, medical interventions, sensationalism and ignorance, it was these that seemed to go missing.

The seventeen people I interviewed for the book give a very authentic and down-to-earth account, not only of times of great suffering and difficulty, but also an extraordinary wealth of wisdom, insight, depth, resilience and courage.

In the months following its publication I was interviewed several times on radio and also spoke at a number of functions.

One of those functions was in a large country town. I was guest speaker at a dinner dance that showcased the mental health services of the region but also created an opportunity for service providers and service participants to get to know each other a little better. I spoke about my book and the people I had interviewed, but also the fact that my own life had been one of difficulty and suffering.

After the talk, many people came up to me to chat, ask questions and buy my book. Standing off to one side I noticed a woman a little younger than me. She watched me very intently but didn't approach.

Later, as I ate dinner, I noticed she was still watching me from across the room.

Then after dessert, as I was briefly sitting on my own, she hurried nervously over and asked if she could talk with me. I smiled and indicated the seat next to me. She thanked me for writing my book and told me how much she had enjoyed my talk.

Then she said, "You know, the hardest thing for me is that nobody understands what it is to *suffer*. Like *really* suffer*!* But when I listened to you talking about your book and your life, I sensed that *you* understand! That's all I've ever wanted. Someone to understand. *Really* understand. *You* understand, don't you? Don't you?" I took a deep breath and felt an all-too-familiar niggling of self-doubt. Did I understand suffering? And did I understand *her* suffering? I wasn't so sure. I asked her to tell me a little about her life.

She shared a life lived behind closed doors. It was a life of isolation and frequent despair. But it was also a life of frustration and grief at not being able to express her considerable intelligence and creativity into this world.

Then looking earnestly into my eyes, she said, "... but *you* have made it out the other side haven't you! You've suffered, and now you've written a book and you're talking to lots of people at a function like this. Please. Tell me. How did you make it out the other side? How did you do it? "

I sat dumbstruck. How did I do it? My journey had been so vast, so multi-faceted, so all-encompassing. It had entailed so much internal exploration, so much clearing away, so much questioning, so much transformation. What could I possibly say to her that would sum up what it was that had brought me through my suffering?

I thought back over all the deeply suffered years of my life when I too had searched for an answer to that very same question. I thought back over all the times I had browsed through bookshops or libraries, looking for that one book that might contain within its pages the ultimate punch line: "*This* is how you bring your suffering to an end." I thought back over all the times that I too had listened to the stories of others' lives and wondered *wondered,* "How did you make it out the other side?" And although there had been much inspiration and insight, countless maps and techniques, and many tastes and intimations, I had never found just *one* thing.

I looked at the woman in front of me. "Hmmm. That's a very broad question," I said. "I'm sorry but I don't think there's a neat-and-tidy answer. It's just not that simple."

The woman looked away from me and I could see tears forming. I knew my words fell woefully short. I frantically cast around inside trying to think of something a little more substantial to say. But then suddenly, with a startled jolt, I realized that my answer to her had in fact been quite patently untrue. There *was* one thing. Certainly it was a very big thing, and in defense of my untruth, also a very recently realized thing, but there *was one thing* … and within it was encapsulated my entire journey.

Although I had shared very little about my spirituality in my talk, only six months prior I had 'awoken'…

One morning I was sitting at my computer sipping a cup of tea and checking my emails, when all of a sudden I 'awoke' out of my everyday self and into my true identity as the vastness of Consciousness or Spirit. It was as though the tightly held contraction of thoughts, feelings and history that I had always assumed was somehow 'me', simply let go. It wasn't any sort of mental conceptualization or understanding, nor was it an altered state of consciousness or mystical spiritual experience of any sort. It was simply a profound shift of identity into a *lived* recognition of my true nature. The actual experience at that time was of moving into an infinite spaciousness, stillness, peace and freedom, which all at once was both the background of everything as well as the substance. I saw what reality was and I saw that I had truly never been apart from it. What I had spent my whole life searching for was closer than close.[1]

But I also knew without a doubt that the awakening was only the very beginning. I still had so much more to learn and so much more to live my way into. And also, attested to by the fact that I still suffered from time to time, I knew there was a lot more internal work and 'cleaning up' to do. But as I looked back to the woman sitting next to me, I also knew that I could unequivocally say that I *had* made it out the other side; perhaps only just, but I *had* made it.

I knew I had to find the words to share this with her.

I suspected that it probably wasn't going to be the answer she expected and certainly at that time, it wasn't an answer that I felt in any way comfortable in articulating to others, but all the same I knew it was the right one. And so I said, "Find out who you are. On the deepest level possible, on the *spiritual* level, find out who you truly are."

She looked at me a little stunned, nodded slowly a few times and was silent. I wasn't sure if she'd understood me or whether my words sounded like the worst sort of spiritual mumbo-jumbo. Perhaps I was just one more person in a long line of people who gave her disappointing answers. We sat together a

---

1. I will describe this more fully in other parts of the book.

little while longer and I held her hand in mine. I hoped that even if she hadn't understood my words, perhaps in that simple gesture of sitting together, she might find her way into my answer.

My deepest wish in writing this book is that those who are suffering will know that not only do I understand, I have also made it out the other side.

There will always be people along the way who tell you it can't be done, that it isn't possible. They will tell you that it's too difficult and too arduous, that there will be too much pain and muddiness to work through, too much torment held in the darkest recesses of your body and soul. There will be those who think you are quite strange or mad to pursue 'all that spiritual stuff' or even 'all that therapy stuff'. There will even be those who say that awakening and spiritual realization are not the stuff of very ordinary lives lived in ordinary suburbia.

But I am writing this book to say that it *is* possible. It *is* possible to move from desperate suffering to peace. And to contentment, sanity, freedom, wholeness and joy.

This book is the story of my journey *into* Life. Into Truth. It is the story of my journey Home. And truly it is everything, *everything,* I could ever have wanted.

I have long forgotten that woman's name and I will never know what became of her, but this book is for her and also for the woman I once was.

Dear soul, precious soul, *this* is what I did to come out the other side.

***

some comments on this book

This book is not a chronological autobiography of my life. However, I *have* tried to place the chapters in the order of my deepening insight and understanding as it was lived over the years. At times this was a difficult exercise and I am aware there is some overlap between chapters. The chapter *The Body*, does however give a roughly chronological overview of the autobiographical details of my life that are relevant to this book.

Each chapter is written on a specific topic or theme that was essential for my movement out of suffering and into a lived experience of my True Nature. For example, it was essential for me to learn how to question deeply so I wrote a chapter called *Questions*. It was vital to know how to work out which therapists and teachers could help me and which couldn't, so I wrote a chapter on *Therapists and Teachers*. It was important for me to deepen into and understand my lived experience of 'edges' and 'darkness' and 'soul' for example, and so I wrote a chapter on each.

This book can certainly be read cover to cover, but each individual chapter also stands quite well on its own. The things that were important for me on my journey, may well not be important for you, so I invite the reader to delve into the subject matter to which they feel drawn. However, there may also be material in this book that is difficult or uncomfortable to read. Rather than gloss over or immediately discard such material as irrelevant, I would encourage the reader to move through it more slowly, allowing an open, but very gentle and compassionate curiosity. When there is discomfort there is almost always something to learn, something into which we have not yet been born.

Contained within this book are some topics that aren't often touched on in writings on suffering and spirituality, but were significant for me. For instance, when I was young I had a very powerful intuition that there was 'something else' going on other than the consensus view of the world. This intuition was a persistent and powerful voice and one I did not see mirrored in the world around me. And so I wrote the short chapter *There's Something Else* not only to articulate and validate that intuition for those who might have it, but also to serve as an inquiry for those who haven't.

I do not in any way intend this book as a self-help prescription for divesting one's life of suffering forevermore. In fact, I would cringe at that idea. Rather I see it very much as an invitation, a question, an inspiration ... and perhaps also a bit of a challenge if that's what's needed. Throughout, however, it is written with the deepest Love, for you, for myself and for all that we *are*.

I wish to emphasize that this book is only *one* person's journey. Each person on this planet and each journey, is utterly unique and beautiful. *Each* movement towards our True Nature, whether it entails awakening or not, is a movement closer to our true healing. There is no prize and no failure. There is only the dance.

ooo

I have previously had two other books published. Each marked the end of a quite distinct period in my life. My flute book, *Flute with a Twist* was written and then published at the end of my flute playing and teaching career. My book *Seventeen Voices* was written in the years leading up to awakening and was a very fitting end to my life of deep suffering and questing.

In the course of writing this book I have become aware that it too marks the end of a period in my life. As the book has progressed there has been an increasing urgency to get it finished, because all that I have lived and remembered from the point of view of the everyday self is fading away as I increasingly look out at this world and see only the indivisible Whole.

But the journey never ceases. Some, I know, would say that there is no journey. Perhaps in one sense they are right. But I do know that as I continue to meet life moment by moment, there is no end to the deepening ...

Here I am rejoicing in this glorious effulgent Universe ...

***

comment on my use of the word 'God'

There was a time in my life I made a point of *never* buying a book with the word 'God' in it. 'God', I thought, was only for poor misguided souls.

If I took a book off the shelves, leafed through it and saw the word 'God', I put it quickly back.

At that time I thought 'God' was either a paternalistic patronizing Christian sort of God or a New Age angelic light-filled God and I wasn't interested in either. I wanted the Truth and I doubted very much that Truth, if ever I was to find it, had anything to do with such Gods.

But now, here I am writing a book, and that book definitely *does* have the word 'God' in it.

However, despite my use of that word, the reality is that what I am trying to convey is impossible to convey with words. For millennia, people have tried to do so, and ultimately they have all failed, as indeed I will fail.

Just as it is impossible to adequately describe the taste or texture of an orange or an avocado to someone who has never eaten one, so it is impossible to describe God. God is always a direct experience, a lived knowing. God can only be known through the tasting, never through the mind.

But even though I will fail, I also know I have to try.

And so I have used the word 'God' for that ineffable, unnamable Totality, Ground or Source that we *are*. But I have also used many other words: True Nature, Truth, Spirit, Essential Nature, Life, Reality, Presence, Awareness, Consciousness, Love, Knowing, Life, Home, Ultimate Intimacy, the Infinite, All That Is, One, Emptiness. Each of these words conveys a slightly different awareness or facet of God, whether that be of depth, nuance or quality.

There are times I have also chosen to use upper case when I am writing of the particular qualities of our True Nature as it is expressed through our humanity. For instance, our True Nature actually *is* Love, it *is* Knowing, it *is* Peace, it *is* Truth. I use lower case, when I use those words in any everyday way, for example, my love of silence or telling the truth.

I am well aware that some of these words are overused and have become hackneyed or charged. But I have still used them. I must use the word 'Love' when it is Love that I know. I must use the word 'Spirit' when it is Spirit that speaks through this body. I once sat with a teacher who never used the word Love because he felt it had been overused and misunderstood. But in his teaching, it was Love that was missing.

However ultimately it is important to remember that the 'something' to which I am pointing, is *between* the words, is carried *through* the words, is *beyond* the words.

It is so vital to let my words and my writing move into you like a smooth mellow wine. Its fragrance is there to be breathed in. Its colors and textures to be tenderly apprized. Its subtleties felt and caressed in the mouth. Its warmth allowed to spread and deepen through the body and the resonances relished long after the glass is empty.

But just like the glass that holds a good wine, my words must be put down after you drink of their contents.

***

comment on 'spirituality'

There's a great deal of confusion about what spirituality actually *is*. And for many years I shared this confusion.

People around me spoke quite matter-of-factly of being 'spiritual' and yet I could see they all understood something quite different by it. Astrology, chakras, meditation, crystals, Wicca, ecstatic dance, premonitions, Christianity, angels, kundalini, Reiki, Buddhism, psychic phenomena, positive affirmations, altered states of consciousness, all congregated under that word, but so did my quest for Truth.

My puzzlement only increased when one of my therapists spoke of 'spirit'. It seemed that at the end of the pursuit of self-development, the 'me' that was now able to function in the world, would also be a partially spiritual 'me'.

The spirituality of which I write in this book, is not a hobby or a pastime. It is not something I am 'interested in'. It is not something I am doing so that I can 'feel good'. It is not an airy-fairy notion with which I hope to escape or avoid the everyday world, my suffering or the traumas of the past. It is not an altered state of consciousness of any sort. It is not a conceptual framework with which I am trying to keep life mapped and under control. It is not the pursuit of a perpetual state of bliss or some lofty spiritual ideal. It's not about becoming the world's best meditator. It's not about being unfailingly 'positive'.

Spirituality is about as 'real life' as it can possibly get. Spirituality is a very deep inquiry into the nature of Truth, into what is *real*, and into who or what I actually *am*. It is a movement beyond the thoughts, feelings, beliefs, ideas, conceptual veils and conditioning of the everyday mind, and deeper and deeper *into* my humanity, *into* my body, *into* my suffering, *into* my life. It is utterly grounded, utterly down-to-earth, and utterly present. It is about what it is that is *here* in my direct experience, in this very moment.

Spiritual inquiry can at times be an extraordinarily difficult and uncomfortable process; all the accustomed byways and beliefs of our lives will be called into question. And yet it is when we come to see reality as it actually *is*, that we are truly set free from our suffering.

***

comment on 'ego' and 'awakening'

I don't like the word 'ego'. As with the word 'God' it carries a lot of baggage. However, in writing this book it is necessary for me to have some sort of descriptor for what it is I am trying to convey. And so I have used the word 'ego', and also a couple of others: 'everyday self' and 'everyday mind'.

Ego is a bit like the operating system of the mind, perhaps a bit like Microsoft Windows for a computer. Like Windows, this operating system can run a lot of different programs: emotional programs, relationship programs, work-related programs, opinion programs, identity programs, but also programs that might reflect a history of trauma, abuse or difficulty.

Over time we might download 'better' or 'more-updated' versions of the operating system (and its programs), and so find we can function in the world with greater efficiency and ease, but despite that fact it will always remain just an operating system.

The ego is not bad. In many ways it does the best job it possibly can, and at times that job is most definitely a life-saving one. But the problem with the ego is that it doesn't know it is just an operating system. Like a goldfish in a pond, it believes that *its* world is the *whole* world. It is incapable of understanding that there is an infinite expanse beyond itself that it can never ever know anything about. It is this expanse to which we give the name God, Spirit or the Totality.

Although there may be times when the ego glimpses or tastes Spirit, it can only ever understand such glimpses from within its own worldview, and so believes them to be some sort of spiritual program it has downloaded and is in control of.

However, unlike a computer, we as human beings *are* capable of stepping beyond that operating system. We *are* capable of stepping beyond the everyday mind. This is called 'awakening'. When we awaken we literally wake up out of that operating system and *see* the truth of what we *are*: our True Nature. This waking up is an unmistakable and very real shift in identity.

Although essentially this awakening can never be 'caused' and is quite often spontaneous, there is much groundwork and dissolution that can be done to prepare and clear the way for opening Into the enormity that lies beyond the accustomed operating system. In my experience this 'clearing the way' is essential and cannot be shortchanged.[2]

It is also worth noting that just because we wake up, doesn't necessarily mean the ego operating system through which we have functioned much of our lives, immediately stops. It may take a long time for it to wind down and eventually step aside.[3]

***

---

2. This 'clearing the way' is the 'stuff' of much of this book and can take place before and after awakening.
3. After awakening it can seem as though one has arrived at some sort of 'end state' of infinite peace, but I found this to be a 'honeymoon' period. As outlined in this book, there can still be much internal work to do and increasingly subtle levels to move into. Awakening is just the beginning … our deepening never ends.

comment on Mal de Debarquement/Disembarkment Syndrome

A number of times throughout this book I mention the fact that I live with a condition called Mal de Debarquement Syndrome (MdDS) or Disembarkment Syndrome.

Disembarkment Syndrome is a poorly researched and poorly understood neurological condition usually brought on by a passive motion experience such as travel. There is some evidence that travel when combined with severe life stressors increases the likelihood of its onset. Although it is certainly a life-altering condition – a very tiring and often debilitating one – the condition is not life-threatening. There is no cure, although people do go into remission. Medical 'treatment' is aimed at symptom alleviation, usually with benzodiazepines. It is not a condition of the inner ear.

MdDS is characterized by a constant sense of inner movement that includes bobbing, rocking, swaying and also sudden plunges and surges; my world is in constant and unpredictable motion. There are times I have very little balance or equilibrium and so find it difficult to walk. There are also times when it is challenging to speak or have conversations; it is as though I am on a wildly rocking boat in stormy seas, trying to stay balanced, while at the same time attempting to have a coherent conversation. It's challenging.

I describe the events surrounding its onset more fully in the chapter, *The Child and the Fundamental Abandonment.*

***

comment on my park bench

Several times in this book I mention a park bench.

Almost daily I go for a walk. Roughly halfway through my walk is a bench that overlooks a playing field and park. I often take the time to sit on that bench, sometimes for only five minutes, sometimes for a lot longer. Sometimes people join me, sometimes they don't. I've been sitting on that bench over many years.

As I sit, I watch life as it moves by. I watch people walking, dogs playing, children running. I watch the clouds, the trees, the birds and the cars in the distance. I meditate, contemplate, question, sit in stillness or plan my writing for the day. I feel the pain in my knee or a deep joy in my heart. And it is in this simple act of sitting, that many times I have been opened to a new insight, to a broader understanding or to uncharted depths.

That bench is a favorite spot.

Sometimes
I stop
and sit
on a bench in the park.

And in the warmth
of a gentle summer morning
there is nothing
that is a stranger.

***

suffering

This is my suffering.
Suffering is the starting point.

I have suffered silently.
I have suffered loudly.
I have watched the overflow of my suffering in a flood of tears or the redness of my blood.
I have painted my suffering with solid lines and bold colors onto canvas.
I have written countless words about my suffering in journals, poetry and prose.
I have spoken of my suffering to others, in the hope that I might find insight and healing.
I have hidden my suffering out of shame or fear.

I have wanted to bring my wretched suffered life to an end.
... and yet I wanted so desperately to find a way to live.

***

journal 1988

I want to die.
I have no reason for continuing with this miserable existence.
I am worse than ever.
I hurt in my head and stomach but most of all in my being.
I need help. I can't do this on my own.
But where do I find that help?
Nothing makes sense.
Everything is confused.
There are only bits everywhere that don't add up.
It is time to leave but I am too cowardly to kill myself.
If only there was some purpose or meaning to it all, I wouldn't go.
I have ruined this life.

I so much wanted to make a go of it but now I don't have any strength left.
The pain is extreme.
I thought I had seen all the pain I could ever see but apparently not.
I thought I had been as anxious as I could ever be but apparently not.
Perhaps death will be a relief.
I want relief. I want an answer. I want a way out that is bigger than all of this.
I can't fight any more.
My little world of lovely precious things no longer equals out the pain.
... I want to go ...

chains of depression, acrylic[1]

journal 1991

I went out this morning to run a few errands, but have returned home
with none of them done. Even a simple shopping expedition is becoming
difficult. I am increasingly nervous and agoraphobic. I am increasingly
avoiding everything. My head spins and my chest is tight. My feelings are
very raw and I become angry or cry at the very least provocation. I am
unable find a center within myself. My whole body is shaking. I feel like a
sub-species of human being. Once again, I wish only to hide myself away.

1. All artwork and photos in this book are my own. Color versions of the artwork included in this book
can be seen at www.truehomebooks.com

I am losing all confidence and hope. What am I to do? I need ONE thing that will work. One thing that I can stick to.

journal 1992

I cry like I have never cried before. It is a wrenching full-voiced crying, that comes from deep within. The pain threatens to tear me apart. There are no words that do justice to its force. I am grieving for what my life could have been, grieving for what was taken from me and grieving for what was destroyed. I am grieving for my very fundamental personhood. It seems I was damaged beyond repair and it hurts like hell. I lie on my bed screaming and crying. The more pain I let out, the more there seems to be. It is never-ending. I can't write any more for fear of tearing this book and myself apart. I have never cried so much. I hate, I hate …

journal 1993

There is a student knocking at my front door outside of lesson times. She is an adult student and she lives nearby. It's night-time. Why is she knocking at my front door?

I have just been bawling. I have been screaming some desperate agony the reason for which I can no longer remember. My eyes are puffy and my face is red. I wonder how long she has been standing at my front door. It is unbearable to think that she may have heard my screaming.

I don't know what to do. I feel pursued. I feel overwhelmed. The confident, calm and eloquent teacher only functions during lesson times. Outside of lesson times I am anxious and fearful. When I have no defined role and persona I have no clue who I am.

I run out the back door. I stand under the back porch with my heart thumping. I listen. My partner has answered the door. I can't hear what is being said. But then I hear my partner calling me: "Marianne! Marianne! Where are you?" Why doesn't my partner understand that I can't talk to the student if I have a red face and puffy eyes? Why didn't she tell the student that I was out, or that I was sick in bed, or in the bath? "Marianne! Marianne!" Why is she calling me? My partner knew I wasn't in any shape to talk to a student. Why doesn't she understand? What is she doing?

I race out into the darkness of the backyard. I am fleeing. Fleeing from attack. I want to run away and never come back to this awful life, but I have nowhere to go. I run around to the old rainwater tank. I huddle against the hardness of the iron. I am screaming inside. My insides are bursting with this pain. This is horror. Horror. I hear my partner at the back door: "Marianne! Marianne!" If I run down the path my student will see me. Why does this feel like I am fearing for my very life?

I must hurt myself physically to take myself away from this horror. I grab a piece of broken brick from the ground. I feel for a sharp edge on the brick and scrape my arm with it. I want this world to go away. I want this horror to go away. The pain in my arm feels good. There is only pain in my arm. The sharp sting of an open wound is a bearable pain. It is a small pain that doesn't overwhelm.

journal 1995

I have been trying so hard to keep moving ahead despite the setbacks. At the beginning of the week, I had felt that regardless of whether life was going well or not, I was still taking my place in a fullness of life that could contain all opposites. It felt like I was finally stepping out to face the world. But at some point my paintings started to feel stupid, my thoughts of writing a flute book felt stupid, I didn't feel strong enough go to a talk on Buddhism. Once again the horror that I am not doing anything with my precious life and talents overwhelms me. I am trapped by myself and my past into some horror netherworld of existence.

What is to become of me? What is to become of me?? Pain. Despair. In am in the car, trying to run away, but I have nowhere to go. I want to smash and destroy. I want to run the car into a tree ... but then I feel sad that I will wreck my little red car. My little red car has done nothing wrong. I come home. I huddle hard into the corner between my dresser and the wall. I push myself in there. Safe. Between a hard wall and a hard wooden dresser. And then I start to moan a little tune of pain. Over and over. The tune is comforting and releases the pain somewhat. In a way, it feels good to be this unwell again. At least I have a task: to get well. But even this 'getting well' isn't really an attractive option, because once I am well again I will still have to DO something with my life.

Oh god, where do I go from here? Can I make a go of my life? I must. I must. I must will myself on. I AM SO VERY VERY SCARED.

journal 2000

I am living the minutes: one and then another one, one and then another one. I am so sick of this life. Why was I born? I can do nothing that the world asks of me. I am never good enough. I am never good enough. If I judge myself by others' standards then I will never be good enough. I will never be a good enough friend, a good enough teacher, a good enough lover ... Where will I find the standards that are my own? Where?

The leaves outside look exquisite. I see them in all their insignificant and yet wondrous glory. They are enough. All on their own they are enough. The deeper I feel this gloom, the more precious each small and unacknowledged speck is. Why can't I ever let the sun shine on me and have that be enough? Can I too be insignificant and yet glorious?

Nothing suffices. There is nothing that will fill me anymore. Nothing. The good fuck, the good life, the good thing. They will never be enough. I am so low. Is there anything to tell me that life is anything but a profound disappointment? A war waged and then death? What is this life? What is this life? Why do I wish only to die?

***

the questions of suffering

Implicit in our suffering are the very deepest life questions and inquiry.

It is often only those who are suffering greatly, who are prepared to question in this way. For most people and for society at large, such questions are usually too real and too confronting.

As I was putting together this chapter, I was surprised to find that buried within the desperation of my journal entries, were just such questions and yearnings:

If only there was some purpose or meaning to it all, I wouldn't go.
I need help. I can't do this on my own.
There are only bits everywhere that don't add up.
I want an answer. I want a way out that is bigger than all of this.
I am unable find a center within myself.
I need ONE thing that will work. One thing that I can stick to.

I am grieving for my very fundamental personhood.
Where will I find the standards that are my own? Where?
Can I too be insignificant and yet glorious?
Nothing suffices. There is nothing that will fill me anymore. Nothing.
What is this life?

Within my words there is a desire for meaning, a longing to find a center and to find wholeness, there is a realization that the deeper answers of life cannot be found in the everyday world, there is a need to know the true nature of my existence, there is a desire to reconcile opposites and move beyond black-and-white thinking, and there is also the recognition that I need someone to stand by my side.

But it surprised me that implicit in my questions was also a profound truth which at that time I was completely unaware of: I was suffering because of the loss of my fundamental personhood, 'center' or wholeness.

It is this disconnection from our 'fundamental personhood' or what I would now call True Nature that is indeed at the root of suffering.

We suffer because we are cast adrift from who or what we truly are.

***

in times of most desperate suffering

The poem that follows was my first piece of writing specifically for this book.

In it, I was asking a question: Will this book be helpful to others during their most desperate times? But I was also asking that question of myself: Would such a book have been helpful for me when my suffering was at its worst?

And the answer that came back was "Yes." Only those who have truly suffered can know what it is to suffer. Although others' intentions may be good, at times their advice may be ill-considered, discouraging or even downright injurious.

I hope my voice is an antidote to those who in their ignorance, limitation or fear, would dissuade you from believing that it is possible to come to a place of deeply lived peace. The journey is already difficult enough without them.

In times of most desperate suffering,
Does it help to know
That you are
Peace,
Stillness,
Magnificence?
Beyond anything you can imagine?
Beyond anything you can ever find words for?
Does it help?

You are peace.
Beautiful woman.
Beautiful man.
Peace.

Truly.

I too, have wanted to tear at my skin,
Scream my pain into the cosmos,
Break my tainted soul into a million pieces.
I too, have lain for weeks in a wordless stupor.
I too, have wanted to end this horror life.

Would it have helped me then,
To know that I am peace,
Stillness,
Magnificence?
Precious child that I was.
Precious woman.
Loved. Loveable. Whole. Free.
Would it have helped?

Looking back now,
I realize
That somewhere
I *did* know.
Even in times of most desperate suffering.
Somewhere I *did* know.

Deep, deep down.
Deep.

Deep.
Down.
Somewhere I knew
I wasn't broken, I wasn't tethered,
I wasn't damaged, I wasn't torn.
Beautiful child that I was.
Beautiful woman.

Was my suffering so great,
Awful tearing torment at the madness of this life,
Only because I *did* know?
Only because I could sense in my deepest soul,
That there was a place I might be cherished?

Would the ache
And the longing,
Have been quite so desperate,
Quite so unrelenting,
If I had had no inkling whatsoever
Of the Love that is my birthright?
Of the Depth of what I truly am?

Precious woman.
Precious man.
In this lifetime,
It is possible.

Peace.
Stillness.
Magnificence.

It is possible.
Truly.

You are that peace.
Beloved Peace.

***

there's something else

Have you ever had the sense that something isn't quite right? That things aren't quite as they are meant to be? That there's something missing?

Have you ever had the sense that there's something else going on? Something other than just 'this'?

And have you ever tried to ignore those feelings and get on with the job of belonging and fitting in? ... all the while still wondering ...

***

the unwelcome gift

When we are little, we are sometimes given a gift, but at that time it doesn't *feel* like a gift.

Gifts are usually wrapped in bright-colored paper or tied with beautiful bows. But this gift has no fancy packaging and no accompanying excitement.

Instead, this gift may come with an unadorned jolt or creep up with a nagging unease. It can unsettle, bewilder and disturb. This gift can even seem like a curse. And so we try to hide it away in the bottom drawer or in the back of a cupboard. We hope that with time, it might go away. Disappear.

Some people are very good at forgetting that gift. Or so it seems. But others aren't.

When I was very young I knew that something wasn't quite right with the stories people told about the world, about themselves and about me. I sensed that there was something else going on. Something *more*. Something *deeper*. At times this knowing left me feeling very lonely and bewildered; the people around me and society as a whole seemed disinterested in or even fearful of that 'something else' I sensed.

And yet, whenever I felt very low or suicidal it gave me a reason to stay alive: "If you kill yourself today you'll never find out what this 'something else' is, will you!" It was a handhold of sorts, a promise.

Eventually I realized that the intuition of 'something else', was the call or the pull we all have within, to know who we truly *are*.

***

follow it, follow it

> when you feel a hint
> that you are more than just
> the empty shells
> offered so easily
> on throw-away paper plates
>
> then follow it
> follow that hint

***

whose make-believe is it?

The first time I recall the sense that something wasn't quite right, was when I was about four.

My parents wanted me to try a new food. They assumed I wouldn't like it, so decided to use reverse psychology. They told me that the food they were eating was a very *special* food that was only for adults and not for little girls. I knew immediately what they were trying to do, and yet when I pointed this out, I was told to stop making up such silly stories.

It was a minor incident, and yet it puzzled me. Although I didn't have the words at that time, my sense was, "But why don't you just tell me the truth? Why don't you offer me some of your food and let me decide for myself? Why is it necessary to play a strange game and for me to play along with you?" I couldn't understand why they would make up a story in order to manipulate me into liking a food, and then tell me that *I* was the one making up stories.

Over the years, I came to realize that some version of this strange game was going on in lots of places. People invented a story and then tried very hard to make sure that other people went along with their story too. It was a make-believe world; they made up the script, they produced it and then they acted in it. It was like a stage play to which they had given the name Real Life.

I quickly learned that it was very important not to let on that I could see through these stories. If I did, other people didn't like me very much, or worse still, I got into a lot of trouble. And yet it baffled me (and still does), that for all the energy they put in, these stories actually seemed to make people quite miserable and sometimes even angry.

When I was nine or ten I heard my parents discussing religion; they were criticizing another religion while saying that their own was the right one. I thought that saying, "I am right and you are wrong" was a very peculiar thing indeed. I could see that the religion which my parents thought was wrong would probably say exactly the same back to them. I thought that surely there must be a bigger truth behind both religions that wouldn't make anyone right or anyone wrong. I wondered why they couldn't see that.

By this time in my life, I knew I had to be very careful about what I said, and yet I thought religion was quite a reasonable and even grown-up thing to wonder about. So I asked my mother, "But if you think that your religion is right, and that other person in that other country thinks *their* religion is right, then how do you know that *yours* is the right one? Couldn't *you* be the wrong one and they be the right one? Couldn't you both be wrong or both be right?" I was told to stop talking such utter rubbish.

Questioning whether there was a world in which nobody was right and nobody was wrong would of course have cut Real Life at its very foundations.

A couple of years later, I started to wonder about Jesus. I recall so very clearly standing on the steps that led downstairs; I asked my mother, "If the point of Jesus was that he was just a man, doesn't that mean that we could all be just like Jesus? Doesn't that mean that *I* could be just like Jesus?" With fury in her eyes she leant down to me and said: "I don't want to hear you *ever* say anything like that again!" It seemed that the games of Real Life were played with very high stakes.

Even then, when I was very young, I could sense that there was something bigger going on. It was something that was true and real and had no agenda but to tell the truth and to be real. But in the world of Real Life I wasn't supposed to talk about this, and I certainly wasn't supposed to speak words that originated from this place. I had to play along like everyone else. I felt like I was the adult and I had to learn the rules of the game in order to keep all the children happy.

However, try as I might, I could never *ever* learn all the rules. And until recently, I never *ever* stopped trying.

***

out on a limb

In my early twenties I moved out of home and with two close friends found a big old art-deco flat near the train line and all amenities. We spent three wonderful years living together, laughing together, arguing and finding our feet as adults.

At some point during this time I read Shirley MacLaine's book *Out on a Limb*. I can't remember how I came across the book, but I do remember that the title appealed to me; I had felt out on a limb much of my life.

I found some sections of the book a tad questionable: extra-terrestrial life, ancient civilizations and affairs with politicians weren't exactly the stuff of my life. And yet in MacLaine's use of the words of spirituality, I realized I had been right to suspect that there was indeed something else going on.

Although there was a time I would have been embarrassed to admit it, that book was pivotal in my life; it made my journey to a lived spirituality, conscious. Despite the mainstream voices to the contrary, it seemed that it might after all be possible to live a life that made sense and to find what was true. I felt a tremendous upsurge of energy and curiosity.

Around the corner from where I lived, I discovered a small metaphysical book shop. I had walked past it countless times but never noticed it. Into my life came the words of spirit guides, yogis, learned writers and spiritual masters, many of whom Shirley MacLaine had mentioned in her book. Buddhism, reincarnation, death, soul and Spirit all became my reading matter.

Rather than the strange pretend world into which I had to squeeze and contort myself, I now had a world into which I could expand and grow; the 'something else' I had sensed was actually far far bigger than I could ever have imagined or hoped for. It was the beginning of an extraordinary journey.

Never, ever, stop wondering if there's 'something else' going on.

***

the call

What is a call?

A call is our inspiration, our flame. It summons us to express our unique beauty, brilliance and strength into this world.

Even through the most suffered times, a call remains as our beacon, as our guiding light and sometimes even as our salvation.

A call is Spirit's voice as it speaks itself into our lives.

***

A call comes from deep within.
It is not a call from society, our parents, our friends, our mind or our ideas.
A call doesn't come over the phone.
A call is not a demand from the everyday world.
A call can seem in direct opposition to the evidence or map of our lives.
A call pays no heed to a time frame.
A call can be of a moment or of a lifetime.
A call follows only its own path and its own wisdom.

I can understand that some have seen it as a call from God.
That is what best describes it: "I must do this. I must follow this."

We ignore a call only at our own peril.

***

the call to write

It was 1978. I was 18 years old and in my first year of a Bachelor of Music degree at University.

I had just eaten lunch and was sitting alone on a bench under the trees, waiting until it was time to go in for a history lecture. Around me, people chatted casually in groups. I watched them but knew I didn't belong. I felt lonely and displaced at university. Something was wrong, but I didn't know what that something was. Why had I chosen Late Modern European History as an elective when it didn't interest me in the slightest? Why did it feel like I was living someone else's life?

I sat for a while, glancing at my watch from time to time. And then all of a sudden, like a blast from an internal loudspeaker, I heard the words, "You're meant to be a writer. You're meant to write books." I was stunned, but by the intensity with which the words had been spoken, I knew without a doubt that they were true.

After the lecture I walked down the road to the university bookshop. I went inside and wandered around. I stroked the covers of the books. "This is what I am meant to do". The feeling of rightness persisted.

And yet there were also questions: What would I write about? I had absolutely nothing in my life to write about. And what did I know about writing anyway? I might have been passably good at writing structured essays, but I had never, in any way, been creative.[1]

And then, almost like that loudspeaker's addendum, the voice told me that the task of my life from then on, was to go forward and gather the experience and skills that would eventually form the backbone and guts of my writing.

I continued my music degree and became a professional musician. And although the call to write went underground at times, it never went away. I wrote in journals, I wrote poetry, I wrote prose, I wrote humorous rhyming verses for my friends, I started a number of books but never completed them, I had articles and interviews published in music magazines. Eventually I had two books published, one admittedly a music book.

And now, years and years and years after that first call, I sit here writing and I know without a doubt that that call was wise in its persistence.

It is the dance of my words that is calling me always to life.

***

---

1. For further discussion of the importance of writing in my life, see *Opening into Creativity* in the chapter *Creativity.*

journal 2002

I tried to write a piece on spirituality during the week – I had a strong impulse to do so and thought I'd follow it. As I progressed I spent more and more time looking up other people's opinions and ideas, trying to compare them to mine, and finding mine always sadly lacking. But now I see that I was doing something quite different to what I thought I was doing ... and it is goose-bumps stuff ... it is 'fuck me!' stuff.

I was learning about the very essence of what it is to write, the very reason I MUST write ... the very reason it has called me over and over and over ... it is because writing is the very thing that is most difficult for me. Because to write, I must put my *very own self* on paper ... not someone else's opinions, not someone else's life, not stuff that the majority of the population will agree with, not stuff that will please anyone ... and to be able to do that, I know, is the task of this lifetime for me. In writing I must find my own voice. I must speak my truth into the world. Nothing short of that will do ... I must write.

***

the call into homelessness, the call to the priesthood

In my book *Seventeen Voices: Life and Wisdom from inside 'mental illness'* both Patrick and John describe a call.

Patrick powerfully conveys his call into homelessness and alcoholism. Although he doesn't explicitly use the word 'call', he describes the characteristic sense of feeling pulled to follow a path that might make no sense whatsoever to others:

> I had to follow something in me that I couldn't deny. It was like a magnet. If I denied it I wouldn't be Patrick. I had to follow something that homelessness is a part of. It was a drive within me that took me to jails, to rehabilitation clinics, and detox centers. It led me to meet criminals, addicts ... people you would never meet in so-called normal life.

So there was some overarching sense moving you through everything?

Yes. It comes from somewhere in the lower belly section. In the lower abdomen. It is almost like you know something but you don't know what it is. It is a different sort of knowing, like an instinct and you have to follow it. My life would not be worth living if I didn't follow it. But people certainly get hurt in the wake of it. I left my wife without a husband. I left my young son without a father. How can I explain to my son that I left home and became a homeless alcoholic because I was following my instincts? So sometimes I ask if it was all worth it, but I know that I had no choice. It was so strong. Something was happening through me …

John describes his lifelong calling to the priesthood, a call which, even when I interviewed him at the age of 74, had in no way dulled. That call persisted despite a lack of support from his family, his difficulty with his studies, and an episode of deep depression.

I recall a Christmas midnight mass when I was a teenager – the words from the prologue of St John's Gospel spoke of John the Baptist, but I felt that they referred to me too:
There came a man, sent from God, whose name was John. (John 1:6)

My lifelong calling to the priesthood jumped out of that moment. I've never forgotten it. It hooked me in and on reflecting back on it, I know that I'm called to bless. I have spent my whole life looking forward to the priesthood. That calling has never left me.

***

roll call

I asked those around me what it is that calls them:

My partner feels a call to make a difference and gave up her music career to do so.
An acquaintance is called to help others.
A friend is called to teach, even though she has a very successful career in an unrelated field.
A family member is called to raise her young family.
An acquaintance is called to work for an agricultural machinery business rather than work as an artist. He felt a call to be engaged in the world in a more tangible and concrete way than that of creative pursuit.
Another friend is called to live a life of quiet contemplation and solitude.

***

the call of Truth

Long before I had heard about inner journeys, self-development and therapy, the Truth had called me. Long before I had heard words like enlightenment, liberation, Buddhism, spirituality or meditation, the Truth had called me.

It was a call from a mysterious inwardness. It was a yearning: "There is something else, there is something more." It was a seemingly inborn response to the strange dissonances, tensions and unhappiness I saw in the world around me. It was the call of a knowing much deeper than the desires and ambitions of my everyday self.

At first that call was barely perceptible. In a single moment there was a fleeting question. A spark. A watchfulness. What is going on here? Why do others brush my questions so hastily aside?

And so a spark kindled a quiet flame. Why is it that in my home I feel no heart, and yet deep inside my heart I feel there is a Home? Where will I find wisdom? Where will I find grace?

And so that flame ignited a fire. Others held my hand, others held my soul, others nourished me and fed me, but the call remained that of my heart alone.

Through suffered and difficult times, the fire of that call sometimes dimmed and yet it never died. It drew me always to its warmth, to its glow, to its sustenance, to its power. This too. Yes this too is Truth.

And as I looked around me at the hardened questions and hardened bodies I wondered: Why are we not *all* called to our deepest maturity and humanity? To peace? Why are we not *all* called to know what we truly *are*? To our True Nature? Why is that spark so often destined to flicker but briefly and then die?

Forever I am called to Truth. That call has no end.

***

the call to stop

A call is not just a call of a lifetime. A call can also be the call of a moment. It can be a call to sit still, to meditate, to go for a walk, to move into depth, to make contact with a friend, to get up and write in the middle of the night ...

I wrote the following poem at a point in my life when I knew I had pushed my body, and indeed my entire being, too far. It is written for myself, but also for a society and a world, in which that relentless forward motion is increasingly the norm. When do we stop?

Every cell of my body is calling me to stop.
Every lived moment is calling me to stop.

I am not despairing. Not depressed. Not unhappy.
But my life. My body. My soul. They are calling me to stop.
Pleading with me to stop.

I can no longer push forward.
To the next moment. The next amusement.
The next holiday. The next job.
The next delight.
The next …

Why do we push forward until our minds and bodies are screaming?
Or until they are forced into a mute or hellish torpor?
Relentless pursuit.
Of what?

So many words for moving forward:
Ambition. Success. Fame. Gratification.
Instant dating. Instant wealth. Instant messaging. Instant noodles.
All there in front of us.
Waiting.
Will they make us happy?

I once had ambition. Lots of it. I once had success. Lots of it.
But here in the very belly of my life
They are so empty.

For me, now, there is only a call to stop.
Cessation. Stop. Please stop.
In every moment. Stop.

Does the world cater for this stopping?
Or does it label it and medicate it?

Is it possible to completely stop?
To want nothing? To desire nothing?
No thought as to what that next moment might hold?

What would I find there?

Would I find myself?

***

what if there is nothing wrong with me?

What if there is nothing wrong with me? What if there is nothing wrong with you? What if?

***

I am not good enough. I am not worthy enough.
I am not perfect enough.
I am bad. I am miserable. I am lazy.
I am too fat. My legs are too big. I should pull my stomach in.
I don't belong.
I'm not sociable enough.
I can't think. I don't know what to say.
I feel sad. I feel angry.
I feel sick.
Surely there must be something wrong with me.
Surely.

***

an insidious legacy

Many times I have thought that the most insidious legacy with which I was endowed was the belief that there was something intrinsically wrong with me. Somewhere in the fact of being alive and walking on two legs on this planet, I had been presumed guilty. It is as though I emanated a foul-smelling odor of which I could never find the source, and which seemingly defied even my most valiant attempts to wash it off.

And yet, as much as I believed that I was unworthy and flawed, on another level, deep within, I knew this simply wasn't true.

It was a contradiction I carried with me like a gnawing ache in my side, like an itch I would forever need to scratch. I knew that there must be another way to live, where the perfection, wholeness and brilliance I sensed were my birthright, could finally find their Home.

***

bad girl good girl, woodcut

***

from where does this wrongness come?

I look back through my life. From where comes the belief that there is something wrong with me? Can I locate its source? The moment of its instigation?

Memories and sensations flood in. There are so many of them. They are mine and yet are they not everybody's, even in some small measure?

My body is bad. How far does that go back? It is beyond my recall. I feel ashamed that I am a little girl. I am in some way tainted. Impure. At fault. Responsible. There are parts of my body I must not touch, parts of my body I must not name. They are wordless, and so without words they are beyond my reflection, beyond my reason, beyond my questions. Without a language they exist only in obscurity. In muddiness. In the shadowlands of someone else's mind. They have been taken from me long before I knew I could claim them as my own.

My very being is bad. How far does that go back? Again it is beyond my recall. As I speak myself into this world, with my anger and my tears, with my doubts and my questions, I am declared a problem. A threat. A burden. I must be rendered voiceless. Violence and punishment are in the nature of the universe. Aren't they? Where is my innocence in the face of an undeniable guilt? Where is my beauty if others see only a misery and a sorrow? Where is love in the face of tyranny? I have nowhere to rest, and nowhere to come Home.

Religion only confirms for me that I have done something terribly terribly bad. The House of God is saturated with the heavy discomfort of scratchy Sunday dresses, hard wooden pews, boredom, and a Sunday School filled with God-forgiven children who seem to know when to talk and how to move. I don't doubt that it is a foretaste of the Hell for which I am destined. Long before I have heard of Original Sin, I am living out its legacy. I await a redemption that never comes. I don't have a clue how to do any better.

In school I am grateful for the rules. I color carefully inside the lines, I print my tidy words in tidy sentences in tidy exercise books. I am polite and quiet. I stand up very straight and always do my homework. But my rigidity and awkwardness betray me and the taunts of my classmates follow me. I try to join in their ease and laughter, but my attempts are only poor imitations and I am caught out as rude or tactless. The whip of a cane and the sharp ache in my stomach tell me that for all my trying I will never fit in and I will never be good enough. Why am I here? What have I done wrong?

In the suffering of my adulthood there comes confirmation of my badness. In a litany of labels and techniques it seems I must surrender up my body and my humanity. I wonder how it is that I have become little more than a fleshly machine. Religion, my family, my society, my world, hold up their hands to proclaim their collective surprise and blamelessness.

How did she end up so bad?

***

the recognition

It was many years ago.

I had just come home from a therapy session. I had walked in the back door and through into the kitchen and then it suddenly hit me: "There is actually nothing wrong with me." My therapist, Mollie[1], had tried many times and in many different ways to communicate this fact to me, and although I had nodded in acknowledgement, "Yes, yes, yes", while impatiently thinking to myself, "You're *repeating* yourself!" I had not understood that reality as my own.

Now I could feel the truth of those words in my body: "There is actually nothing wrong with me." It was such an overriding shift in identity and belief that I started to shake uncontrollably. I could not think who I was, nor remember who I had been, past that single transparent recognition.

---

1. I describe Mollie and Radix body-centered psychotherapy more fully in the chapters *Beyond the Battle* and *The Body.*

The words repeated themselves: "There is actually nothing wrong with me. There is actually nothing wrong with me."

I dropped down onto the solidity of the wooden floorboards and propped myself up against the kitchen cupboards. I sat on that floor for a long time in utter astonishment. My suffering hadn't come about because I had done something bad, because my life was a mistake, or because I was innately wicked or evil. My suffering hadn't come about because I had screwed up my life or because I hadn't tried hard enough. I wasn't ill. I wasn't sick. No. None of that was true. None of it. My *life* made sense. It was *all* meaningful. *All* of it. There was absolutely nothing wrong with me. My suffering made complete and utter sense in the light of everything that had happened to me.

There is a misconception, or perhaps it is a hope, that such moments can sweep away the beliefs and functioning of a lifetime. This may well be the case for some, but it has never been the case for me. I have found that these moments, although extraordinarily powerful, are only the beginning; I now have to go back and learn how to function and understand life from a completely new vantage point. At times that period of adjustment is challenging and disconcerting, both for myself and for the people around me.

How do I operate in a world that is in many ways based on the belief that we are fundamentally flawed?

It took me many more years to live the realization of that day. But it was a profound beginning.

***

but it's good for me

There were many ways in which I kept the sense of my 'badness' alive.

The most obvious were those that criticize my body ("I'm too fat") and those that criticize my actions or responses ("You're just hopeless and nobody will ever like you if you say/do things like that.").

But one of the ways in which I kept the sense of my 'badness' alive was hardly noticeable: "But it's good for me."

With these words, I pushed myself relentlessly forward, always towards a 'perfect somebody' I would eventually become if only I could do better. There were many times I pushed myself to the limits of my endurance simply because I believed I would be a better or stronger person because of it. I truly believed I was pushing myself "for my own good".[2]

> If I wasn't comfortable driving long distances, I would force myself to do it anyway, believing that not driving long distances was a bad thing: "It's good for me to force myself to drive longer distances."

> When I suffered from panic attacks I frequently forced myself to confront my fear and go into the very situations I feared most, even though a ten-minute outing exhausted me for days afterwards: "It's good for me if I don't let my fear get the better of me".

> If I didn't like loud noise I would force myself to endure it, because I thought it was bad to be so sensitive to noise: "It's good for me to put up with this noise."

> If I found it painful or difficult to be around my family, I would force myself to make contact with them, believing it was bad not to be in contact with my family: "It's good for me to talk to my family."

> If I didn't feel like being sociable I would force myself to chat with people or invite them over for dinner, believing that it was bad to be on my own too much: "It's good for me to balance time alone with time in company."

But this pushing towards an ideal of perfection kept alive the idea that the person I am, in this moment, is somehow bad; that this person, here and now, needs to be fixed, manipulated, punished, pushed and goaded.

Slowly I have come to see that I am a person who quite simply doesn't like driving long distances, I am a person who doesn't like loud noise and busy-ness, I am a person who doesn't fit in with her family in any deeper or satisfying way, and I am a person who prefers being on her own for longer periods than most. That is how I am in the world. That is how Spirit expresses itself through *this* human form.

***

---

2. I write these words with Alice Miller's powerful book *For Your Own Good: Hidden Cruelty in Child-Rearing and the Roots of Violence* in mind. It is no surprise where these beliefs come from.

what happens when we realize that nothing is wrong?

What does it mean, if I no longer see myself as flawed? What does it matter if I realize that there is nothing wrong with me?

When we believe ourselves to be bad or flawed, broken or sinful, wrong or worthless, we are believing the stories of others: our parents, our teachers, our society, our religious leaders, our doctors, our psychiatrists.

Their stories come from a belief in humanity's intrinsic flawedness and deficiency: the badness of the child who needs to be tamed, the badness of the body with its wayward urges and meaningless illnesses, the worthlessness of the sensitive soul who does not fit in, the shame of those who are mentally suffering, the overarching sinfulness of humanity.

But those who tell us these stories are not immune from their own beliefs; in their quest for power, control, fame and unquestioned rightness, they betray the fact that they too feel deficient, powerless or unworthy.

The deficient have no choice but to convince you of your deficiency. The broken have no choice but to convince you of your brokenness.

These stories are deeply entrenched in our Western narratives, and as such, we rarely call them into question. We assume that it is in the nature of reality that we are in need of fixing, purification or punishment. And so we continue striving for more success and money, we pray harder and meditate more, we go to doctors and gurus for advice and healing. We try to be better people. We *want* to be worthy, we *want* to belong, we *want* to be well, we *want* to be loved. We don't want to be bad.

But we are locked in an endless cycle: at what point will we ever be good enough, perfect enough, normal enough? When exactly will that be? And who will tell us when we have finally made it? Nobody. Never. It will never ever happen. Why? Because in this moment there is absolutely nothing whatsoever wrong with us. There never was and there never will be. In this moment we are *complete*. We are *complete* for this moment. We aren't bad. We aren't wrong. The badness is a fabrication. It is make-believe.

But how on earth can I be complete in this moment when I have a headache, I'm tired and I feel like being on my own? Surely if I am complete I no longer have headaches, I have boundless energy, and I wish to clutch the whole of humanity to my infinitely compassionate bosom!

When we believe in badness we oppose it to an ideal we call 'goodness' or 'perfection'. Just as the idea of our badness is an invention or a construction, so is the idea of this 'perfection'. In this moment, there is no 'good or bad'. There is simply what there is. And this 'Is-ness' is called Life or Truth. It is Spirit as it is expressed in Life. *Your* Life. *My* Life. It is Life as it is in this moment. Life doesn't happen tomorrow, or in a year's time, when we finally match up to an ideal. We don't start this thing called Life, only when we have perfected it. That sort of perfection is never going to happen.

The *true* Perfection[3], the *Divine* Perfection, the *Sacred* Perfection, is in this moment. I am sitting at this computer engrossed in my writing, my neck is a bit stiff, I have a stain on my t-shirt and I am hungry. And nothing about it is 'wrong'. Stiffness is stiffness, hunger is hunger, a stain is a stain. And it is complete; it is perfect. It is Divinity as a sacred work of art with all its light and shade, all its textures and clarity, even all its grubbiness.

This moment of my Life does not need to be fixed or altered or perfected or added to in any way. In five minutes time I might go and eat something because I'm hungry, I might get up and go for a walk because my neck is stiffening from being at the computer too long, I might even throw my t-shirt in the wash, but those activities are not a reflection on the perfection or completion of this moment. When I get up and eat something, then that will be another moment, and that will be perfect. When I get up, walk around and stretch my neck, then that too will be perfect. When I wash my t-shirt that will be perfect.

When we see Life as a Divine Creation, something changes. We see that Life is inherently intelligent, wise and meaningful. And as human beings, we are not separate from that Life. We *are* Life. That is our Truth.[4]

Our suffering too, is part of Divinity and of Life, and as such, it is also intrinsically meaningful.

Our suffering has not come about because we have done something bad, or because we are failed and miserable human beings. Nor is our suffering that of a machine-like body with parts that can break down and are in constant need of oiling or fixing.

---

3. I use the word 'Perfection' here with reticence. I am aware that this word is too often charged with the very judgements and beliefs of which I am writing. I have, however, capitalized it to indicate that I am writing of Divine Perfection. From the vantage point of our everyday self, perfection is an ideal based on judgement. From the vantage point of the Divine, Perfection is Completeness. Divine Perfection includes everything: my weariness, my wrinkles, my anger, my love. Nothing is missing, nothing needs to be changed or added to. Everything is happening exactly as it is.
4. Also see chapter *Life*.

Our suffering makes sense. Our suffering is valid.

When our suffering is seen as part of life, we can begin to be truly curious about it: we can ask questions of it, follow it, move with it, feel it, embody it. We no longer fight it.[5]

We no longer despair that we aren't perfect. We no longer get frustrated and upset that life is somehow different to how we thought it should be. We aren't disillusioned or disappointed. We no longer feel the need to prove ourselves to anyone. When we open ourselves and our lives to interest and to exploration we are creating the opening through which insight and self-awareness can emerge.

There is a belief that when we stop pushing, fixing and berating ourselves, we'll sit around on our backsides and say, "Well this is Divinity regardless of what I do, so why not just eat chocolate donuts and watch television." But that simply does not happen.

When we see the Perfection of this moment, the opposite happens: there is a natural upwelling of momentum as Life is given its freedom to flow through us unimpeded.

***

---

5. Opening to suffering is discussed in greater detail in many other chapters throughout the book.

stories

Stories carry power. At times that power is inspirational and vital, but at other times that power can be limiting and even crippling, particularly if we aren't aware that a story is being told.

***

the paradox of my story

This story is a fairy tale.
It is a dream.

And yet it all happened.
And it is all true.

This story has no beginning.
And it has no end.

And yet there *is* a beginning.
And there *is* an end.

I always knew where I was going.
I was never lost.

And yet I had no clue where I was going.
And I was so completely lost.

These are paradoxes.
And they make perfect sense to me now.

There is an end to suffering.

There is an end to suffering.

***

telling our story

In how many ways can I tell my story?

Undoubtedly we have all met people who believe there is only one way of telling their story.

I have an acquaintance who only ever tells her 'angry story'. And she tells it to everyone she meets. One day she is angry with her neighbors, the next she is angry with the council, the day after that she is angry about the barking dogs across the road. It is no surprise that her 'angry story' communicates not just in her words, but also in her face, her body and her entire being.

Another acquaintance only ever tells his negative story. Even a beautiful sunny day is a problem for him because it won't last.

But our stories can be told in countless ways.

In writing this book I'm aware that I can account for my journey both as a pursuit for Truth and as a quest to find an end to my suffering. Both are equally valid.

I can tell the story of my inner life or the story of my outer life. Both are true.

Throughout this book I recount stories from a suffered past. But I also include stories of joy, of inspiration, of insight and of humor.

Other people also tell my story. I know that the stories some family members would tell of my life, would correspond very little to the stories I would tell of myself.

People in the helping professions have also sought to tell my story. Some have told my story as a narrative that I can retell in the manner of my choosing. Some have told my story as a series of learned responses that I must relearn. Some have told my story as that of repressed feelings which I can release. Some have told my story as that of a skin bag of blood and bones, the cells and brain of which have somehow gone awry. Some of these stories carry a degree of truth, but some don't.

People in spiritual circles also tell stories: Hindu stories, Buddhist stories, Christian stories, stories of the power of meditation, stories of unfolding kundalini energy, stories of light and bliss, stories of angels and crystals, stories with which they have sought to elevate themselves to saintliness or guruhood, stories of the quest for Truth. Some I have pursued for a time and some I haven't.

The stories I have included in this book are stories from my life that I hope might carry power for those who are suffering. Stories paint a picture that can easily come to mind when times are tough and we need something to hold onto. Strategies, practices and self-help techniques don't necessarily have the power of a simple story and its associated images and meaning.

But the Ultimate Truth is not something I will never be able to tell a story about; I can only hint at it, point at it, work around the edges of it. Anything that can be put into words is not the Truth.

Look for that which has no words …

***

the power of a very good story

Even as a child I wasn't much interested in stories of make-believe. I didn't sit on the floor watching *Yogi Bear* or *Astro Boy* with my brother. I thought the story of *Alice in Wonderland*, with its white rabbit, blue caterpillar and smiling cat, was silly and childish. I preferred a picture book on jungle animals or jungle eco-systems to a book of Kipling's *Jungle* Stories.

But although fantasy and fiction were never my 'thing', I more than made up for any story shortfall in my fascination with other people's lives; I *loved* reading autobiographies. I have been carried to exotic peoples and places. I have relished insights into journeying and suffering and hardship. I have been fed and inspired by courage, tenacity, resilience and all that can be lived through this human form.

In the early 1990s I read Sorrel Wilby's account of her 6,500km traverse of the Himalaya, *Across the Top*. To all appearances my life could not have been more different from Wilby's: I was unfit, I was overweight, I suffered crippling fear and anxiety, and some days I struggled to walk even to the letterbox. And yet, there was something in Wilby's account that spoke to me. Her journeying, her hardships, her doubts, her resolve and her ups and downs may have taken place in the awe-inspiring Himalaya, but in some ways they were not so different to the struggles that I quietly lived out in suburban obscurity.

At one point in the book Wilby describes walking through a gorge in Pakistan. The heat was so extreme that her lips and her skin blistered, and her tongue swelled. It was 55 degrees (Celsius) and it was hell. For someone who quivered with anxiety when the temperature rose above 30, I was stunned but also immensely inspired by the fact of her endurance and her simple survival. But her experiences also allowed me to acknowledge the extremes of my own inner landscape and my resolve to traverse them: the searing wildfires of open wounds, the courage of blazing honesty, the valleys of unrelenting fear, and my unremitting determination to continue to put one foot in front of the other. Whether an inner journey or an outer one, it seemed that the steps one must take were not all that dissimilar.

But in addition to that, after I read her story, I started to walk. And I will always be grateful to Sorrel Wilby for that. I thought, if she can walk 6500km, if she can walk when it is 55 degrees in the wilds of Pakistan, then I can walk one kilometer when it is 22 degrees and there is a major medical facility only ten minutes down the road.

And that's how it began.

One day I drove my car to a nearby national park, parked in the car park, and with fear pounding in my chest and thoughts of imminent personal calamity running riot through my mind, I started to walk the kilometer-long loop track around a small lake. At times panic rose, but with a quick glance back to the cocoon of safety that was my little red car, I kept going.

Although to any onlooker that walk would have appeared spectacularly unexceptional, for me it truly was one of the greatest feats of my life. Soon I was able to walk around that small lake three times, then five times. Then I gradually added in slightly larger loops, exploring the different trails through the national park. Then I walked for one hour, two hours. Walking became my sanity. My great joy. Then I bought my first pair of hiking boots, and proudly looked back to admire the tracks I left behind me in the mud or in the sand. And then I started to dream of all the places that those boots might take me. I walked snowy tracks in New Zealand, red rocky tracks in Central Australia, boggy tracks in the Tasmanian wilderness. I walked along wild and empty beaches, breathing in the delicious thick salty air. And countless hiking boots later I am still walking.[1]

Also in the early 1990s, I read a book called *Grey is the Colour of Hope*, the prison (gulag) memoirs of Russian poet and dissident, Irina Ratushinskaîa. I picked up her book one day in a bookshop solely because it was an autobiography; I knew nothing of the author and very little of life in the Russia of those times. I can't readily recall many of the details of the book, but there was a small section that stayed with me.

In winter, in the cold of her cell, Irina attempted to keep warm by lying down lengthways against pipes that ran along the floor. Intermittently the guards would remember to stoke the fire, and then for a short time the pipes carried a little warmth, perhaps just enough to briefly rekindle some of the circulation in her blue and icy fingers. For me it was a description of life lived on the edge and the capacity we all have to take advantage of even the smallest moments of grace. But it was also a standard by which I sought to invite gratitude into my life: as desperate as times were, I wasn't imprisoned for my poetry and I wasn't lying in a cell clinging to a metal pipe in order to keep blood moving through my body.

It was also in the manner of picking up any autobiography that I could lay my hands on, that I found the writing of Alexandra David-Néel. I held up her astonishing life as an inspiration for my own. Despite physical limitation and discomfort, this explorer, writer, lecturer, photographer, Buddhist authority, Sanskrit grammarian and spiritualist led an extraordinary life of travel, adventure and esoteric investigation. She famously spent many years in Tibet at a time when it was closed to foreigners, but she also travelled widely through China, Nepal, Korea, Japan and India, often by foot, wagon or on horseback. At times when I thought, "My life is over, I have nothing left to do", I thought of David-Néel, who, even when many many years older than I was, continued a full engagement with life and with adventure, writing and research. She famously continued to renew her passport until she was 100 years old. She died in 1969 aged 101.

There have been so many other stories: there are diaries, travel journals, stories of time spent in nature or in mental institutions, there are accounts of spiritual

---

1. As I was writing this chapter, I wrote to Wilby to express my gratitude and included the section of this chapter in which I mention her. I was thrilled to receive a reply which in part read: "I'm absolutely floored by what you've written and totally humbled to know my early adventures had an impact on your life ... I hope you continue to find your zen in every step - forward or back - on the path you have laid before you! And yeah - don't forget to stop and smell the roses - literal and figurative!" Yes.

or personal unfolding, stories of lives lived through war or political turbulence, there are stories of desperate illnesses and of dying. They fill my bookshelves and their words and accompanying images fill my storehouse of inner wealth.

There is such power in a very good story read at just the right time.

***

the stories that encircle

The first time I became aware of how a story can encircle, limit and even cause harm, was very early in my journey.

It was a time when I was suffering greatly; anxiety and panic attacks were increasingly crippling my ability to function. I went to my doctor for advice and she recommended I see a psychiatrist. I didn't want to see a psychiatrist, but at that time I wasn't aware of any other healing modalities and so assumed it was my only option.

I recall sitting rigidly on a shiny black-plastic chair in the psychiatrist's office. After initial introductions, he asked about my life: my family history, childhood, relationships, sleep patterns, thoughts about living, feelings, work history, plans for the future, my panic attacks and my anxiety. He took a long time and wrote detailed and careful notes as he went. As he did so, I slowly relaxed back into my chair with relief; I felt listened to and cared for. I was certain that by taking all of my life into account in this way, he would be able to uncover the deeper meaning of my suffering. I felt hope rising out of what had previously been deep distress. I was confident that things were going to be okay.

When he finished his questions, he glanced thoughtfully through his notes and then sat quietly for a moment. He then looked across at me and said, "Taking into account everything you've told me, it is clear to me that you are suffering from depression. You have a chemical imbalance in your brain and we can prescribe anti-depressants for that." I can still hear those words coming out of his mouth and I can still feel the effect they had: I was gutted, stunned, I struggled to breathe. It truly was one of the most damning, demeaning and shattering moments of my life.

We tend not to think of psychiatry or for that matter, medicine, New Age healing, Cognitive Behavioral Therapy, aromatherapy, herbal medicine or acupuncture[2] as stories. But on one level, that is exactly what they are.

---

2. This list is not exhaustive.

All theories, systems, cults, philosophies, sciences, jargons, and even spiritual teachings, are stories.

Each practitioner is a specialist of their own 'story': they learn the words, learn the ins-and-outs of the plot and learn the role of the characters (human beings/patients/clients). Each story is only specific to its own framework; a psychiatrist would never use the words of aromatherapy, a doctor would never use the words of New Age energetic healing.

My psychiatrist's task was not to listen to my feelings and thoughts, it wasn't to look at my life as a whole, it wasn't to attempt to heal the traumas of my life or to bring the light of understanding into my world of suffering. His task was merely to account for my suffering within the jargon, diagnostic categories and terminology of his 'story'; only words like 'diagnosis', 'neurotransmitters', 'Generalized Anxiety Disorder', 'Clinical Depression', or 'anti-depressants' were in any way useful or valid. By accounting for me within that circle of words, he believed he had explained what my suffering actually was: a chemical imbalance in my brain. And he believed that he had the cure: antidepressants.

By the breadth of his questioning I had assumed that the psychiatrist was relating to me *as a whole person*. I had shared many aspects of my life that were painful, hidden and intimate and I had expected that he would use that information to come to an informed understanding of my suffering. When I realized that he had only been listening to me within the framework of what he wanted to hear, I felt humiliated, reduced and even dehumanized. I felt as if I had been made a fool.[3]

At a time in my life when I had very little sense of who I was and even less of the fact that I might be a person of value, it felt as though any remaining self-worth I may have had was stripped from me. Within the 'story' of psychiatry I wasn't a human being and my suffering had nothing whatsoever to do with a meaningful expression of my humanity and history. I was merely a defective skin-bag of blood and bones and brain. Nothing else mattered. *I* didn't matter.

I returned home feeling confused and defeated. I took his anti-depressants for a little while, but the hazy blur of side effects stripped me even further of any sense of self I might have had. Previously I had not been overly depressed, but

---

3. After that visit the one thing that replayed itself over and over in my mind, was the fact that I had told the psychiatrist how much I loved my partner. I had spoken to him from a place of tenderness and intimacy, thinking that in his overview of my life, he might care to know something that was of such importance to me. When I realized that this was not the case, I felt that something sacred within me had been violated.

now I lost all will to live. Day after day I lay in bed: "What's the use?" My life was already difficult but now it had been made substantially more so.

And yet, amidst the mire, there was the tiniest glimmer of hope: I knew the psychiatrist was wrong.

ooo

I don't for one moment believe that psychiatrists, doctors or healers of any persuasion, leave for work in the morning with the intention of harming people; I think the opposite is very much the case. But it is also the case that over and over, in my search for answers and healing, I found myself in situations such as the one above in which I came away feeling narrowed and distressed.

For me, healing has entailed a gradual process of inclusion; it is a deepening, a broadening and an opening into *all* that I am. It is a process that asked of me an exceptional degree of honesty, vulnerability, resilience, courage and sincerity. Understanding and peace were hard-won, although in the end, utterly worth it. To then come up against the storylines of medicine and psychiatry[4], which reduce the human *being*, its healing processes and its profound spiritual depth, to the human *body*, was extraordinarily painful.

There was nothing whatsoever in their languaging that could allow me to account for the processes I was living; there was nothing that could have given me any traction to account for my value or worth. Whether it be my unswerving sincerity or my distress, within their storylines these were at best irrelevant or at worst, symptoms of a 'disorder'.

Ultimately, it became a very important part of my healing to understand that their stories are just stories, and not an incontrovertible truth of which I necessarily had to partake.[5]

It was also vital for me to not allow myself to be defined or labelled within their storylines. If I needed their help, I certainly asked for it, but I learnt never to expect that their help would come from anywhere but within the parameters of their narrative.

---

4. Although I use medicine and psychiatry here as examples, there are many others.
5. I feel that this is particularly important considering that our society, our media and even our government is becoming increasingly medicalized, and that pharmaceutical companies (Big Pharma) wield ever-increasing power.

Over time I also learnt to be very specific and very careful with what I shared and what I didn't. If I needed to hide my feelings or needed to appear one-dimensional for a time, then I did so. If I had to be a little 'creative' in order to get what I needed, then I did that as well. But nonetheless, those interactions were never easy, and to this day they remain, to some extent, challenging.

But it also taught me something else: that the sign of the truest healer, or the truest philosophy, or the truest path, regardless of which field (or storybook) they come from, is the one that above all, values *YOU*. It is vital to find that person or that healer who above all, *believes* in you, *values* you and acknowledges the profound Knowing, meaning, depth and validity that *you* have within.[6]

It is only when we find our true identity in Spirit that stories collapse altogether, but from time to time, we will still need to see a doctor, an acupuncturist or a naturopath.

And here I sit writing a book, and that too is a story. Hopefully it is a useful one, but it is a story nonetheless.

***

the stories we tell ourselves

What stories do we tell ourselves? What stories do we choose to believe? Which stories will trap us? Or trap others?

journal 2001

On the weekend, I shared my plans for my flute book with a friend. She was very negative about my ideas and the prospects of getting such a book published. I have so many ideas but when I share them, I let people shatter them to pieces. Why do I even bother thinking that I can write a flute book? I'm always trying to please everyone. I'm always trying to be good. Good girls will never be able to do anything. I won't ever be able to move. I won't ever do anything with my life if I'm trying to fucking please everyone. "Stupid, stupid, stupid", is pounding through my head. I am stupid. I am worthless. I don't belong in this world.

So often we live our lives by virtue of a story in our mind.

---

6. Also see chapter, *Therapists and Teachers*.

The story that I am worthless and stupid has reverberated through my life in one form or another for a very long time. Most of us probably carry some version of this story.[7] We damn ourselves, we get in our own way, and then as I did in this case, we spiral down into self-loathing and thoughts of suicide. But as we do so, we ignore the reality of what we actually have in front of us in this very moment. If the same incident happened now, I might be a little curious and nonplussed by my friend's negativity, but I would recognize that this negativity was part of *her* story, not mine, and I would trust my impulse to write a book.

As an aside, this story proved to have no validity. Only a couple of years after writing the above journal entry, my flute book was published with relative ease, and shortly after, it was included in the Australian Music Examinations Board syllabus. I lost touch with my friend.

But the stories I might tell myself are everywhere:

I might tell myself a story about an acquaintance I meet on the street: "He's so grouchy and not very happy to see me!" But perhaps the reality is that he has recently lost a dear friend.

I might tell myself a story about my partner's bad mood: "She's so angry with me!" But perhaps the reality is that she has a bad headache and doesn't want to bother me by mentioning it.

As I increasingly moved to a place of Truth, this sort of storytelling lost its power. My everyday self, with its needs, desires and demands, was increasingly taken out of the equation. I was no longer worrying so much about how the events in my life affected 'me'. More and more I simply noticed what was in front of me without any need to tell a story about it: here was a friend who looked sad, here was a partner who appeared troubled. Without a story I could simply be present for my friend and I could feel compassion for my partner.

I recall an occasion when an old acquaintance from interstate dropped by unexpectedly. At the time I was in the middle of a seven-day meditation retreat but my partner contacted me, told me of his arrival and asked if I wanted to meet with him. My history with this man had been a difficult one. In the past he had often been demanding and argumentative far beyond what was necessary or reasonable, and frankly I hadn't expected to ever see him again. However, now he was here and he wanted to see me.

---

7. Also see the chapter *What if there is nothing wrong with me?*

I doubted anything had changed between us, but decided to come out of the retreat and meet with him in his hotel room. From the moment I sat down with him, I was stunned to realize that the story of our history, the story of how testing any interaction with him could be, even any story about how I would rather be meditating than meet with him, was simply *not there*.

It wasn't that I tried hard to be nice, or tried valiantly to make the stories disappear, they simply *did not exist*. All that existed was what was happening in front of me: here was man and I was sitting with him in his hotel room making polite conversation while we drank tea. That was it. No stories. No mental overlay. No dramas. No angst. He still wasn't someone with whom I would have chosen to meet regularly, but that was just fine. I sat with him for an hour and then made my way back to the retreat.

***

the longing for home

Do you want to go Home?
Do you want to be at Home?
Come walk with me,
Come walk in this field we call 'life'.
Home is closer than you can possibly imagine.

***

we are not at Home

We know we are not at Home. Somehow we simply know it. Or I certainly did.

At some point we have been cast adrift. We have been forced to leave. We had no option. We had no choice in the matter. We had to survive.

When did it happen? When were we cast adrift?

Was it at the moment of our birth? Was it the moment we realized we had feelings and thoughts that were different from everyone else? Was it the moment we were told we were bad? Was it the moment we decided it was necessary to be what everyone else wanted us to be?

When was it? When were we cast adrift?

In my most suffered times, when death truly seemed the only option, the cry that emanated seemingly unwilled from deep in my soul was: "I want to go Home! Please, please let me go Home."[1]

---

1. Throughout this book I have capitalized the word Home, when I refer to our true Home in Spirit as opposed to a physical home/house. Although in some places in this chapter the sense of 'home' was as yet undefined, I have still chosen to use upper case, Home, as it proved too confusing to do otherwise.

It was a primal cry, a cry that acknowledged that *somewhere*, somewhere, there was a place that I might call Home. I could feel it deep in my bones. I could feel it as my birthright. I could feel it as I stumbled around in bewilderment, tripping on the sharp rocks of my life and bloodying my knees and my heart. It was pulling me, calling me, "Come hold my hand. Come with me. Do not be afraid."

And I knew, that were I to unexpectedly stumble upon this place called Home, I would recognize it instantly, not because I'd visited it before, but because I had never been separate from it in the first place. From time eternal it had been always been mine.

When I was twelve years old I wrote a poem. I doubt its words were wholly mine. At that age I would not have been capable of such insight, and yet, I must have sensed that they contained a truth.

> If I were strong,
> Of mind,
> Of body,
> I would build a Home for me,
> That no one else could see.
> It would be solid
> And impenetrable.
> I'm not me now,
> But perhaps one day I can rebuild as I want,
> And then I can truly be me.

Isn't our greatest longing, the longing to simply go Home?

***

looking for Home in all the wrong places

Growing up I had a friend, Jennifer, whose life from the outside looked close to perfect.

She came from a wealthy and successful family, was gifted in sports and academics, and was well-liked and admired. She seemed to know what to say, how to act, and how to move. She wasn't awkward, puzzled and fearful as I was. As she grew into adulthood her life seemed to fall neatly into place: a successful career, a husband, a family, a beautiful house.

Our everyday self or ego has no clue what 'Home' might look like. It might, however, sense an underlying dissatisfaction, an emptiness, a feeling that the life one is currently living is a lie. And so in lieu of any better ideas or deeper understandings, we imagine that if only our lives looked a bit like that of Jennifer, we might feel a whole lot more comfortable. Replete. At Home.

In this perfect 'Jennifer' sort of life, we would want for nothing: our kids are lovely, our partner is perfect, our career is fabulous, we have our health, we have a great sex life, we have enough money, we have lots of friends, our family is supportive and everything goes along according to plan.

And so, some of us set about trying to create that ideal: we work hard so we have more money, we buy a new car or a new house, we urge ourselves to be a better person, we read self-help books, go to relaxation classes, we try to please everyone. We surround ourselves with busy-ness and industry. We imagine that there will be *something* we can do to make ourselves feel more at Home in the world. And as long as we're doing this 'something', we feel okay about life, because one day, *one day*, we imagine we'll have everything we want … and we'll finally be at peace.

For others, however, that ideal seems like an impossible task. We might truly *want* to feel comfortable, happy and complete, but when we look at our lives, it seems a hopeless cause: our car needs new brakes, the roof is leaking, our knees are wretched, we never have enough money, we are cranky and miserable, and our teenage daughter has just presented us with a tattoo of her boyfriend's name emblazoned across her chest. It's all too hard. We'll never be at rest in this world. And what does it matter anyway? There's nothing else beyond this everyday sort of life, is there? Perhaps we'll just have another drink, play another computer game, watch another hour of TV. Pass the time.

Do we ever consider that the Home we're looking for, or the Home we've given up on, might not be where we think it is? Could we be looking for Home in all the wrong places?

***

tastes of Home

Throughout the years I have been given many tastes of Home. These tastes were never willed and could never have been concocted by the mind. As if by grace, I simply fell into them. And each and every time, in instant and joyous recognition I knew, "This is Home".

The first experiences I had of that distinctive feeling that I came to know as 'Home', were spontaneous but brief openings into peace.

Typically these occurred as I sat or wandered in the tranquility of nature and felt no need for my experience to be any different than it was. To outward appearances nothing changed, the world 'out there' was still exactly the same, but in my inner world, everything was different: *this* moment, here and now, felt whole and complete. It was as though in the simplicity and openness of nature I was remembered momentarily into my own essential simplicity and openness.

journal 1988

> *When I am here with the sun and the birds, sitting under the yellow umbrella in the backyard I am content. There is a wordless space that feels so whole and peaceful.*

Undoubtedly we have all had these moments, but often, without a deeper context or understanding, our mind steps in to interpret them: we might see them as a brief relaxing respite from the hassles of everyday life, we might cling onto them as a yardstick of our specialness or spiritual prowess, or as I did, we might minimize or dismiss them.

Even when my spiritual search became conscious, I remained oblivious as to what that sense of peace and wholeness was actually showing me; in its simplicity I believed it was in no way relevant to my search for an end to my suffering. I certainly didn't recognize that it might be possible to deepen immeasurably into its mystery and eventually live from its depths.

One of the defining qualities of the experience of 'Home' is its timelessness; it feels as though it could go on forever. Each time I dropped into its peace, I assumed that from that moment forward I would no longer suffer and life would now move along smoothly.

journal 1989

When I am loving the trees and the plants everything makes sense. I can really BE. Certainly there are still some trials and traumas, but I come through them now and I know that this space is always there for me. It is inside, and I know that I shall keep it with me forever.

On rereading my journal entries from around this time, I wince a little at the certainty with which I repeatedly declare that my struggles are now over. In hindsight I recognize that this assumption was not surprising; I was being given a short glimpse into the Infinite, and as is the nature of the Infinite, it definitely *does* go on forever. From the Infinite, we can only see the Infinite and so there is no doubt that it will always be accessible. But at that time I did not question *why* it was that I believed my suffering was now over; I did not understand its meaning.

However, as time passed, I came to resent the extremes of contrast between the short episodes of profound peace and the often months-long periods of distress and suffering. It was painful and confusing to return, over and over, to anguish and suicidality.

journal 1990

I relish this feeling of sitting with the parrots in the trees, the sun shining and a cool breeze. It is a feeling of completeness. I know there is nothing that is more important than this, but often now I find myself avoiding it. There is such an intensity in my experience of this completeness and it becomes increasingly disheartening and painful to come back to the real world. It is too much.

Brief tastes of peace did not magically wipe away my pain and the wounds of my past; I wasn't being given a get-out-of-life-free card. Rather, I realized that I was being called to look ever more deeply into the nature of my suffering. And so I began to question: Why did my peace so rapidly give way to torment? Why was I suffering so much?

I started to wonder if there was a 'whole picture' that might include both my suffering and my peace. Increasingly it was the only way of looking at life that made any sense to me.

journal 1990

There must be a way of living my life with the <u>whole</u> person in view – a way of life that takes ALL into account. How else is it possible for me to be whole? Increasingly it seems that to be whole, I must live with the whole and be that whole. Is that possible? Perhaps it is only ever possible to be part of that whole – no, I think it must be possible to enter into the wholeness ... but how do I do that? How do I include it all?

The only setting in which I found mention of this 'wholeness' was in the words of spirituality. But the bigger-than-life stories I read about in spiritual books didn't seem to match, in any way, my very ordinary life and its humble little openings into peace. Enlightenment, out-of-body experiences, Indian sages and channeled higher beings made for interesting reading, but I dismissed them all as having little relevance to me.

I longed for wholeness but didn't know how to piece all the bits together.

ooo

As time went on my experiences of Home expanded beyond the uncomplicated peace of sunshine and nature.

One day as I was concentrating intently on driving a steep and very winding road nearby, I spontaneously opened out into a world of extraordinarily blissful wholeness that was beyond the road, and the car and the driving, but that included it all. What was I seeing? What was I knowing?

Another time, friends from interstate had just arrived to stay with us, when I received a phone call that my partner had been injured at work and taken to hospital with a suspected broken shoulder. I raced to the hospital worried about my partner, but also worried about how I was going to play hostess to our house guests while at the same time tending to the needs of a partner with a broken shoulder.

I recall sitting overwrought in the hospital waiting room with thoughts racing through my mind: "How serious are my partner's injuries? Why are they taking so long over the x-rays? How am I going to get through the next week?" All of a sudden, I expanded back into a place of rightness, wholeness and peace. I was taking part in exactly the same scene of life as a few moments before, but now I knew without a doubt that I was held in a far bigger reality. A hospital waiting room and anxiety felt like Home. House guests and a partner with a broken shoulder felt like Home. And from that Home I had the unshakeable knowing that it would all turn out just fine.

There were also times I was brought to an even deeper place, that although seemingly beyond this everyday world, I still instantly recognized as Home.

journal 2005

I woke in the middle of the night with a quality that is very hard to describe – all at once the most all-encompassing compassion, awareness of all suffering and loss, and yet abidingness within that. After a while I felt immense surges of energy roaring up through my body, twisting, writhing and at times acutely painful. It was black. It was electric, extraordinarily powerful. I wondered whether it was some sort of kundalini experience but I am not sure, because I don't know enough about such things. I got up and walked around but the experience did not abate, so I went back to bed. After a while I was exhausted and this rising 'stuff' just didn't stop, so I decided to go down into it, while it was rising up. I used the pathway of its upward motion to follow it back to its source … and I could do so quite easily … and here was a blackness that was Home. My Home. Warm beyond all belief. Exquisite.

I found these 'spiritual experiences' interesting, but I continued to minimize what I was being shown.

Although I had approached spirituality in many different ways and from many different angles, I still did not have an all-encompassing context for understanding them; I had not found an explanation that was completely satisfying. What was this 'bigger reality' I was experiencing? And why, when I frequently expanded into extraordinary peace, was I still catapulted back into such immense suffering?

My longing for Home was now in earnest.

ooo

Then at some point early in 2008, life circumstances brought me once again face-to-face with a pocket of deep anguish. I was dismayed that even after all the work I had done and all the insight I had gained, I still found myself in a place of such distress. I knew I needed help and sought out a counsellor.

The counsellor was helpful with the issue at hand and it was quickly resolved. However, off to one side, a rather interesting subplot was taking place. With increasing queasiness I heard myself recounting the same details of my life as I had recited to other therapists, I heard myself using almost identical words, and I realized I was thoroughly sick and tired of myself. I was fed up with my suffering, my stories and my search. It felt like boring, mind-numbing, tedious and repetitive drivel. I knew I could not keep repeating the same material over and over and over. I'd had enough of it all. Completely and utterly enough.

Then one night a couple of days later, while having a hot bath, in utter exasperation I pleaded, "How do I stop this? Please God, how do I stop this? I am so tired of it! *Please* God, give me a break! Give me a break!" And then all of a sudden, it was as though God really *did* give me a break. He broke me open.

Parading in a line in front of me, I saw all the identities I had ever been: the fearful child, the searcher, the nature lover, the young woman in desperate pain, the woman who wanted to kill herself. I saw all my patterns of behavior through the years: the words, the tears, the defenses, the dissociations, the contractions, even the most subtle hand or eye movements. And I felt how each of them was held in my body with its own particular bearing and its own unique awareness. And in that instant I knew without a doubt that I was none of them and never had been.

It was a profound experience but I didn't yet grasp its full significance; I didn't yet understand what it was showing me.

Then, one morning, a few days later, I spontaneously 'awoke'. One moment I was sitting at the computer checking my emails and then the next moment it was as though the tightly held contraction of thoughts, feelings and history that I had always assumed was somehow 'me', simply let go and I awoke into the vastness of Consciousness as the reality of what I am. It was the Home for which I had always been longing. Quite literally, '*I*' was Home.[2]

***

---

2. I describe the awakening itself and also its significance, much more fully in the preface and in other parts of the book.

48

flatland and the dilemma of 'normality'

Oh to be 'normal'!

I would have loved to look normal, fit in with normal people, say normal things, think normal things, write normal things, do normal things. Normal. Normal. Normal.

Normality would have been so good ... wouldn't it?

For how many people, is 'normality' a struggle, a question, a burden?

***

flatland

Many years ago, I read a book called *Grace and Grit*. It was written by Ken Wilber[1] and describes the journey through his wife Treya's illness, their search for healing, and then finally her death.

Inside the cover I had carefully printed my name and then underneath, "March to May 1995". It was a book that was well worth the three months I took to read it. Not only was it one of the most moving books I have ever read, it also greatly informed my journey into spirit and depth. There were many times I had to put the book down and take a few deep breaths.

After I finished reading it, I was eager to explore more of Ken Wilber's work.

---

1. Ken Wilber is an American writer, theorist and philosopher who has written widely on spirituality, philosophy, ecology, psychology, and mysticism. He formulated Integral Theory, which was an attempt at a 'theory of everything'. In including as many different viewpoints as possible, including those of Eastern religious traditions and Western psychological development, he hoped to integrate the enormous breadth of human knowledge, experience and thought into a single, coherent system.

It was a thought-provoking exploration and I learnt a great deal, and yet I felt mostly uninspired and occasionally irked.

One of the most boring Sunday afternoons I ever spent was at a talk on Wilber's Integral Theory. After four hours of quadrants, holons, lines, levels, exterior, interior, collective, individual, I walked out the door into a pre-dusk light and was transfixed by its simple beauty. I was so grateful that the glorious teeming abundance of life remained intact despite the afternoon's attempts to map and contain it. Wilber's map of life may have been extraordinarily vast and clever, but it was a *map* nonetheless. I realized that the terrain of life could never be reduced to an ordered sum of its parts. For me, life was *already* whole and it was up to me to *uncover* that truth, not to try to construct it. Life was *already* meaningful and meant.

But somewhere in my reading, I did come across something I found valuable: Wilber's term, 'flatland'.[2] I doubt that I fully understood the complexity of Wilber's use of this word, but I still found it an enormously useful term.

'Flatland' gave a word to something over which I had puzzled and fretted for much of my life.

Our society, in many respects, is a flatland world. Flatland denotes the surface of life, the exterior, the horizontal plane. In Flatland it is assumed that there is only one playing field of life: the flatland playing field. Just as a fish in a pond could never conceive of a bird flying in the sky, so flatlanders cannot conceive that there might be another way to live or other things to know. It is assumed that flatland is "just the way things are".

In flatland the observable, the tangible, and the material are valued.[3] In flatland the human *being* is reduced to the human body, and suffering is reduced to illness. In flatland there is a horizontal gathering of bigger, better and busier experiences: new fashion, overseas travel, the latest gadgets, new lovers, spiritual highs. As long as there is a constant and excited movement over the surface, flatlanders feel that life is meaningful.

---

2. Later I discovered that the term 'flatland' predated Wilber by a century or so. An English schoolmaster and theologian, Edwin Abbott Abbott, had written a novella, *Flatland*, in 1884.

3. For the purposes of this chapter, I am writing about flatland in black-and-white terms ie. I am opposing flatland to a 'land' of depth. I have no doubt, however, that most people live on a continuum somewhere between those extremes, and feel the dilemma of 'normality' to a greater or lesser extent.

In flatland there is virtually no understanding or languaging of depth, or for the processes through which one might descend into and inhabit that depth. In flatland 'conformity' and 'normality' are the bywords. In flatland, 'difference' is seen as a threat, a strange thing, an evil thing, an abnormality, a disease. In flatland 'difference' must be reduced, eradicated, belittled, fought, punished or medicated.

I came to realize, that as much as I lived in a flatland world, I was one of the 'different' ones. I was different from the very first day I came out of my mother's womb. I was different in my family. I was different at school. I was different at university. I was different when I played tennis. I was different at dinner parties.

That difference was sometimes hinted at in other people's words: "you're too sensitive", "you're too clever", "you're too deep", "you're too intense", "you get too upset", "you're too difficult", "you're eccentric", "what's wrong with you?", "why don't you just try and fit in?" At other times that difference was inferred by a charged silence, a look of puzzlement, a tone of judgement and also by violence.

It seemed that when I was just being myself, I would always be a 'problem' for flatland. And yet for many years I really didn't understand why. Because the fact was, I never *wanted* to be different and I never *tried* to be different. I *wanted* to fit in and I *tried* to fit in. I *wanted* to be able to say the right things at the right times. I wanted to move my body just like everyone else. I *wanted* to laugh and chat with the effortless ease of the in-crowd. I *wanted* to be embraced with unconditional acceptance and love by my family.

But my attempts would always be in vain. I might have walked around in flatland, I might have been able to see the world of flatland all around me, I might have looked exactly the same as any other flatlander, but I *wasn't* a flatlander and nothing I could do would ever make me into one.

From day one, my world was *not* flat.

The landscape in which I lived was immeasurably varied.[4] It was rich, finely tuned, and full of tones, textures and qualities. I sensed shapes and edges and furrows. I delved into depths and soared with the birds. I drank in the consolation of solitude and of nature and of art. I loved stillness and peace. I reveled in the simple innocence of animals. I touched a tree and I saw its light. I rejoiced and wept as my boots trod ageless desert tracks. I sensed the inner fire or inner ice of those around me. I watched before me as the world joined

---

4. Also see chapter *Soul*.

as one, a flower no different to a cloud or to a chair or to a feeling. It was a world and a language I understood. Within it was contained the very essence of all that I truly felt myself to be. In my senses and in my sensing, in my soul, in Spirit, in my touch and in my Knowing, in Truth and in Beauty and in Love, my world was *deep*. Deep.

I tried my very best to live in flatland. I learnt to speak their languages and kept the deeper reality of my life carefully hidden, but such a life could only ever be one of oscillation and impasse. I assumed that one day I would eventually make a comfortable-enough home in flatland, but in speaking and acting to the flatland scripts, the words that came from my lips were hollow and my performances always paper-thin.

Would it ever be possible to live from depth in a flatland world? I held that question for many many years.

The following poem was written at a time when I felt the dilemma of living in two worlds was killing me. Even after awakening, when I knew my entire life as that of Spirit and Depth, I was still trying to 'fit in' with flatland and be a 'good-enough' flatland person. The poem is addressed to God.

> All my life I have searched for You,
> Yearned for You.
>
> Without You, I had felt death stalking me.
> My soul dying. My body dying.
>
> And now You are here.
> Through me. Inside me.
> Never having left me.
> Never having abandoned me.
>
> So why do I not proclaim my love for You
> Openly?
> Why do I not shout my joy
> To all who come near?
> What am I waiting for?
>
> Am I sparing them the discomfort?
> Or myself?
> Did I hope to mold You and shape You

Into an acceptable presence?
Amenable. Comfortable. Conforming.
Did I hope somehow to fit You in
Quietly,
Too quietly,
Into our stiflingly normal daydream world?
How could I ever have imagined that
Your vastness and Truth could be contained?
How could I ever have imagined that
I could squeeze You
Into this narrow plane of surface life?

One day, I was sitting alone on my favorite bench at a local park. In the distance I watched a dog running after a ball and a child playing on a scooter. Then all of a sudden I knew that I could not go on living that dilemma for another moment. It was too painful. Too difficult. I had tried doggedly for so much of my life to bring the two worlds together and it had proved to be an impossible task.

Out loud, and to no-one in particular, I announced, "I can't do it anymore. I *really* can't do it. I've tried all my life and I've had enough. I've *really* had enough. I give up. *I give up!*" And seemingly by admitting my defeat and articulating my surrender, I had stepped out of the dilemma I had believed was inescapable.[5]

I realized I had indeed given myself an impossible task. It can never be done. It *really* can never be done. The gap between flatland and my world of depth can never be bridged, fixed, resolved or 'made better'. There is *no* solution to the dilemma of 'normality' because Spirit and Depth cannot be contained within flatland. Rather, it is flatland that is contained within Spirit and Depth.

Spirit doesn't deny flatland, it doesn't brush it away with clever spiritual words or a swipe of God's almighty hand, it just understands that it is one small part of the infinite and glorious whole.

***

---

5. Although I chose not to give it a separate chapter, this episode illustrates an aspect of my journey that I call 'the path of failure'. At times it was simply in the act of 'wearing something out', of trying over and over and over to 'make something happen' but never succeeding, that it would spontaneously open or surrender into a bigger picture.

out of body, acrylic

I painted this canvas at a time when I felt overwhelmed by the flatland world. I had spent several weeks living in inner-city Melbourne and felt as though I was dissolving in its all-pervasive clamor. I longed for stillness, bush paths, trees and deep rich earth. I longed for a rootedness in depth.

***

beyond flatland healing[6]

For many years my question has been: How do I seek help and healing in a world in which the majority of counsellors, therapists, psychologists, psychiatrists and doctors are flatlanders?

When I have a nail through my foot, a ruptured appendix or a broken arm, the answer is easy: a physical injury requires a physical (or surface) solution.

But if my heart is breaking, if my sensitivity feels like a curse rather than a blessing, if a lump of grief from my childhood is caught in my throat and defies all my attempts to cough it free, if a wretched fear courses through my veins,

---

6. For further discussion see the chapters *Stories* and also *Therapists and Teachers*.

then how will I find that person who can offer me more than just a surface solution: anti-depressants, behavior modification, throat lozenges, blood thinners? Where will I find that person who can meet me in the depths of my soul, hold me and then set me free?

As I looked for psychological or emotional healing I always sought out those who had a spiritual dimension to their work. For some this was only an added-on and little-understood extra, but for others it was a profound underpinning to their personal as well as professional lives.

When first making contact with a practitioner, I asked not only about their practice and training, but also about their relationship to depth and to spirituality. A practitioner's capacity to meet me and be met on the fundamental level of Spirit I found essential for healing. It is True Nature that is the ultimate healer.

In seeking help from the mainstream medical profession a query as to their spiritual orientation was generally not practicable and indeed, usually inappropriate. In going forward with treatment, I found it vital to recognize that the care received would be on a surface/observable level (i.e. symptom relief, bandaging, excision) and not to expect otherwise. There were many times when this level of care was entirely appropriate or a necessary step in a process of exclusion. However, there were also many times when treatment left me feeling invalidated, uncomfortable, objectified, traumatized or even sicker.

Particularly when approaching the mainstream medical world, but also *any* practitioner I didn't know, I found it vital to be vigilant and cautious, to remain guided by my intuition, to take control if needed, to ask questions and most importantly, to listen to myself[7]: Is this what I need right now? Is this treatment working for me or do I need to go elsewhere? Is this doctor/counsellor actually listening to me? Am I being met on the level on which I need to be met? Frequently, that process was a wearing and laborious one. Unfortunately I have never found an easy solution and there continue to be times when I come away feeling uncomfortable or reduced.

As we seek treatment or help it is essential for each of us determine for ourselves what is 'right': will flatland healing suffice, or is it necessary to move beyond the surface and look more deeply? We are multi-faceted beings.

***

---

7. Also see chapter *Listening*.

exiles from flatland

So often I hear of people who suffer, people who are tormented, people who find it "hard to be on this planet".

An acquaintance tells me about his adult daughter who is depressed and is withdrawing from life; she is "too sensitive" to deal with the demands of earning a living. A friend tells me about her nineteen-year-old son who is "so talented" and yet has no friends and struggles to live in the everyday world.

After listening to their stories I frequently ask, "What is your son/daughter like? What sort of person are they? Are they deep?" And each and every time, the answer that comes back is something along the lines of, "Oh yes! Very deep. She's certainly much deeper than I am. She thinks a lot. Perhaps she thinks too much. She worries so much about the state of the environment and cares so much about other people. She's so sensitive. She's so lovely. But she's so depressed. So miserable. I can't understand it. The doctor has given her anti-depressants."

When I hear these stories I wonder, are these the people who don't fit into flatland? Are these the exiles? Are these the souls, who just like me, are different? And I wonder, how many people are out there, how many people are reading these words, who live lives of quiet desperation, suffering their sensitivity, their creativity, their intelligence and their depth, because our society values only the surface of life? And I wonder how many out there feel that their only option is to seek out a flatland cure, the sole purpose of which is to bring them back into the 'normality' of the flatland fold, so that they can partake of the world which sent them mad in the first place?

For many, 'normality' is not only a dilemma, it can all too easily become a living death.

***

suicide

Why am I still alive, when so many are not? Why didn't I kill myself when so often I desperately wanted to?[1]

***

journal entry 1993

I can't stand being alive. The only thing that goes through my head is that I want to die. I feel like bashing my head in over and over. What's wrong with me? What's wrong with me? Why is this my life??? Why??? I am so scared. I am so very very scared. I am a pathetic attempt at a human being. I'd be better off dead.

***

the darkest day, lived till tomorrow

In my book *Seventeen Voices*, Eva starts her interview with a quote by 18th century English poet, William Cowper: "Beware of desperate steps; the darkest day lived till tomorrow, will have passed away." It is a wonderful quote. I have lived my own particular version of it many times over.

When I was desperately suffering, it was the period just after going to bed that was most difficult.

---

1. Beyond the material in this chapter I discuss suicide and feelings of desperation in a number of other chapters. For a discussion of the power of art and writing both in my healing and as a way of moving through suicidal feelings, see the chapter *Creativity*. Also see the chapter *Beyond the Battle* for a discussion of the power of poetry, art, journaling and writing as means for moving into an engagement with current experience, which includes that of suicidal desperation. I also found it enormously valuable to see episodes of suicidality within the larger context of a journey; for further discussion see *The Journey*.

As soon as I put my head on the pillow it was as though the floodgates of hell opened. Swirling thoughts and feelings surged in. I was taunted by merciless self-admonishments for the day that had been and filled with fear at the day to come.

Many times, the only thing that kept me going was the knowledge that if I just stayed alive through those very darkest of hours and managed to sleep for even a couple of minutes, I would inevitably wake up with a new perspective on life. Lying in the fetal position, tears streaming down my face, throat rasped raw from bawling, I would repeat to myself, "If you just stay alive until tomorrow, things will be different. If you just stay alive, things will have changed." Sometimes that change was only very subtle, but it was there nonetheless. And it was there each and every time.

As much as we might sometimes wish it to be otherwise, change is the very fabric of the universe. Everything is change. Life is change. Our bodies are change. Our thoughts and feelings are change. Moment-to-moment is change. And we don't need to *do* anything for that change to happen.

We might feel annoyed that our enjoyable times change into difficult ones, but those difficult times will just as surely transform back into joy.

I learnt that the intensity of my suffering was often directly proportional to the degree to which I clung onto either difficulty or ease. It was when I tried to force life to go the way I wanted it to, that I froze myself into a tight-fisted ball of torment. There were times, even though I woke up feeling refreshed and renewed, that I would remember myself back into the anguished thoughts of the previous day and once again find myself caught in the web of their cruel misery. There were also times when I felt well and content, that in my almost frantic desire to 'stay happy', I created the very despair that I was trying to avoid.

Over time, I learnt to trust that feelings and thoughts (including those of suicide) inevitably change. In doing so I was able to align myself more and more with the natural movement of life … its ebb, its flow, its rise, its release.[2]

***

---

2. For a diary of this natural flow of life, see the section *Music Informs Life – the Glorious Symphonic Composition* in the chapter *Life*.

the embrace of Spirit

From the time I was very young I had the sense that the world of outer appearances wasn't the whole story; I felt that something bigger and deeper was going on. At times this was a very lonely position to hold; the people around me and society at large seemed disinterested in this depth.

However, it was this sense of bigger-and-deeper that on many occasions kept me alive.

Even when filled with the most intense thoughts of suicide, a faint but irritatingly persistent voice would rise up above my despair: "If you kill yourself you'll never find out if there actually *is* something deeper going on, will you! What if you kill yourself and there *really* is a place of depth and wholeness and peace and freedom? And what if you miss out on that? What if? What if? Do you really want to take that chance? Do you?"

And the reality was, that I *didn't* want to take that chance. I truly *did* want to know what it was all about. I didn't want to kill myself, only to look down afterwards from some otherworldly abode, and think, "Damn! I was on the right track after all!"

Eventually this bigger-and-deeper became the knowing that essentially we are *all* spiritual beings. Spirit is our Home and we are held in the embrace of its depth. We swim in that depth, we are immersed through and through by it.

I know that depth when I am in pain, I know it when I am walking the dog, I know it when I am cooking dinner. That knowing is not confined to an elite few, the best-of-the-best, the most accomplished meditators or the most articulate religious scholars. It is the birthright of everyone. I wasn't special in any way. I wasn't particularly gifted. I suffered and spluttered and stuffed around like everyone else. People laughed at me, got angry with me, misunderstood me. But I continued doggedly on my path. I *wanted* to know, and I *wanted* to know with a passion.

The embrace of Spirit isn't something that disintegrates the moment life isn't going so well. Holding and support are there all the time, even if we might only sense it in the vaguest of intuitions or in the fleeting flutter of a moment's grace.

We are held.

***

get some help

Often we carry within us, parts that have been hurt or traumatized.

These parts may be very young, very sensitive and very fragile. Particularly when confronted with situations that parallel the original injury, they may be unable to cope. Over the years I was able to heal these parts, but I needed help in order to do so.

When grappling with all that lay unhealed within, the pain was often intense and unbearable. Any extra demand from the outside world quickly overwhelmed me. There were times I felt I had no option but to kill myself. By the intensity of my distress, I learnt to recognize when I wasn't able work through my suffering on my own. At those times it was vital to acknowledge, not only that I needed help, but also that it was up to me to set about finding it. Nobody else was going to do that for me.

Sometimes that search for help was a laborious process and sometimes it was relatively easy.[3] But at all times it was important to be proactive, not only in finding the sort of help that was useful but also discarding that which wasn't. Some therapists or counsellors were quite clearly inexperienced when working with the complexities of traumatic injury and suicidal anguish. I came to value those therapists who themselves had come from a place of suffering and at some point had voluntarily undertaken their own therapy or personal work. Such an understanding was invaluable and could never have been acquired solely through an academic qualification or professional experience. Of a couple of therapists I even asked, "Have you ever thought of suicide?" I felt relief when the answer came back, "Yes".

When I was suicidal it was a very lonely place to be, so it was essential to have someone in my life who was genuinely able to listen. Most people find it hard to truly listen, and even more so when there is a mention of suffering, death or suicide. The fact of not being listened to can feel like deep rejection and can also lead to additional traumatization and despair.

I found therapy a profoundly important medium for that listening to take place. It was always immediately apparent to me if a therapist was capable of deep listening; there was something in their manner that spoke of acceptance, care, openness, lack of judgement, depth of understanding, and a capacity to

---

3. For a detailed discussion of finding a therapist, see the chapter *Therapists and Teachers*.

bear with me through my deepest pain. This sort of listening felt immediately healing, holding and validating.[4]

It was also immediately apparent if a therapist (or medical professional) was unable to listen or was merely using their listening skills as a technique for gathering the information that *they* wanted to hear. As damning as this at times felt, it was crucial for me to see this as *their* failing (or the failing of the professional framework within which they worked) and not in any way a reflection on my self-worth or grounds for falling into further self-loathing or self-destruction.

For me, a trusted therapist was a very powerful ally, mentor and spiritual midwife through the most tortured times.

***

"what is it within you that wants to die?"

I can't remember when I first heard this question. But I do remember that it pissed me off!

It sounded like one of those appallingly unhelpful comments that people make when you're feeling desperate or suicidal: "Do you think you might be overreacting?" "Why don't you do some gardening or make a cup of tea?" These comments come from a complete inability to understand the depths and reasons for pain.

In any case, the question, "What is it within you that wants to die?" stayed with me.

It had a vague ring of truth about it and I wondered if it had any validity. It certainly continued to piss me off from time to time, but over the years, I came to appreciate the insight it offered: when I felt suicidal it was often because there was a very young or 'ego' part that continued to confound or overwhelm me despite the fact that it was now a long way past its use-by date.

But I also realized why the question had pissed me off so much. It didn't address my pain and it didn't help me to distinguish which particular part it was that wanted to die. It also didn't address the fact that recognizing a part

---

4. See chapter, *Listening*.

as obsolete did nothing whatsoever to transform or heal that part; wanting something to die, did nothing to help it die. If anything, it only increased its power and my sense of helplessness in the face of it. On top of that, it denied the reality that this part may, once upon a time, have played a crucial role in my emotional or physical survival.[5]

And yet, where this question *was* helpful, was in the fact that it acknowledged that the desire to die might not necessarily be a desire for a *bodily* death and as such, the end of my life.

Our language is extraordinarily limited in conveying our very complex inner workings (see the section that follows), so when we feel a sense within of "I must die", our immediate assumption is that this dying must be that of the body.

But there are so many different sorts of dying: our thoughts die back into the place from which they came, this moment of my love dies into the fun that might follow it, boredom dies into interest, interest dies into boredom, loneliness dies into connection, this moment of the sunrise dies into the day, the day dies into the night, the defenses of my childhood die into the freedom of my adulthood, youthful skin dies into the wrinkles of middle age, peace dies into torment, torment dies back into peace, my sitting dies into my standing ... moment by moment we are dying ...

What is it within you that wants to die?

***

'wanting to die' – an exploration

There are a number of words in the English language for the actual act of killing oneself, 'suicide' of course being the most common. If I look up a thesaurus I can find a few others: self-murder, hara-kiri, self-destruction, self-immolation, self-slaughter, ending it all, topping oneself ...

But there is virtually no word or even understanding for the *feeling* of 'wanting to die'.

We simply assume that when someone says they want to die that it means they

---

5. To reflect deeply on such young parts, usually requires the mirroring and empathic holding of an experienced therapist. This sort of exploration is virtually impossible and often far too overwhelming to carry out on one's own.

wish to kill themselves. Even when we utter those words to ourselves, we think, "Yeah, I want to end it all, slash my wrists, take some pills, get it over and done with." And so, naturally enough, any mention of death or 'wanting to die' quickly becomes a *big* problem. We are looking the ultimate taboo in the face and in our panic and fear, we rarely consider that we might take the time to look a little closer.

What are we actually *feeling* when we say we want to die?

Reflecting back over my life I can see that there have been countless sorts of 'wanting to die':

> I am so tired and I long to rest.
> I don't have the skills to deal with the complexities of life and I want to run away.
> I find people's needs overwhelming and I wish everyone would disappear.
> I sense such emptiness within and I assume this means I am worthless and may as well die.
> The pain of childhood memories is unbearable and I don't have the skills to cope.
> I want to escape the voices from my past that harangue me mercilessly.
> I hate myself and can't stand to live with myself even for one more day.
> I am too sensitive/soft for this world and I don't belong.
> I can feel one stage of my life coming to an end and I can't yet see a way forward.

The piece that follows is an exploration of a particular sense of 'wanting to die'. It was a quiet voice, quite different from the desperation of the past. The process I describe took place over a couple of weeks and I made notes as I went along. Eventually I came to rest in my spiritual 'self'. I was still at least three years away from a full and lived understanding of that 'self' as my *true* self, but in retrospect I realize it was a powerful precursor of awakening nonetheless.

In sharing this piece I hope to show how we can consciously deepen into and follow a process such as this, but I also hope that it serves as an invitation to question the immediate assumptions we might make when we feel, "I want to die".

I want to die, 2005

I want to die. It's a familiar thought. *I want to die.*

I'm not crazed with desperation. I'm not about to fling myself off a cliff. I won't run my car into a brick wall. I won't swallow a bottle of pills.

No, this is much quieter.
As I walk the familiar pathways of my life, there is a simple and very quiet
I want to die.

I stand where I am.
I want to die.

I look around me at the pavement, the trees, the clouds.
They will continue on after I die. I will be gone but they will still be here.
What will that be like? To no longer be here?
I want to die.

But to say I want to die is a problem. *I want to die*. It is a problem.
Friends will be worried. Family will tell me to stop being silly. Doctors will give me pills.
Nobody will listen.
I want to die.

Perhaps I must listen to myself, because when I listen to myself,
I know that it isn't a problem to say such words.
I want to die.

I look inside. Reach inside. Listen inside. It is still there.
I want to die.

I listen in more closely. *I want to die*. I *feel* it. Tentatively. Around the edges.
It is an ache in my forehead. An ache in my belly. I allow the ache to simply be there.
I ask the question:
What are you aching for? What are you aching for?

I ask it many times and then softly softly the answer comes:
It is a longing. A longing for it all to stop. A longing for it all to end.
I want it all to stop. I want it all to end.

But what is it that I want to stop?
I don't know.
I ask the question again, letting it dwell within: What is it that I want to stop?
What is it?

The answer comes:

This. Here. Now. I want it all to stop. I want this life to stop.
This life. Not *my* life. *This* life.

I want this whole life to stop. I want this whole life to die.
I want this *doing* to stop. I want this *wanting* to stop.
This whole thing. I feel burdened by this life.
I am tired of it. I don't care about it. I don't want what everybody else wants.
I can't move in the ways that everybody else moves.
I don't see the point of all of *this*:
This chatter. *This* movement. *These* ups and downs. *This* pleasing.
This everyday life wants to die. It is so empty. It is so superficial.
But the only words I have for this are
I want to die.

Is there any other life?
I ask the question, feel the question: Is there any other life?
I whisper the question, plead the question, yearn the question:
Is there any other life?

Suddenly a space opens up inside. I feel that space. I *know* that space.
Tingles of recognition race through my body. The ache in my belly opens.
My eyes look inward and the ache in my forehead has gone.
This is *me*. This is *me*! This space. This open space. This is *my* life. This is my life.
It is more *me* than anything I could ever describe in words.
It is deep. Solid. Precious.

Does this *me* want to die?
No.

***

into the depths of despair

Regardless of the fact that over and over I had been shown quite the opposite, each and every time I felt suicidal, each and every time I dropped down into the pits of despair, I did not doubt that *this* time, *this* piece of suffering in my life, was a stupid, pointless, pathetic waste of time and energy that served no purpose whatsoever; I was useless, my life was useless, and this wretched suffering was useless.

And it makes sense that I thought this way; that voice is the voice of despair. The voice of despair is not an upbeat one. The voice of despair can only speak about the depths of despair.

But it is also the case that each and every time I was suicidal, each and every time I felt myself dragged down to the very limits of what I found bearable, that in some way I could never rationally account for, I would find myself breaking open, breaking through, breaking free, transforming, deepening, maturing.

It was in the depths of my despair that I found the depths of my humanity and my soul waiting for me. In those depths I found extraordinary insight. In those depths I found compassion and wisdom, peace and love and beauty. I found meaning. In those depths I found myself.

Where else could I have found depth, but in depth?[6]

***

talking about suicide

We are bombarded in the media by images of death, war and brutal murder, and yet it seems that it isn't all that acceptable to talk too much about our own inevitable death. On occasion I have asked other people, 'Do you think much about death?' Almost invariably, with a slightly queasy look in their eyes, they reply, 'No, not really.'

Suicide and death are uncomfortable subjects for most. How many people have faced their own mortality, let alone feel comfortable talking with someone who is distressed and contemplating suicide. Understandably, people struggle with what to say and what to do.

When I felt suicidal what I needed most was someone to bear with me in my pain; to simply *be* with me, to listen, not to say or do anything in particular, and not to minimize my feelings or try to placate me with "I'm sure you'll feel better tomorrow" or "We've all had bad days".

In retrospect, if I were ever feeling suicidal again, I would ask for what I needed, whether that be of someone else or of myself. Of someone else I would ask, "Please could you just sit with me in my pain? That is what I

---

6. Also see chapter *Depression and Descent*.

need." Of myself I would ask, "What do I need right now? What is it that I need to do?"

The following poem was written at a time when I was growing into a deep acceptance of the fluctuations and opposites of life. I felt okay with the fact that I both wanted to live and wanted to die, that I was both mad and sane, beautiful and crazy, both a body and a soul. Within me I could feel an almost glorious push/pull of living and dying; it was the pulsation of a life that I was increasingly embracing and inhabiting. There was such tremendous energy and expansion coursing through me, and yet people's reactions were the same as they had been when I was in despair: people were fearful and uncomfortable, they sought to placate me, they minimized or infantilized my feelings. I felt frustrated and limited by the narrow and 'acceptable' pathways to which the mainstream world sought to confine me and confine that which might be considered to be 'beyond the norm'.[7]

This poem was not written for anyone in particular. It was simply a plea for someone, anyone, the world, perhaps even for myself, to bear with the breadth of *all* that I am. We can contain it all.

an invitation to empathy, 2003

Crazed. Crazy. Thoughts. Feelings.
I want to die.
I want to live.
I'm not supposed to write things like this.
Am I?

Hormones. Yeah it's probably just hormones.
Wretched fluctuating nuisances.
Or it could be my past.
Or my soul. Or my relationships.
Or?

I don't want to be fixed or healed any more.
I don't want to be silenced or comforted.
And I don't want to say:
"I'm sure I'll be fine tomorrow."
Always placating. Pleasing. Appeasing.

---

7. See chapter *Flatland and the dilemma of 'normality'*.

Here and now.
In this awful, wonderful, terrible life.
I want to die. And I want to harm.
I want to dance and I want to live.
All of me. Now. Here.
Not just tomorrow. Not just yesterday.
Not just potentially. Or spiritually.
Or calmly. Or rationally. Or quietly. Or.

I can't remember. I really can't.
Was I a foe or was I a friend?
Was I a leader or was I a follower?
Was I a body or a soul?
Was I sitting? Standing? Fucking?
Can I bear all of this?
Can I bear this fluctuation?
This wondrous intelligence and beauty?
This wretched, monstrous madness?
Can I?

Can you?

***

a life sentence

One of the most important decisions I made in my journey, was not to kill myself.

What follows is a journal entry that describes the internal process that brought me to that point. As I wrote, I was more and more desperate, closer and closer to feeling I would kill myself, and then, as often happened, at the very lowest point, at rock bottom, I seemingly broke through to a new understanding and a new way of living my life:

<u>This is my last entry</u>[8] -
ENOUGH IS ENOUGH.
ENOUGH IS ENOUGH.

---

8. Formatting is as it appears in my journal. Upper case letters were gouged with large letters into the page.

These pills[9] will take me out of this miserable world.
ENOUGH IS ENOUGH.

Increasing financial hassles. I just want to die. I have locked myself in the bedroom and threatened to take pills. I am aware that I just want someone to come and take care of me. *I WISH SOMEONE WOULD TELL ME THAT THEY WANT ME IN THIS WORLD. I WISH SOMEONE WOULD PLEAD WITH ME NOT TO KILL MYSELF. SO THAT THEY TELL ME THAT IT IS OKAY TO LIVE. SO THAT THEY GIVE ME THE RIGHT TO **EXIST***. But everyone always gives up. Why is that? Why is that? What the fuck is wrong with me. I am aware that I am furious. I AM SO FURIOUS. I WANT SOMEONE TO PLEAD WITH ME TO STAY ALIVE. BUT NO ONE WILL COME. NO ONE WILL EVER COME. I WANT SO MUCH TO DIE. SO MUCH. SO MUCH. I WANT TO DIE.

And now, all of a sudden, inside, I realize that the decision to live is up to me. I can't live for anyone else. Living for someone else will never ever be good enough. Ever. I can feel something guiding me but I don't know what it is. I have to want to live. I have to want to pursue my life. I hate having to make this decision, because it means that I will have to look after myself now, and that I have to be stronger than I have ever been. The child in me is crying so desperately … but if I kill myself, will somebody come and take care of the child? If I commit suicide will anyone care? The answer is NO NO NO NO NO NO. STAND UP. NOW. STAND UP. And live. I wrote that 'enough is enough' meaning that my life was at an end. Perhaps it meant that I have had enough of thinking about killing myself, and now I can choose to live. I have to choose to live, because nobody can live *for* me. It is *my* life. I must have been given this torturous task that is my life for a reason. I have to work out how to live it.

In my book *Seventeen Voices: Life and Wisdom from Inside 'Mental Illness',* Glenda, who lives with spinal muscular atrophy, had spent much of her life believing that she would die young. However, in her early 40s she found out that she would have a normal life expectancy. In my interview with her, she astutely remarks, "… the drawback of realizing this, was that rather than a death sentence, I now had a *life* sentence. I felt robbed of a certain self-righteous sookiness: 'Oh shit, now the joke's on me!'"

When I made the decision not to kill myself, I did indeed now have a 'life sentence'.

Despite my desperate desire to escape my suffering through death, I actually felt enormous conflict about ending my life; I *wanted* very much to stay alive.

---

9. In my journal I had specified the drug by name.

I even wanted someone to plead with me to stay alive. Driven to realize that nobody was going to do this, I suddenly knew that the movement towards life could only ever come from *me*. It was up to me alone to live my life. No one else could do that for me.

It didn't mean that I no longer *felt* suicidal, because I certainly did, many more times. But when I decided that I would never *act* on that feeling, I opened myself to possibility. As long as I was always giving myself the 'out' of suicide, then I would never have to figure out how to actually stay 'in'. I knew that as a reasonably intelligent, insightful, creative human being, I *had* to be able to find a way forward other than that of suicide. And so I started to question: "How do I go on living? How do I truly *live* this messy human life?"

It was an oh-so-necessary step. I didn't yet know *how* to live, I only knew that I was going to stay alive and somehow work it all out.

***

contemplating death

Many years ago I was visiting an acquaintance who knew nothing of my personal struggles. She told me a story about a friend, David, who frequently visited her when he was feeling suicidal. She had tried numerous things to help him: she had listened to him for hours on end, she had suggested he pursue professional help, she had let him know that she didn't feel emotionally equipped to deal with his distress, she had hugged him, made him dinner and let him sleep on her couch.

However, eventually she had grown weary of his continual threats of suicide and also the chaos this created in her life. So one day she had said to him, "Well, David, it seems that you are intent on killing yourself, so how about tomorrow we go to the funeral home and have you measured up for a coffin."

Apparently there were a few moments of charged silence between them, before they both burst out laughing. But her statement had a profound effect on David. He realized the practical reality of what he was continually threatening: he would die and someone would have to measure him up for a coffin. He also understood the burden he was placing on his friend's shoulders, and sought professional help.

But the story also had a lasting effect on me. I began a deeper contemplation of death.

The reality was that if I killed myself, someone would indeed need to measure me up for a coffin. I wondered: What would it be like to lie dead in a coffin? What would it be like to have my precious body burn up in flames or rot into the ground? And if I killed myself would death really bring my suffering to an end? Or would I have to come back and do it all over again? And what is it that would die? Was it my body? Was it my soul? And what of Spirit?

I also reflected on the people in my life who had died. A dear friend Richard had died of cancer when only quite young. I put a photo of him up on my wall and frequently looked at it. Was there something in his experience that might have hinted at the fact that he would not grow old? Why was I still alive when he was not?

There were also times, when I was very sick, that faced with the very real fragility of my body it became starkly clear to me that I *didn't* want to die. I wanted very much to stay alive and I fought mightily to do so. I didn't want to think that there would be nothing left of my precious memories and joys. Who would look after my dogs? Who would cook my partner lovely meals?

Whenever I wandered out into my garden, I could see clearly that nature seemed to take death in its stride. I wondered if I too would slip into death with the same ease as did a leaf or a blade of grass. I took innumerable photos of dead birds, dead fish, dead flowers, dead grass. Death was everywhere.

And yet, so was life. Soon enough I would be dead. Soon enough I would flutter from my mortal tree and wither away. But in this moment, with blood coursing through my veins I was very much alive. I wondered if perhaps my contemplation of death was not separate from a contemplation of life.

I started to look around me, in supermarkets, in the park, or when I was out walking. Why did I so often see a mask of lifelessness in people's eyes? Their bodies were certainly alive, but where were *they*? Had they ever contemplated their inevitable demise? Had they ever contemplated their wonderful lives?

I realized that each time I had felt suicidal, inherent in the intensity of those feelings was the question, "But how do I truly live? How do I live with this mess, this pain, this torment?" but also, "What does it mean to be *alive*?" I wondered if it was possible to truly *live* even when I was out shopping or sitting in front of my computer. I wondered whether suicidality was perhaps a privilege of sorts; could suicidality be the very coal face of my decision to wholly engage with life?

I knew these questions could never be answered intellectually. Nor could they be answered by someone else. They were the deepest questions of life, *my* life, and as such they could only be answered by me. And neither could they be answered by trying to look into the future or reflecting on the past, for the only life I saw happening was the one I was living *right now*.

Over the years, I was able to engage more and more fully with the play of life as it moved through me. On occasion that play still contained the intense feelings of suicidality. Other times it was joy or excitement or love. But regardless of its intensity or its form, I was increasingly able to simply feel its movement in my body without contracting back, withdrawing, fighting or clinging on. And in doing so, I began to truly *live*.

Life is *never* anywhere else than here. Life is not in our heads, it is not in our imaginings of how it should be. Life doesn't just happen when we are happy and things are going according to 'plan'. Here. Now. Sitting at a computer, writing these words, in the delicious silence of the early early morning, this *here*, this *now*. This is *life*. I am here. And there is nothing whatsoever blocking my path to that.

> And for *all* of us, that is our journey …
> to work out how to truly live.
> Whether we know it or not.
> And whether we are suicidal or not.

***

life

Life[1]. It's what we all are.

The common usage of the simple four-lettered word 'life' belies how extraordinary life is. Life is all at once so achingly beautiful and so wretchedly tragic, so exuberantly joyous and so heartrendingly sad.

So frequently we only labor on the edges of life, hoping, hoping that one day we might find a way to truly dance in its glory. If only we knew how …

As I embraced more and more of everyday life, I suffered less, but I also came closer and closer to knowing myself as the Truth of Life itself.

Can I include it all? Can I?

***

dance of life, drawing

***

---

1. I have used the word 'life' in this chapter both with capitalization and without. Although this can be a little tedious on reading, I felt it was necessary to distinguish between everyday 'life' and 'Life' as the entirety of existence which includes the lived knowing that we are in no way separate from that.

this chapter

When I write a book, I 'feel' its existence long before I have written a single word.

I felt the existence of my children's music book, *Flute with a Twist*, years before I sat down to actually write it. My book *Seventeen Voices* was the same. And in both instances I even 'knew' who the publisher would be. It was as though in the realm of potentiality, the books already existed and my job as their author was to bring them to life.

It was this chapter *Life* that first alerted me to the fact that *this* book was waiting to be written; its subject matter pressed ever more urgently in on me. I tried to ignore it by telling myself it was probably just a passing whim but then as I was out walking or as I was going to sleep at night, a voice insisted: "This must be written. This must be written."

The content of this chapter was pivotal in my movement out of deepest suffering and it needed to be written.

But as much as it needed to be written, when I sat down to actually write it, the words didn't come. Rather, it was the titles and content of other chapters that appeared. And so I began to write the other chapters first, and slowly a book grew. At times I would feel my way back to this chapter, thinking that if only I could find a title for it, the words might start to flow. I came up with many possibilities: *Accept Everything, And this too, Embracing it All, Can I include this?* But they all felt wrong, and the chapter remained unwritten.

Then recently, a conversation with a spiritual teacher came to mind; it was early in 2008, shortly after I had awoken. I asked the teacher, "How would you best describe enlightenment?" He thought for a moment, looked straight at me and then said, "Life". I don't know what I had expected him to say, but it certainly wasn't that one simple word. It was far too ordinary. I wanted something more substantial, more special. And yet, my disappointment at his reply, set me to wondering: What had he meant, when he so simply had said, "Life"? What was it that I didn't yet know?

And now I am writing this chapter. And I understand his answer completely.

Life. Yes, Life.

***

red flowers

Years ago, an older couple from the UK moved into the house across the road. Their lifelong dream had been to live in Australia after they retired, and so they had spent their entire working life, saving the money to make that possible.

Shortly after they moved in, I saw them busy in the front yard, so thought it was a good time to go over and introduce myself. As I walked across the road I was shocked to realize they were sawing off the branches of a beautiful old callistemon[2] that shaded their driveway. I introduced myself and we chatted. At some point I casually inquired about their intentions for the tree. They told me that one of their first tasks when moving into any house, was to remove *all* red-flowering plants; they detested any plant with red flowers.

I can't recall what I said in response, but I certainly recall how I felt: I was dumbfounded. What! You've got to be kidding! I couldn't fathom chopping down a decades-old tree, solely because of the color of its flowers. I looked at that callistemon, with its striking red bottlebrush flowers and I felt grief on its behalf. As I walked away, I offered it a silent benediction and an apology on behalf of the human race.

But in my feelings, there was such an intensity, that I knew there was something in the incident for me to learn. Why was I *so* shocked? Why had my reaction been *so* strong? Did I perhaps have an equivalent of 'red flowers' in my own life? Was there something that *I* felt a need to chop down, remove, or destroy?

As I looked within, I realized with a grimaced queasiness, that there were countless upon countless 'red flowers'. They weren't as visible as that tree, but they were there all the same. It seemed I was lived by them, moved by them and breathed by them: she's a nice person/she's not, get rid of that/keep that, that looks good/that looks awful, that feels nice/that feels uncomfortable. Perhaps I wasn't so different from the red-flowers-are-horrible people after all.

Around this time, I came across the spiritual teaching of acceptance: to allow what is present in one's experience to simply be there, without rejection or preference. Although on the surface this sounds very simple, it is, in actuality, an extraordinarily difficult thing for the everyday self or ego to do or to bring about. The everyday self keeps itself alive, and indeed thrives, on push/pull, black/white, yes/no activity. But this sort of activity also keeps our suffering alive. We suffer when we fight

---

2. Australian bottlebrush

something in our experience that we believe shouldn't be there: a headache, a nosey neighbor, the hum of a chain saw at dawn, a traumatic memory, a troubling world event. We all have our own particular demons with which we struggle. And it is a misery. After the tree incident I decided that I truly didn't want to be a person who had to chop down all my 'red flowers' in order to live happily in this world. There had to be a better way.

I later learnt that complete acceptance can only come about when we realize all life as truly one Consciousness, but after the red-flower episode, something profound changed in my approach to life.

At first that change was only very small. I recall seeing a tree with dark and untidy bark that I didn't particularly like. So I asked myself: Would I remove that tree simply on the basis of its bark? Or could I include this tree in my life? In my garden? What would it take for me to do that? Then I saw a dog I didn't ordinarily warm to: a bull terrier. So I asked myself: Could I grow to love that stocky build, the small triangular eyes, the curved nose? Then there was a day of heavy rain that ruined my plans. Can I include this rainy day in my life? Can I allow its raininess? Can I perhaps even *embrace* its raininess?

Then with increasing depth, I looked to the pain and the anguish that I held within. Could I tolerate this wretched anxiety in my body? This desperate fear? Could I bear it and include it even if just for a moment? Could I feel it without immediate thoughts of self-destruction or self-criticism? Could I embrace it in even the smallest of ways and dare to look at it with interest and curiosity? Or, one day, even with love? What would it take for me to do that? Could I eventually embrace all of my inner life, my outer life, the ups-and-downs of my relationships, my spiritual life?

And so my exploration began: How much of this enormity that is Life could I include? How much of myself could I open to? It wasn't a self-help program to make myself into a perfect person. It was just a quiet question; it was a background inquiry lived gently within my days.

And nor did I immediately go out and buy a rough-barked tree and a bull terrier, or perform a celebratory dance every time it rained. Nor did I freely and easily go within and embrace my fear, anxiety and pain, without asking for a *lot* of help to do so. It was simply that I no longer automatically fought my experience in this moment. I looked at life with more openness and curiosity, and questioned the almost mechanical knee-jerk reaction we have when we say, "No. Not me. Not mine. Too awful. Too hard. Too ugly." Life was no longer something that had to be rigidly defined or defended against. Life was no longer so much the enemy. For someone who, at that time, was suffering deeply, that change in perspective was very profound.

What are my 'red flowers'?

***

red-flower postscript

Shortly after the red-flower episode, I felt a rather mischievous impulse to buy a plant with red flowers in full bloom. The only plant that was available was a protea. Interestingly, I had never liked proteas all that much. But despite that fact, I still bought it.

I brought it home and planted it just behind the letterbox, in full view of the couple across the road. Every day when I looked at that plant, I felt a dissonance within. A discord. Not only had my reasons for buying the plant been of a not altogether honorable nature, I had planted a plant that I didn't really like and now I had to tolerate the conflict it created in me. I began to realize, in some small way, what the couple across the road must have felt whenever they saw a plant with red flowers.

But the protea became a question for me. What exactly was it about proteas that I didn't like? Was it their growing habit? Their leaves? I wasn't sure. I often looked at that protea, feeling its particular 'protea-ness' in my body, and slowly it grew on me; I could tolerate it a little more. And then a little more again.

And now, when I come home and see that protea flourishing behind the letterbox, I rather like its angular different-ness.

Our lives are a constant invitation to take on more and more of the Life that we truly are.

***

music informs life – the glorious symphonic composition

Music can convey a vast array of emotions and moods. Even a single piece might span cheekiness and seriousness, joy and sadness, boldness and calm.

When we listen to music we feel ourselves touched or altered by these emotions. If we feel sad, listening to a melancholic piece of music might deepen us into our sadness. The power of a Beethoven symphony might open us to our own capacity for strength or for action. A teenager cruising along in his car playing loud music with the bass turned to full volume, might feel his power or invulnerability. A love song opens us to our capacity for loving or reminds us of someone we love. There is endless variation. And we *expect* that variation; we *like* that variation. It's the reason we listen to music. We'd quickly get bored if music expressed only one feeling or mood. Why would we bother?

In our everyday lives we have within us that same scope for emotional expression and feeling. But whereas in a piece of music we might welcome and delight in its variation and breadth, when it comes to our day-to-day lives, we limit ourselves. We divide our emotional life into good and bad. We block our anger and our sadness. We fight our gloominess and even sometimes our joy. We tell ourselves stories about who we are and what we are capable of: I mustn't show my anger, grief is a bad thing, I'm too sensitive, I'm too exuberant.

The range and variation of emotion that we like in our music, we don't necessarily carry over into our lives.

As a music teacher I always tried to bridge this gap between music and life. In 2003 I had my children's music book *Flute with a Twist* published. Many of the pieces in the book were written with particular students in mind; through my music I hoped to demonstrate that all their experiences of life, even those commonly deemed 'unacceptable', could be welcomed and enjoyed.

And so I wrote a piece of music called *I'm SO bored* for a boy who was often bored in his music lessons. I wrote *Answerin' Back* for a girl who liked to disagree with me. I wrote *Simply Sad* for a girl about to have major surgery. Both *Angry Attitude* and *Can't Sit Still* were written for a wonderfully fiery and vivacious teenager. I also wrote musical games for students who liked to experiment and try new things. In seeing themselves reflected in the music, my students began to appreciate that all of life, even feelings of boredom or anger or sadness could be expressed and celebrated.

In preparation for writing this chapter I decided to keep a diary of my emotions on one random day. As I jotted down my entries, the variation truly astonished me; it came as a complete surprise. Here was the flow of life as it moved effortlessly from fury and grief to ecstasy and joy. In the past I might have clung on to some of these emotions while resisting others, but when opened to and allowed, they really are just like the harmonies, melodies, tonalities, nuances and rhythms that might make up a glorious symphonic composition.[3]

6.30 – **Concern.** I wake up tired. I've had another restless night with pain in my hip. I am concerned that the pain will stop me from finishing up some work in the garden

6:45 – **Peace.** Quiet peace as I sip my morning cup of tea and watch as the first rays of sunlight touch the trees.

7:20 – **Fury, grief and pain.** I check emails and Facebook. I see a photo of a family gathering in which I haven't been included. A comment underneath says, "So good that everyone was here!" I am furious. Furious! Everyone? Everyone? Really?! *I* wasn't there!! Only last night I had dreamt of not being a part of my family. Tears come and I walk around the house, unsettled. I long to be part of my family but know I am different from them. This family stuff is *sooo* painful and the desire to belong, so strong.

7:30 – **Acceptance.** A lingering anger. I look out the window. It's a beautiful spring day. Life can contain my sadness and fury.

7:40 – **Joy and lingering irritation.** I share a joke and a cuddle with my partner in the kitchen. There's still a lingering irritation but it has become part of the fabric of the day.

8:30 – **Laughter.** I feed the dogs chicken necks for breakfast. I laugh when the larger dog wants the small chicken neck, the small dog wants the large chicken neck. I shower and dress.

8:45 – **Sadness. Emotionality.** Lingering sadness remains that I am not part of my family. A clinging emotionality tells me that I am pre-menstrual.

9:00 – **Sadness. Questing/questioning.** I feel an edge of questioning implicit in my sadness. Why is the pull of family so strong? Is it merely an idea that entrances us with the unachievable notion of 'belonging'? Perhaps being enveloped in the bosom of one's family is like our ultimate worldly Mother.

9:15 - 10:30 – **Joy. Ecstasy. Compassion.** Acceptance. I go for a walk. I take such pleasure in my rhythmic footsteps, my breathing and the movement of my body. I am not separate from the life around me: sunshine, a cricket match on the oval, people gardening, fresh air and delicious smells. There is still a remnant sadness and questioning. I feel a rush of uncaused ecstasy when I see a bank of flowering nasturtiums near the creek in all shades of green and orange. I feel compassion as I chat with an older

---

3. My capacity to allow the flow of life in this way, although informed by my musical and spiritual life, had its foundation in the body-centered psychotherapy, Radix. For further discussion on Radix, see the chapter *The Body*.

woman, whose husband has Alzheimer's Disease. This is the movement of existence. There is room for it all.

11:00 – **Simple pleasure.** Drinking fresh vegetable juice in the garden with my partner and dogs. We chat and laugh and enjoy the dogs' contentment in the morning sun. I drive to the nursery to buy plants for the front garden.

11:40 – **Peaceful tiredness.** I come home with a selection of plants. I am tired after the restless night, but peaceful. I make a decision to sit quietly in the sun before lunch rather than push through the tiredness and work in the garden.

12.10 – **Annoyance. Gratitude.** I have an early lunch in the garden with my partner and dogs: a salmon and salad sandwich. I feel a little annoyed for no particular reason except perhaps my tiredness and PMS. I decide to take a nap to catch up on sleep.

1:15 – **Grumpy. Angry.** I wake up too soon, still feeling tired. I stay in bed a while. A few angry thoughts about this morning arise and then subside. They are left to flow through.

1:30 –**Grumpy. Tired.** Concern. Love. I get up and have a cup of tea in the garden. I am still so tired. I wonder what is wrong with me. PMS? MdDS? Sore hips? I never once had sore hips before I went to the osteopath. Now I have sore hips. I cuddle my beautiful dogs.

2:00 – **Contentment. Resentment.** I sit down to write. It always surprises me how complete I feel when I write. I resent jotting down this emotion diary a little, because it keeps me from my writing but I decide to persist with it.

2:45 – **Ambivalence.** My partner calls out to me. I knew that once I settled to write, my partner would have time away from her study to help me with the gardening. I feel the dilemma: I wish to write *and* I wish to finish the garden.

4:00 – **Satisfaction. Anxiety. Peace.** We have planted the new plants and they look fresh and lovely. I feel some anxiety at the thought that my partner is now studying on top of full-time work. There is always so much to do around the house. I know I can't do any more than I already do. I feel a peace that I can now sit to write.

5:00 – **Contentment. Engagement.** Continued writing.

6:00 – **Mild anxiety.** My partner calls out she is hungry. She begins to heat up the left-over vegetable soup from last night. I always feel some anxiety when my partner is in the kitchen. She is not a good cook and too often in the past has created a small catastrophe. I decide to get up and take charge of the soup.

7:00 – **Contentment.** Humans fed and dogs fed. I am writing again.

7:50 – **Tiredness.** Dissatisfaction. I am too tired to continue. My partner wants to watch television. I find the television tedious, but decide to sit with her for a while and go to bed early.

8:00 – **Fun. Laughter. Surprise.** We spontaneously start to play with the puppy in the living room, tugging on his toy and then throwing it. He is cute and clever, and we both laugh. He is so much more entertaining than a television program. He is so sure of his place in the world and so sure he is adored. My partner reads this emotion diary. I am surprised that she is interested. It is a revelation to her that emotions change and move as they will. She laughs at my mild anxiety at 6pm.

8:30 – **Interest.** My partner is watching a program she recorded on 'Friendship'. It asserts that most people have a network of 150 friends. Hmmm … I don't! Still I'm interested. I listen as I do some simple exercises and get ready for bed.

8:45 – **Lust. Fun.** I have a lusty cuddle with my partner in the laundry. We both laugh.

9:00 –**Worry. Mild annoyance.** Peace. It is bedtime. I worry that I will have more hip pain in the middle of the night. I have exercised the painful areas tonight. I feel mildly annoyed when I see a small dog dropping near the kitchen door. The puppy has had an accident. My partner offers to clean it up. I get into bed and relax into peace.

***

the sticking point and silence

The sticking point is the place where we can't embrace life. It is the place where over and over we get stuck. Where we resist life.

The 'sticking point' is the place where we encounter the demon we would prefer to keep hidden in the cupboard, and realize how utterly powerless we are in the face of it.

My sticking point throughout much of my life has been noise. From the time my brother's rock music first thumped through the walls of my bedroom, I hated noise. And then there were my father's footsteps stomping down the hallway. My parents' arguments. Later there were barking dogs, chain saws and neighbors who played loud dance music late into the night.

I have always loved the freedom and refuge silence offers. I celebrate it. Silence doesn't draw my attention. It doesn't demand that something be done. Silence simply *is*. In silence the trees and the flowers grow. In silence the stars and moon move slowly over the night sky. In silence I wander freely between my inner and outer worlds. In gentle silence I find wisdom and strength. In silence I connect more deeply with another than I can with words. In silence I have found my depth and my True Home.

Noise, on the other hand, jangles, disturbs and disrupts me. It clamors for my attention. It mocks the peace I might have enjoyed only a few moments earlier. I harden and clench my body against its burden. I want noise to disappear, go away. Noise pisses me off.

Over the years, I have voraciously devoured those books in which the author describes their own particular sticking point. I wanted to know if they eventually found resolution, and if so, how.

I recall a book in which the author bought a secluded house with a beautiful view over forests and rolling hills. Only after she moved in did she notice that there was a power line strung across that view. She became obsessed with the power line and her aversion to it. She closed the curtains so she could no longer see the view. In another book, the author retreated to a quiet mountain village to spend the summer writing a book. Only when he settled to write did he realize that just out of sight below him was a girls' school with all its accompanying bells, hooters, screams and laughter. He was so consumed with his dislike of the noise that he was unable to write. Both of these authors mirrored my own battle: the all-powerful obsession with the 'thing' that shouldn't be there and the internal battle of suffering that ensues.

As my journey to Truth became conscious, noise became my leveler, my spiritual reality-check. I couldn't kid myself, because I unequivocally knew that if I couldn't know noise as God, then I didn't fully know God. But I also suspected that if a time came when I *could* include noise then I might be close to the end of my journey.

And so noise became my teacher. How was I to include the very thing that I simply couldn't include? How? I held that question for many many years.

As can be so often the case, it was at the very point that I felt pushed beyond what I thought I could reasonably cope with, that the tide changed.

There was a time when the house next door was rented out. Every six months, there were new tenants: a teenager who played loud music, a boy learning drums, a punching bag set up under the carport, a man panel-beating an old car. Each time I steeled myself harder and harder against a new onslaught of noise, while still determined that somehow, somehow, I would find a path through to acceptance. I made small gains, but a drawer full of ear plugs and a set of industrial-strength ear muffs, attest to the fact that my success was only rather limited.

Then the house was sold, and I had great hopes for the new neighbors. But two couples both with small children, moved into the house. Perhaps they had hoped to save money, but the house was far too small for all of them. Arguments ensued, cars careened off in anger, people came and went at all hours of the night, car doors slammed, people yelled. I knew I would have to move out of my beautiful home if the racket continued.

One day as I was sitting quietly, I knew I could not take another day of the noise. I hated it with a vengeance. But even more than that, I hated the battle I created within my own body and mind: the hardening, the clenching, the relentless circling thoughts. I decided, "Okay, I haven't come up with any better alternatives, so I'm going to sit here and feel this awful torment and listen to this bloody noise, until I find a way through it."

And it was somewhere in that decision to go willingly *into* the whole situation rather than attempt to fight it or run away from it, that the solution came. I was inexplicably surrendered into a bigger view of reality. It wasn't yet to the depths that awakening would bring, but still, it was an expansion into a vast and silent space that was beyond my current experiencing while still paradoxically containing it; my struggle with myself and with the world could cease, because now I could *include* it all. That Silence was not an absence of noise, rather it was a Silence that could contain both noise and everyday quietness. It was a taste of God, and God, of course, wasn't trying to get rid of one bit of reality in order that another be given preference. God was all of Life, including noise, and I wasn't separate from that.

The realization of that day didn't bring about a miraculous conclusion in which I lived happily ever after; I still struggled with noise from time to time. But it was a beginning. It was a vision of what was possible. It was an understanding that by embracing an experience, however awful, the answers would come. The ego or everyday self has only one way to do things, and that is to fight against what it doesn't want, or grasp at what it wants. The ego assumes a winner and a loser. The bigger answers, however, never come about through that sort of polarization.

The only way to find the truth is to move *into* the Truth, and that Truth is always always what is *here* in this life under our very noses, right now. It is never *ever* anywhere else.[4]

Interestingly, in the 'sticking point' examples from books I gave above, both the woman with her power line, and the author with his girls' school, came to a similar understanding. Both were pushed beyond what they thought they could bear, and in that moment, something let go within. The fight was surrendered into a bigger and more inclusive reality. The woman could enjoy the view while still seeing the power line. The author embraced the school noises as a welcome companion to his writing.

I would still prefer silence over noise, much as I would prefer to eat a mango over tofu, but there is no longer the struggle there once was. I can go to a teenager's birthday party, and feel myself as the deepest Silence while the rock music thumps loudly in the background. I no longer feel an immediate knee-jerk contraction when a chainsaw starts up. But I also have a quiet and adult discernment within, from which I am able to give myself permission to effect change: "Excuse me, I would greatly appreciate it if your dog doesn't bark after 10pm."

And sometimes I do still wear ear plugs.

***

beginner's mind

There is a Zen teaching called beginner's mind.

Beginner's mind is a 'not-knowing'. It is a way of looking at the world with freshness and newness, and without our internal lines, boxes, conceptual constructs and assumptions in the way. From beginner's mind we approach each moment of life as though we know absolutely nothing about it. It is as if we become children again, and see things for the first time … as they *are*.

I had come to my own home-grown and rather modest version of beginner's mind prior to hearing of the Zen teaching, but knowing of that centuries'-old understanding, gave depth and buoyancy to my own.

---

4. As a postscript, the noisy neighbours moved out a few months later.

Undoubtedly we have all had times when we hear a noise and make an instant assumption about what it is. We then react to that noise according to our assumption rather than to the actual experience.

I recall one evening when I thought I heard the neighbor's chainsaw starting up. Instantly I thought, "What! A chainsaw at this time of day?!" A few moments later I realized, "Whoops, it's only the chirping of crickets." Immediately the 'awful' sound became a 'nice' one. Only a few nights ago, I heard a loud and rhythmic thumping as I was going to sleep, and I thought, "Oh no, a loud party! I won't be able to sleep!" Then I realized it was the fireworks from Australia Day celebrations and I lay in bed listening to the thumping with a smile on my face.

No doubt we have all approached life in this way at some point: letting our assumptions, our fears, our past categorizations and past experiences get in the way of interacting with life as it is. We assume we know what is going on; we assume we are already experts on this moment even though it has never happened before.

But what if we respond to life from beginner's mind? What if we truly see and feel the moment of life we have in front of us as if we know absolutely nothing about it? What if we imagine that never ever before in our lives have we had this particular experience?

Yesterday I felt inexplicably sad. Initially I cast around for 'reasons', somewhat puzzled by its sudden onset. But then I asked, "What would my *actual* experience of that sadness be if never before had I felt 'sadness' and so had absolutely no conceptual construct or context in which to place it? What is *actually* happening in my experience in this very moment?" I noticed:

> an impulse to stop and sit, to stay in one spot and not move,
> a desire to simply breathe,
> a lowering of awareness down into my belly,
> a pull downwards away from my writing and my thinking,
> a need to cry

And so I stopped my writing. I let myself drop into inaction. I cried. I didn't go for my usual morning walk. I lay in bed. I slept. I meditated. I sat in the garden. I let myself be pulled down into my body. I rang my partner to bring home fish and salad for dinner so I didn't have to cook.

And that was my life as it was yesterday. Certainly if I had made a whole list of demands on myself – that I mustn't cry, that I must exercise and write every day, that I must cook dinner every night, that I mustn't lie in bed during the day - then yesterday would have been a miserable and suffered day. But as it was, yesterday was just yesterday. Was any of it bad? I don't think so …

As I've written in other parts of this book, there are certainly feeling or emotional states that may be too charged to enter into on one's own. I am also quite practiced at 'simply following' what is happening in my experience. But we can be in beginner's mind in even the most ordinary of ways.

We have all had instances when we unexpectedly see a familiar scene with fresh eyes. There are times I've walked into the garden first thing in the morning and I see it as though I've never seen it before; even a scene that I see countless times each day, can suddenly seem extraordinarily vivid and new. We can also cultivate this capacity. If I go down to the local beach and imagine I am on an tropical holiday and am seeing this stretch of coastline for the very first time, it takes on a completely different appearance: I become entranced by the play of light on the sand, the azure blue of the ocean, the laughter of people walking by. I feel wonder, awe and delight. It is *all* new.

Even if I am waiting in line at the bank I can cultivate beginner's mind. What is it to be waiting in line at the bank for the very first time? What is the simple feeling of 'waiting in a line' if I don't immediately categorize it as a tedious or time-consuming activity? What is *here*? I feel my two feet on the ground, I see my surroundings, I see the people standing in line with me, I feel alive and engaged, someone sees my engagement and smiles at me and we start to chat. A line in a bank is as good a place as any to engage with life.

We can also cultivate beginner's mind in our relationships. I have an acquaintance who likes to plan all conversations in advance. If I visit him I know he will already have decided what we will talk about and he will already have made assumptions about how I will respond. Such a conversation is stale even before it has even begun. There have been times I have sat with him and I can feel his anger rising because the conversation he imagined having with me three hours ago, isn't taking place in the here and now. What if we are simply present to the space that is created when two people meet, and then let life flow from that?

'Not-knowing' is freeing, it is joyful, it opens us into possibility, and above all it is truly alive.

***

everyday haiku

Haiku is a form of poetry inspired by Zen. It has three lines of 5, 7 and 5 syllables respectively. It is an invitation into the immediacy of this moment, without any judgements, constructs or beliefs in the way. Although traditionally haiku is written about the natural world, it can also convey the 'now-ness' in our ordinary everyday lives.

> stains on the carpet
> a dog whines to come inside
> I sit and eat cake

> waiting in a queue
> interest rates are going down
> purse in my pocket

> silence in the house
> I drink water from my glass
> a car passes by

***

black and white: the gift of the awful counsellor

At different times in my life, I sought professional help.

At one stage, circumstances once more catapulted me into a deep anguish. I tried to work through the pain on my own, but it only intensified. As much as I didn't want to enter into a therapeutic relationship again, I knew by the power of my distress that something remained unresolved. I didn't want to spend more money on personal work, so decided to try a free counselling service.

From the moment I met my appointed counsellor, I knew that we weren't going to get along; she giggled a lot, she continually fiddled with her hair and rapport was non-existent. I saw her only twice before finding someone else, but still, she left me with a profound and lasting gift.

At one point she spoke of black-and-white thinking. People had mentioned this to me before, and although I understood it to a certain degree, I had never taken its full significance into my life. I heard her babbling on about 'black and white' and I thought, "So what! I've heard it all before. I don't particularly like you and you're not focusing on the issues I came to you with."

But then a short time later, as can be the case with the things we instantly dismiss, the truth of what she had said, hit me. I *got* it. I *got* 'black and white'. And it had an extraordinary and lasting impact.

I had previously recognized that we divide our lives into black and white, into inner and outer, good person and bad person, yes and no, sinful and pure, nice feeling and awful feeling. I had also recognized that we split our lives into opposing forces that then go to war with each other; one part wants to go one way and the other part wants to go the other, one part wants to lose weight and the other wants to eat chocolate donuts every afternoon.

But now I could see that there was only *one* thing happening and that one thing was *Life*.

I saw that not only were there infinite shades of grey, there was also room for *both* black and white. There was room for both yes and no, both good and bad. We could create all the boxes and lines and labels we liked, but Life would remain forever as *one* thing. And as such, it naturally included *everything*.

I could love my partner and still feel frustration. I could feel questions without expecting an answer. I could be depressed and not label it as bad. I could feel competent while also feeling weak. I could feel fragile *and* strong. I could have extraordinary spiritual understandings and still feel annoyance when dealing with difficult tradespeople. I didn't have to erase one bit of experience in order that another be given preference. I could entertain the validity of *all* experience.

I saw that there is only the 'is-ness' of Life, without separation; everything is just as it is.

It was quite literally the beginning of the end of 'ego'; only shortly after, I awoke out of its dream.[5]

***

---

5. As an addendum to this story, after two sessions with the 'awful counsellor', I approached the management of the counselling service, and asked for a more down-to-earth and compatible counsellor. They did not question the issue of incompatibility, and went out of their way to match me with an appropriate counsellor.

holding life

We all know what it is like to be held by someone when we are feeling sad or disappointed or hurt.

That holding can be a bodily holding but it can also be the holding of presence as someone simply sits with us or listens to us. In that holding we are given permission to open to and allow all that we are to be present in this moment. And as we do so, our struggle eases and our feelings no longer overwhelm us.

But we can also hold ourselves. We can take ourselves in and allow our sadness, grief or pain. Spirit is the ultimate 'holder', but within that vastness, there are many levels on which we can hold ourselves. The poem that follows describes this process in myself, as I moved from feeling scattered and fearful, to the extraordinary joy of allowing life to simply be as it is.

embrace

I pull all the scattered and scared parts to me,
The small parts,
The pain-filled and tired parts,
The parts that have seen enough
Of the world's angular pushing for now.

I hold them all in softest embrace;
Soft as the caress of my lover's cheek
Or the kindness of compassionate eyes.

My hands, my breasts, my belly, my heart,
Loosen,
And take me in.

I curl myself into the warmth of my own soul.
Smoothing and soothing.

I sink effortlessly into the depths of who I am,
Allowing all of life
Its place in this moment.

Exquisite gentleness.
And indescribable joy.

***

Is Life merely a fairy tale that
never comes true?
Or is Life something so much more vital
and fluid and moving?
A mystery which we are living
in each moment?

***

questions

Questions are glorious.

Questions have carried me from times of desperate suffering to a place of lived and profound peace. And yet it is so vital to know how to question: how to live questions, how to ask questions, how to feel questions, how to let questions incubate and mature, and even how to let one's very self become a question.

Questions are so very much more than just a sentence with a question mark at the end.

***

a little girl with a frown on her face

Once upon a time, there was a little girl.

Her mother and father said to her, "Get that frown off your face. We don't want to see such an angry frown in this house."

The little girl didn't feel like she had a frown on her face and it certainly didn't feel like she was angry. So the little girl said to her mother and father, "I'm not frowning!" But her mother and father didn't like that very much. "Yes you are!" they said to her. "Get that frown out of our sight right now! Little girls look so pretty when they smile."

So the little girl went away. She went into the bathroom and peered into the mirror. Where was that frown? She pulled her eyebrows up and down. She could see that when her eyebrows went up she looked happy and when she put them down it did indeed look like a frown. But still, it didn't *feel* like a frown inside. The little girl tried to put her eyebrows up and smile so she looked pretty. But then the little girl only felt sad. She didn't know what to do.

The little girl didn't know it at the time, but she was asking a question. A very big question.

It wasn't a question like, "What are we having for dinner?" or "Can I go downstairs to play?" It wasn't even a question like, "What will I be when I grow up?" It wasn't a question with words and it wasn't a question with an easy answer.

It was a question she felt every single day in the way she lived in the world, in the way she moved her body, in the way she felt inside, in the way she talked to people, in the way she often felt sad. She was asking: How do I live in this world when this world doesn't make any sense to me? Why don't people understand me? Why are they often so angry with me? Why can't they see that on the inside I'm not really what they think I am? Why do people say one thing and do another? Why don't people tell the truth? It was as though her whole body and her whole life had become a question. It was a very big question for such a little girl.

Her frown was the weight of all the questions she carried.

***

intellectual questions

This chapter is not about intellectual questions:

> If God is good then why is there suffering? If everything is Divinity then is the ego also Divine? Is there a purpose to existence? Is there such a thing as free will? Is the Allah of Islam the same as the God of Christianity? Is everything uncaused? Will meditation free me from the mind? Would I be more spiritual if I became a vegetarian?

Intellectual questions seek to piece together intellectual concepts and frameworks.

They can be an attempt to find a place for oneself in the comfort or security of an intellectual map, story or philosophy. Intellectual questions aim outwards rather than inwards. Intellectual questions come from the head, not from the heart or the gut. Intellectual questions are thought, not felt. Intellectual questions have words and phrases and question marks. Intellectual questions might be asked simply for the sake of conversation, argument or exercise. Intellectual questions might be used to showcase our cleverness or because we're trying to impress someone. Intellectual questions might be used to fill the empty space of 'not-knowing'. Intellectual questions sometimes come from a tacit conclusion, goal or assumption.[1] Intellectual questions don't really have a place in spirituality.

This chapter is not about intellectual questions.

Nor is this chapter about the questions of everyday life.

> Will I go to Bali or Fiji for my holiday? Will I study Agricultural Science or Horticulture after I finish school? Will I buy a new car? Why is my dog barking? What will I cook for dinner tonight?

This chapter is not about the questions of everyday life.

***

answers

Our world is a world of answers. If a question arises we simply type it into a search engine and press 'Enter':

> What is the pain in my right side, just under my ribs?
> Where can I buy composting worms?
> How do I make vegetarian lasagna?
> What is the population of Estonia?

We only have a question as long as it takes us to find an answer.

When we have a deeper life question or problem, we also expect that there will be an answer or solution out there *somewhere* waiting for us. It might take some ingenuity or skill to find that answer and then put it

---

1. I think here of a doctor who may already have decided a patient has 'depression' and only asks questions that will justify that 'diagnosis'.

into practice, but sooner or later we know the answer will be there. Once we find that answer we assume we'll be able to continue on with our life as usual.

If I were to notice a persistent sense of meaninglessness in my life, I could start looking for an answer by typing a question into a search engine:

What is the meaning of life?

In a matter of moments I would have an enormous list from which to choose:

The meaning of life is to give and receive love.
The meaning of life is to find God and then never let Him go.
The meaning of life is to work at something you feel passionate about.
The Meaning of Life is the title of a 1983 Monty Python film.
"What is the meaning of life?" is one the most profound questions of human existence.
Life in itself has no meaning.[2]

If none of these answers appealed to me, I could broaden my search a little. I could browse in a bookshop and find a book called *Ten Easy Steps to Life's True Meaning*. I could pick up a magazine and learn that I might feel better about life if I lost weight, had more sex or adjusted the energy flow in my living room. If I still felt my life lacked meaning I might consider taking a yoga class or an adult education class in philosophy. Failing that I might see a psychologist, a career counsellor or a New Age healer. And if the sense of meaninglessness persisted and indeed intensified, I might even decide to make an appointment with my doctor and explore my pharmacological options.

Just like a supermarket filled with multi-colored packets and boxes, aisle upon aisle of answers await me. But the price I pay for all those answers, is that they will only ever be someone else's idea of how to resolve my sense of meaninglessness. It will be the doctor's answer, the New Age Healer's answer, the magazine editor's answer ...

So how do I work out which 'meaning of life' is truly *mine*?

***

---

2. These are the actual results from a search engine.

to question deeply

The real questions of life are *lived* ones. They are life questions that if followed will bring us 'life' answers. They are questions that fire our journey and speak their urgency into our soul. They are questions we hold in our hearts until we are slowly ripened into their answers.

They are not intellectual questions or questions of the mind. Rather, they are *felt* in our physical body and within the body of our lives and our living. They are experienced as a discomfort, as a pressure, as a burden, as an empty space, as a not-knowing, as a sensing, as a yearning, as a questing.

It is in our very experiencing of these bodily sensations, the allowing of them, the coming closer and closer to them, that the questioning itself is carried.[3]

> I sense deep down that I am so much more than a shallow surface persona. And so I ask: What is this 'more' that I sense I am? What is this larger presence that lies beyond my mind? Who am I? *What* am I? Why does it feel so important?

> I feel myself torn apart by an anger or a memory. And so I ask: What is it about this anger or this memory that I don't understand? What are these resonances that lie in its power? Where in my body do I feel this anger? Who is feeling this anger?

> I feel a yearning to know what it is to be a human being. And so I ask: What is this sense inside that defines my very humanity? What is it that takes me away from that humanity? What is the humanity I see in another's eyes? And why am I so drawn to it?

> I want to know what truth is. And so I ask: What is this sense inside that feels true and real? Where is this truth? What is truth? Is truth in my mind or is it in my body? Are my thoughts true? Am I true to this moment? Is there a bigger truth? Is what I am experiencing in this moment the truth? Or is it something else? Is it *somewhere* else?

I follow the questions, and I love the questions and I don't let them go. I live the questions and I allow them their life. I let them waft and press and flow within the activities of my everyday life.

---

3. In some instances, it may be helpful or even necessary to have a therapist or teacher or friend by one's side when one does this sort of exploration.

I take out the trash and there are my questions: What is this 'more' that I sense I am? What happens when I inhabit that sense more fully? What is my experience when I move in closer and closer, deeper and deeper? What do I notice?

I make love with my partner and there are my questions: What is this bigger 'something' of which this love is so much a part? What is it? What is this joy? What is this brief sadness? What is this ecstasy?

And then I leave the questions there. I entrust them into my depths. I don't worry at them. I don't prod and push them. I don't rush them. I don't make assumptions about what the answers might be.[4] From time to time I might check in to see if an answer is forthcoming, but if not, I simply leave them there to incubate a little further. It is as though in simply asking the questions and offering the invitation there is now space for a new knowing, a new insight or a new experiencing, to birth itself into this world.

And then, after a few minutes, or a few weeks, or even a few years, the answers will find me. They will slip in according to *their* timetable, not mine. They will work their way into my life when I least expect it. They will surprise me. They will delight me. And in their wisdom I will come to rest. The questions are my path to Truth. *My* Truth.

And that's how it is to ask a question. A deep question.

***

where do questions come from?

Possibly twenty-five years ago, in a book I can't recall, I read the phrase, "Truth is Love and Love is Truth".

It had a ring of extraordinary profundity about it, but as far as my experience was concerned it made no sense whatsoever. I had no idea what Truth really was, and I had no idea what Love really was. And how they could be in any way synonymous, was even more of a puzzle to me. And yet for some reason I was intrigued. I wondered whether I would ever get to a point in my life when I might understand words like that. Was Truth *really* Love? Was Love *really* Truth?

---

4. Questions have no goal in mind. An inquiry into sadness is not an attempt to have it transform into happiness or come up with a tidy conceptual framework in the mind. It is simply an inquiry into sadness, and that inquiry can lead anywhere.

That phrase became a question for me and I let it dwell within for many years. Occasionally I returned to it, realized I was perhaps a little closer to understanding it, and then moved on again. Then one day, only a few years back, I looked within, and Truth was indeed Love, and Love was indeed Truth. It could be no other way. It wasn't a momentous realization, it wasn't a bells-and-whistles thing. The truth of that small phrase had slipped in quietly under the radar. Would I have come to that understanding without having held that question? I don't know.

Another question that I held for decades was something I had overheard as a child. Two children were talking. One asked the other, "What remains still, even when you're walking?" It sounded like a riddle and yet it caught my attention. Was there really something that remained still even when I was walking? Occasionally when I was out walking I asked myself that question, searching in my body for something that didn't move. Where was it? What was it? Eventually, as an adult, I found that there was indeed something that remained still even when I was walking. But the paradox was, that although it was still, it was also forever moving.

We must allow ourselves to be open to questions. We must allow ourselves to be curious, interested, engaged. We must keep silent and listen. Always listen. Questions can come from anywhere, from anyone, at any time. Questions can come from reading, they can come from an overheard conversation. They can come from childhood. They can come from our lived experience of this moment. What is it about this person, these words, this experience that I don't understand?

Many questions have come out of my experience of suffering. Why do I suffer so much? What is this deep emotional pain? The Buddha asked that question and it is a very good question. And from that question have come so many other questions: How do I live this life? Why do I want to kill myself? Where can I find peace? Is there an end to suffering?

But as I searched for an answer to my suffering, I was also frequently troubled by the notable *lack* of questions. In almost all healing modalities, there was virtually no questioning as to what it was that was actually being healed. It seems bizarre to me now, that this basic question was rarely, if ever, addressed. If 'I' was being healed, then what exactly is this 'I'? Am I a body? Am I a brain? Am I energy? Am I am assortment of behaviors or stories? Am I a conglomeration of parts that can eventually be glued together to form a happy healthy human being called 'Marianne'? And if I fix just one of these parts, will that then alleviate the suffering of the whole? And why, in my search for healing, did I so rarely feel myself addressed in the fullness of my humanity and my potential? Why were there too many occasions when, in my fragility, I found myself even further diminished and invalidated?

People in my life are also questions. It is a well-known Buddhist teaching, to think of every person you meet as the Buddha. The invitation for me in that teaching, is to see the perfection in everyone; this person right here in front of me is perfect, not in any light-filled, beatific, heavenly way, but rather simply *as they are*. This woman in a yellow dress crossing the road is perfect, this thin man with a cigarette hanging out of his mouth is perfect, my grumpy partner is perfect, this person in the locked ward of a psychiatric hospital is perfect. If I react or relate to them with disdain, with withdrawal or with anger, then for me, there is a question. Why do I feel annoyed by this person? What is this person really trying to say to me? What is the look in this person's eyes that so moves me? Why do I have such difficulty with this person? If they are the Buddha, if they are God, Spirit, whatever name *I* choose, then why do *I* then have a problem with them? That's the question. It's a good question. And a big question.

For me there has always been a question inherent simply in being alive. If I sit for a moment and experience this living form that is this human body that I call 'me', then that experience is extraordinary. It is completely remarkable. And it is something the mind can never grasp. I am a living 'something' that is in a body. I am not that person over there, I do not have that other person's thoughts, and I do not have that other person's skin. No, I am *this* person. I function, I think, I can go to extraordinary depths within, and I can travel to amazing places without. Particularly when I was younger, those thoughts, and that experience of simply being alive was fascinating to me. I was *alive*! One hundred years ago I wasn't alive and in one hundred years' time I won't be alive again. What is this life? What is this body? What will be this death?

Slowly over the years, the answers have come. And I have found out that I am that person over there after all, though not in any way I could contrive in my mind. And I have found that life is so much more extraordinary and yet so much more ordinary than I could ever have imagined or thought or dreamt.

Ask the questions …

***

poetry as a question

I often use poetry to explore and experience my questions. Poetry is a bridge between the realms of deepest sensing and the everyday world. In poetry nothing is wrong; nothing is forbidden. In poetry there is room for silence and space and invitation. I write what is there in my direct experience. I move and flow with it. Sometimes a poem will be written in a few minutes. Other times, a poem will be the result of a lengthy process of questioning and meditation. In poetry I sometimes find my answers. And sometimes I don't. Sometimes I know it is enough to simply articulate the question.

not-knowing

can I allow myself
not-knowing?

can I feel not-knowing
in my body?

a discomfort
an ache

an emptiness
an inability to move

not-knowing

here now I feel
not-knowing

between my wholeness and depth
and solidity,
and my neediness and cravings
and desires,
there is not-knowing

am I one?
am I the other?
am I both?
am I neither?
am I a strange fluctuation?

I don't know
I don't have a choice
I don't know where I am in this story.
am I an adult now?
or a child?
am I whole?
or am I damaged?

I am just here
where I am
with my feet on the ground
eating
sleeping
walking
fucking

and not-knowing

***

placing questions into the ether

When I was a child I occasionally prayed to God. I'm sure I was meant to ask for good and wholesome things – global peace, an end to world hunger, happy things for my brother – but I didn't. I asked that my parents stop arguing and I asked for lovely things for myself. As I grew, asking God for nice things seemed a bit like treating God as a wish-fulfilling genie; it seemed like a rather selfish thing to do.

Yet there have been occasions when the charge of a question, or a need in my life, has been so great, that I have 'placed it into the ether'; I have entrusted it into the 'hands of God' (All That Is, Spirit) for safekeeping but also resolution. And it has truly astonished me, that those questions have *always* been given a response, albeit sometimes months or years later.

My most recent experience with this, was my longing for a teacher. I knew to the very depths of my being, that I needed and wanted a teacher. I could feel the teacher there, but when I looked around for a teacher through all the usual channels, I did not feel drawn to anyone, nor to any particular spiritual path. I began to doubt that I would ever find someone, and so at that point I placed my longing into the ether. I felt the longing in my body, I felt the wise teacher and

I asked the All to bring them together for me. Occasionally I lay in bed at night and once again articulated that longing: "Please, please, I feel such a need for a teacher right now. Please bring me a teacher." Then slowly things happened in my life that were unexpected, unplanned, strange even. And yet, as I followed that path, it led me to my teacher. And she is here and she is in my life.

***

the question of meditation

relentless sitting
to rid myself of a miscreant ego
seemed so mindless
mind-numbing

now meditation has become a question:
what is down there?
what is this feeling?
what is this breath?
this body?
this beauty?
this longing?

what is this moment?

and so life becomes
a question
rather than a battleground

***

an end to questioning

Just as there is an art to questioning so is there an art in knowing when to stop. There comes a time when everything is simply as it is, without fanfare or fuss. *Here* is the answer, in the completion of this moment, in this expanse, in this deep, deep silence. Nothing more is needed. It is all here.

A deep silence within.

She does not clamor

To show off her wares
To speak of her finery or beauty
Or holler her fame.

A deep silence within
Has no question
And no argument.

***

the journey

The metaphor of a journey is a redemption.

It is not a redemption from sin or evil, but rather a redemption from the stranglehold of a normality that would see suffering as a problem, as an illness, as less-than-perfect.

When we suffer deeply we may feel that we have lost our way, that we have been abandoned or left by the roadside. And yet, over and over, when we look back on those deeply suffered times, we are astonished to see their perfection in the unfoldment of our lives.

Even if in the moments of our greatest torment we are blinded by our tears, we are not separate from the journey Home. We are already walking its steps.

Everything we need is waiting for us on the path ahead. Dare we open our eyes and our hearts and embrace its gifts?

***

to what are you journeying?
to where does this journey go?

what is it in your heart or in your soul
that would lead you onto this lonely, rocky, windswept trail,
plunge you into the damp and slippery swamps of your unknowing
or the cruel and barren deserts of your nightmares?
what is it that drives you to seek a world
beyond dissatisfaction and restlessness?
beyond the bright lights and easy paths,
beyond the glossy surface sheens on which we so easily slip and slide and then fall?
what are you yearning for, aching for?

***

the richness of the journey

When we are suffering, it is all too easy to believe that our distress is meaningless and there is something fundamentally wrong with us.

Society perpetuates that belief. The 'right' sort of life is portrayed as happy, driven, engaged, friendly, outgoing and busy. It is extraordinarily difficult to escape that image.

We turn on the television and we see happy people doing happy things: they smile and laugh because they have flawless skin or drink Coke. We go to a family gathering feeling a little sad, and our mother says, "Couldn't you make an effort to smile more? You've got so much to be grateful for." Our partner senses our unhappiness and says, "Perhaps you'd feel better if you had your hair done." The voice in our head joins in with that chorus. We berate ourselves for feeling anti-social: "Why can't you be happy and normal like everyone else? What's wrong with you?" We feel we must get back to a happy sort of life as soon as possible. The only framework we are given for understanding our suffering is that of illness, concern, alarm or inconvenience.

But within the context of a journey, all that changes.

In my last two years at high school, there were twenty girls and only five boys in my class. How I managed to nab the best-looking of those boys as my boyfriend, I will never know. He was, however, a devout Christian, and so I tried to become a Christian too.

Perhaps to encourage my conversion, my boyfriend gave me an inspirational little book; it was an autobiography of a woman who had come through difficult times and found peace 'in Jesus'. I can't remember the name of the author, nor its title, but I *can* remember that it was the first time I came across the concept of life lived as a journey of discovery and growth. I found something very real in those pages that suggested to me a meaningful world beyond the sort of 'journeying through life' sanctioned by 'normality'[1]: study, get a job, earn money, get married, have children, retire, have grandchildren, die .... I felt the stirrings of a curiosity that had, up until that time, only flickered on the edges of my consciousness.

Although my Christian phase ended very abruptly when I was dumped by my

---

1. Also see chapter *Flatland and the dilemma of 'normality'*.

boyfriend for using the word 'fuck' in front of his parents, my interest in stories of journeying and unfoldment quickly became a passion.[2]

When I was twenty years old I read Peter Matthiessen's book, *The Snow Leopard*. It was an account of his eight-week trek accompanying zoologist George Schaller into a remote region of Nepal in order to study the mating habits of the Himalayan blue sheep and perhaps catch a glimpse of its elusive predator, the snow leopard.

In the many years since, I have never read another book that portrays the power of journeying with such potency and beauty. I *savored* every page and every beautiful word. There were times I hugged that book to my chest, as though to take its fertile resonances more fully into my heart. I wonder now, whether on some level I foresaw the paths I would follow in life, for contained within its pages was everything I came to value about journeys and journeying.

On a journey *everything* can be included.

Matthiessen's journey included extreme cold, the effects of altitude, physical discomfort, the elation of seeing extraordinary landscapes, the simple beauty of mountain streams and wildflowers, wretched disappointment, sorrow, painful memories, great joy, questions and courage.

I may not have been walking on lonely mountain paths, but with the assurance of a journey beneath my feet I learnt that even when I fell flat on my face, even when I barely had the energy to put one foot in front of the other, even when I felt desperately suicidal, *all* experience belonged. There was nothing 'wrong'. It was *all* part of the journey and wherever I found myself was always exactly the place I was meant to be. On a journey it was impossible to lose my way. Everything I encountered was nourishment and inspiration for my next steps forward.

Journeys invite us to engage with all dimensions and levels of our humanity.

Matthiessen's journey may have had an overarching physical context, but it was also a spiritual, emotional and cultural journey. As his feet trod the mountain paths, he searched for meaning and significance after the death of his wife, he engaged with villagers and their way of life, he contemplated suffering and impermanence, he explored Zen Buddhism and moved ever more deeply into

---

2. Also see chapter *Stories*.

the present moment. None of these levels can be separated; between them lie intricate layers of meaning and reverberation.

Even as I embarked on my unseen and unlauded journey in my very ordinary life, I was invited ever more fully into the breadth and richness of *all* of my humanity; I delved into different spiritual paths, read many books, explored nature, pursued different therapies, deepened into my body, gained insight into my childhood, meditated, travelled overseas, camped and hiked, taught music, painted, wrote books, worked in different jobs, made love, laughed and cried, did the shopping and mopped the floors … and that entire time I was on a journey to make sense of my suffering and find the truth of life.

> **Journeys also call us to reflect on the deeper questions of life and of living.**

On a journey, without the familiarity of everyday comforts to fall back on, we may feel our customary or everyday identity slipping away; we may begin to intuit its limitations and its illusory nature. We may ask: What is life all about when I am alone in the enormity of the natural world or feel lost in the maze of my inner jungle? What is this seemingly small and insignificant speck of life I call 'me'? Why does my everyday life feel so dull or uninspiring and yet I feel so alive when I am putting one foot in front of the other? What is it that gives life meaning? What is it that bears witness to the most glorious and the most painful moments of my life? Who am I most truly? What is my true nature?[3]

> **On a journey we have no option but to embrace change as the moment-by-moment reality.**

Within the framework of a journey we realize that even when we take one single step, our perspective changes; around each corner there is something new to see and to know.

In our everyday lives, change can feel uncomfortable and unwelcome: we don't want our car to break down, we don't want our dog to die, we don't want our body to age, we don't want a happy feeling to contract into a sad one. And so we resist change, we feel angry that we are seemingly at its mercy, and we cling desperately to any sense of stability: money, a particular identity, fixed beliefs or points of view, our partner, our children. But change is the natural condition of life; without change, there is only stagnation and death.

---

3. Also see the chapter *Questions*.

A journey gives enduring meaning to the natural uncertainty and impermanence of life. We learn to 'go with the flow' and dance with life as it appears before us.

On a journey we embrace adventure in both our inner and outer lives.

We are curious, engaged, interested. What is around the next corner? Who will I meet today? Will I have a comfortable bed tonight? What will I eat for lunch? What is this contraction or tension or fear showing me? When will the rain end? Dare I take this risk? Can I sit with this pain through each moment of the day? How does this fit into the primary themes or sticking points that repeatedly confront me as I make my way through life?

Adventuring is not always easy, but if we are open to whatever it offers us, it is always fascinating.

On a journey we are given an overarching context for growth and transformation.

As we are tested and pushed beyond the confines and comforts of what we know, we are given the opportunity to learn and to grow. My journey brought me tremendous insight, healing, understanding, deepening and ultimately awakening. I also found myself increasingly open to qualities such as dedication, humility, sincerity, whole-hearted determination, courage, grace, dignity, compassion, strength, maturity and peace.

Journeying necessitates a ruthless honesty.

Simply living through the day-to-day hardships of the journey there Is no room for 'kidding oneself'.[4] On a journey we must face our failings, our weaknesses, our doubts, our physical fragility, and through them find a true and deep resilience. It is through the utmost vulnerability that we find our utmost strength.

A journey assumes a goal.

A goal gives meaning to the journey. For Matthiessen, the goal was to find the Lama of Shey and perhaps catch sight of the elusive snow leopard. The 'goal' of

---

4. Also see the section on sincerity in the chapter *Suitcase for the Journey.*

my own journey changed over time, although at its fundament it was always a journey Home.[5]

At the end of his book it seems particularly apt that Matthiessen fails in his quest to see a snow leopard. The reality is that when we come to the end of our journey we find ourselves, not at the destination we had imagined, but rather back at the place we started from. However, as we look about us, it is as though we are now seeing that place for the very first time. We realize that the 'goal' was actually a multi-layered metaphor for all that the journey would bring out in us.

What we were searching for was under our feet the whole time. [6]

Shortly after my book *Seventeen Voices* was published I was asked to give a talk at a mental health center. I spoke about my motivation for putting the book together, the process of doing the interviews, the wisdom contained within the interviews and my own life of journeying.

When I had finished a man came up to me and said how much he had enjoyed my talk and in particular, my reflections on my journey. He described his own journey out of suffering and then said, "The journey into peace and understanding is *soooo* rich! People don't understand that! Society doesn't understand it! Our families don't understand it! Even doctors don't understand it! They think that when we get to the end of our journey of suffering and 'get better', we end up back where we started. But we don't. We may look like we're in exactly the same place, but we're looking out at the world with new eyes and we're seeing so much more than they can possibly imagine!"

Yes.

***

---

5. Our goal can also be to answer our fundamental life questions. I recall being in a group in which people were asked to introduce themselves by way of this fundamental question. People came up with: Who am I? What's the meaning behind everything? Is there meaning? Is there a picture/theory that includes everything? How do I find my fundamental uniqueness and sovereignty? Is it possible to be 100% authentic? Is there more than just this? Is there a way in which I can piece together all the bits of life?

6. The teaching in some spiritual circles is that there is 'no journey', because we already are what we are seeking. In some sense this is true. However, there is an enormous journey to undertake before we can realize this as a lived Knowing. We can't just be jumped there, except perhaps as an intellectual exercise/construction or in a moment of transcendence. It is only when we look out with the 'new eyes' of the wisdom, insight, clarity and breadth we have gained on the journey that we can return to the place we started from and recognize its Truth.

your path

as you bear the weight of a grief in your heart
an ache in your marrow
a sudden betrayal
a cruel twist
when all doors close
when storm clouds gather
when you lose the keys you spent a lifetime looking for

please know, beautiful one
that there is a path
a path for you alone
there is a path to paradise
I have seen it and I have walked it
and I have laughed with gratitude as I stood fulfilled

this
beautiful one
this is your path
even if you fall
even if you forget
even if you are tired and for now you must sleep
even if grief tears at your throat
this is your path
and you can never stray from it

the flowers will bloom under your feet
when you are not looking

***

journaling the journey

All my journals bear testament to my journey. Below are some excerpts that speak specifically of journeying.

1993

I never thought this journey of getting better would be anything like this. What did I think it would be like? Certainly not a battle for every single step.

1996

I say it over and over to myself, "And this too, and this too. It's all part of it, it's all part of this journey." I can see that now, but at times the pain is so bad I want to end it all. But perhaps the 'wanting to end it all' is part of it too … yes, that is the key. This wretched 'wanting to end it all' is part of it. Nothing can be left out. Nothing. Why is that lesson so hard to learn?

2002

This whole journey, this learning, this process, never ceases to amaze me. The last week, in retrospect was so lacking in any sort of clarity – I couldn't work out why I couldn't get my head to work – lots of fuzzy stuff. And then it suddenly made sense – the journey is going on ALL the time. It doesn't need to be forced, it doesn't need to be controlled. Once again I learn that I can utterly trust its process. It does not let me down. It is so easy for me think that I am not 'doing things' right somehow and that I'm not thinking the 'right' things, but the fact is that I am doing it all so utterly right. It's *all* part of the journey. On the journey there is never anything wrong!

2004

I don't know what to do, nor how to move forward. I can only go step by step, moment by moment. I don't have the energy to talk or to work. It is so hard, but this is how it is right now. It is just This.

2005

This morning the feeling of death is so strong and I am unable to go into or deal with it on my own. Every step and movement is death and I feel utterly terrified. Yesterday, I felt much stronger and more grounded, went for a short walk, painted some fence, but thought "I am not ready to get better yet, this journey is not complete". There is still something I must learn. What is it? What is it?[7]

***

the spiraling journey

7. On reading this journal entry for inclusion in the book, I wondered whether I somehow foresaw my awakening into True Nature/Consciousness in 2008. There definitely was much more to learn.

As we move forward on our journey, there are times when we once again find ourselves wading through a mire of suffering and confusion.

We look back at all the work we've done, all the progress we thought we'd made, all the difficult times we've come through, and we assume that all our effort and insight was in vain: "Surely if I'd made some *real* progress I wouldn't still be suffering, would I?" We jump to the conclusion that nothing whatsoever has changed ... we're *still* useless, we're *still* stupid and life is pointless ... same old story, same old words. I wrote the following poem about just such a place:

> Can I forgive myself
> That once more
> I am in this place of pain and suffering?
> How often have I been here?
>
> Am I destined to circle around
> Like a chained and footsore bear,
> Wearing a path into the
> Dusts of eternity?
>
> How can I ever step out of this
> Endless wheel?
> There seems to be no solution
> To this wretched circle.
>
> I try to walk faster,
> Strengthen my body,
> Buy new shoes,
> Feel the grief of my fate,
> Pay heed to the urgings of others:
> "Keep going, keep going!"
>
> But it makes no difference.

We imagine that a journey goes along in a straight line; we start from a place of difficulty or anguish and end up with a storybook happy ending. But journeys aren't like that; they aren't linear.

I came to realize that a spiral is by far the most accurate metaphor for the course that a journey takes.

Certain issues, particularly those that were very painful or those that carried resonances from my childhood, came up over and over. I realized that healing these memories or patterns required that they be seen and then resolved on ever-deeper and ever-more-subtle levels. Each time I approached them, my view had changed and it was necessary for me to understand and embrace them from my new vantage point; the outlook from the top of a 42-storey building is very very different to that from the ground level.

Even after awakening and knowing myself as a fundamental deep peace and wellness, it was still necessary for me to revisit many difficult places.[8] It was as though in moving into them and casting the eyes of Consciousness upon them, they could be given their ultimate holding and as such, their freedom.

> The circles within
> Go deeper and deeper.
> We circle around,
> Spiraling,
> Gaining depth each time.
> We meet over and over
> The child we once were,
> Understanding afresh the torment
> And the pain
> Until there is no separation
> And we hold it all in the embrace of Being.

***

---

8. For further discussion see the chapter, *The Child and the Fundamental Abandonment.*

suitcase for the journey

For any journey we pack a suitcase. The journey out of suffering is no different.

What follows is a list of those things I packed, those things I picked up along the way and those things I discarded.

***

courage

There were times people said to me, "Oh but you're so brave to go within and look around. I'm not deep like you. I prefer to stay with what I know." I was always taken aback by such comments; I never felt brave. Rather, I felt that I was doing what I was called to do. It was what I *wanted* to do. And frankly, I've always found the journey exciting, interesting, energizing, and fascinating.

But it was in the small moments that nobody ever saw, that there was indeed a need for tremendous courage.

There were times when I *truly* wanted to kill myself, when I desperately wanted my life to come to an end, when I wanted to hurt myself or take some pills. It was at those times when I lay in bed with tears streaming down my face and said to myself, "No. I will lie here until I go to sleep, or I will lie here all night crying, but I will not kill myself", that were truly some of my most courageous.

It was the courage of feeling the desire for self-destruction and yet continuing to live in the face of it. It was the courage of continuing to breathe. *That* was courage. And it was courage to wake the next morning, get up, have a cup of tea, get dressed and face the day as it was, without remembering myself back into the distress of the previous night. It was courage to simply *feel* what the new day might bring: the tiredness, the ache in my gut, the questions. But it was also courage to go outside and gently witness the dawning of a new day, hug a dog, breathe the air and to go back to bed again if I needed to.

And there was also tremendous courage in facing my own weaknesses, courage in breaking through the twisted chains of my emotional inheritance, courage in having a gentle compassion for myself even when life was difficult and my body hurt like hell, courage in moving forward despite a wretched anxiety or fear, courage in asking for help, and courage to sit with my questions and confusion. It also takes courage to go down a path that society as a whole will not applaud or recognize, that your family will not understand, and that will leave your friends puzzled or even angry.

We call people heroes when they can kick a soccer ball into a net, when they climb a high mountain, or when they can entertain us with their fancy dance moves, but sometimes the truly courageous people are those whose actions will forever remain unlauded and unseen. And yet, I have no doubt that the reverberations and beauty of their simple acts will remain forever etched into the wholeness of our collective Being.

Do we realize how courageous we are in even the very smallest of ways?

***

sincerity

Sincerity is essential.

The journey out of suffering and into the knowing of our True Nature, can be a difficult and complicated one, but without sincerity as its backbone it would be impossible. How could we ever open to a state in which Truth is its very breath, if we do not choose to live it in every moment?

For me, sincerity feels very much like an internal clarity and openness. It is a clear space that in its simplicity and transparency, immediately registers any obfuscation or muddiness in my motivation. It is an unreserved embrace of what is true and real, that finds even the smallest acts of guile distasteful and at times even painful. It is a blistering honesty that burns away all falsehood and artifice.

In my sincerity, I ask myself: Is this true? Am I telling the truth and do I *own* that truth? Is my bearing a genuine one? Are my motivations coming from an uncontrived whole-heartedness? And if not, what is it that is holding me back? What it is that wants to judge, to control, to conceal, or to separate?

In my sincerity I don't run away from my difficulties, I don't lie to myself so I feel more comfortable, and I am prepared to face my weaknesses and my shortcomings without flinching. I am also honest about my feelings and honest about those parts of me that would choose to be less than honest. In my sincerity, I am open to asking any question of myself, open to examining even my most treasured assumptions and beliefs, and open to exploring all the hidden corners of my soul.

In our childhoods, we receive mixed messages about honesty and sincerity. 'Telling the truth' can be a difficult minefield for a child to negotiate. On one level we are told not to tell fibs or be deceitful: if you break something it's important to own up to it rather than try to blame your brother, it's not very nice to steal money from your mother's purse.

But beyond this, we learn that to be honest about what we feel, what we see, or even about who we truly are, is not necessarily welcomed. Honesty and sincerity are often the fall guys in our need to please our parents and get the love and care we need. At times our emotional and even physical survival may actually depend on our *dishonesty*. The price we pay for this is substantial: we lose the capacity to carry ourselves authentically, both in our external and internal worlds. We relate from fear rather than from honesty, we try to please people and 'say the right thing' rather than be true to ourselves, we block out our deepest woundings and pain, we build defensive walls around our carefully constructed identities, and we veil our lives with half-truths and silence.

Therapy is a powerful and important medium in which to explore what is actually true and to learn to speak that truth into the world. The best therapists are those without an agenda, who can allow and encourage that honesty and transparency, and also provide us with a mirror to reflect all that may lie obscured. As with the spiritual journey, effective therapy travels along the path of our deepest sincerity.[1]

***

integrity

I was in my early teens when I first learnt the word 'hypocrisy'. I was rather pleased to find a word for something that had often troubled me: I could never

---

1. For further discussion see the chapter *Therapists and Teachers*.

understand why my parents reprimanded me for things that they themselves *did*. Why were *they* allowed to be angry, when I wasn't? Why were *they* allowed to shout or swear, when I wasn't? Why would you expect someone else to behave in a way that you yourself did not? It seemed obvious to me, that if you were to present yourself as above reproach, then this should be borne out in your behavior. Why would you pretend to be something you weren't?

But of course, hypocrisy was not limited to my parents, and I am certain that I have been guilty of it on any number of occasions. But at that time I made a quiet pact with myself, to attempt as best I could, not to speak or act in any way that was hypocritical; I wouldn't say one thing while doing quite another. And I certainly wouldn't tell someone else how they should act.

I see integrity as being the opposite of hypocrisy. Integrity is certainly a sincerity and an honesty, but more than that, integrity speaks to me of wholeness and undividedness. It speaks of one's actions, words, beliefs, soul and Spirit, all working as one. From integrity, we don't champion the environment and then throw poisons down the drain, from integrity we don't act righteous and worthy in front of our spiritual teacher and then act abusively towards our children. Integrity is how we choose to behave when nobody is looking. Do we pick up litter when nobody is around to praise us? Do we help someone out even if they'll never know what we did? How do we respond to our suffering or our quest for Truth, when nobody is around to give us encouragement, attention or praise?

Oftentimes we will be the only person who knows whether we acted from integrity or not, but it will always be the measure of where our inclinations truly lie.

***

curiosity[2]

Children are naturally curious: "Why do people die? How did a baby get in that woman's tummy? Why do people cry when they're happy? Who makes the lightning?" The curiosity of children is playful. Their eyes are wide open with wonder, interest and possibility. The nature of their questions isn't limited by beliefs or assumptions, and so they are open to whatever answers or outcomes their curiosity might bring. Children are on an exciting journey to discover the truth of what it is to be alive in this world.

---

2. Also see the chapter *Questions*.

But as adults we lose that spontaneous and joyful curiosity about life. Many of our questions from childhood have been answered: we know how babies get in women's tummies, we understand the forces of nature that produce lightning, we know about tears of joy ... and we also know how to use a search engine. We believe we know what's going on in the world, and so we gradually stiffen behind our own particular worldview.

But our journey into life never ceases, and that includes the journey into our inner world. Each moment has never before been lived. Others may have gone before, and can provide us with inspiration and guidance, but it is a path that we must discover for our selves. Just as in childhood, curiosity was vital as we explored the physical world, so is curiosity vital as we travel into our inner realms and find our feet on uncharted and sometimes rocky terrain. We become like a child exploring a forest trail for the very first time: every little stick, every bend in the trail, every toadstool, every bug, is worthy of investigation. Certainly, there are times we might fall face-first in the mud and struggle to regain our footing, but it is all part of the richness of life.

In curiosity we open out into a genuine engagement with what is *here*. We recognize an enthusiastic and childlike quality in our bearing. We feel alive. Absorbed. Fascinated. It is our curiosity that takes us by the hand and leads us through the depths of our forests: What's going on? What is real? What is this feeling of emptiness? What is the richness I feel all around? Why do I now feel at peace when yesterday I wanted to end my life? What is this darkness? What is this love?

***

gifts

Sometimes, even in the most suffered times I was given a gift.

Gifts aren't a big deal. They were simply a way I had of understanding that despite the suffering and pain, there was still beauty, specialness and fun in the world.

Gifts are always there, but only if we look with the eyes that can see them, listen with the ears that can hear them, and hold out our hands and our heart to receive them.

> On a grey and cloudy day, I feel sad and pre-menstrual, but I am suddenly uplifted by the brilliant colors of a parrot in a tree.

I have a very bad headache. I decide to go for a walk because sometimes I feel better after physical activity. I see a neighborhood acquaintance approaching me and my heart sinks: "How am I going to talk to this guy when my head is pounding?" And then somehow, I am captivated by a twinkle in his eye, and I find myself engrossed in a delightful conversation. It lifts me and I forget about my pain for a little while.

I can't get to sleep. It is 2am and I am still awake. I walk into the kitchen and look up at the vast and starry sky. A shooting star surprises me as it streaks through the darkness. It is a moment of sheer delight and I am so grateful that I was awake to witness it.

I have had a rather unsettling phone call with a friend that leaves me feeling ill at ease. I go outside and the enfolding warmth of the sun on my skin gently soothes me.

Some years ago, there was a period when life seemed quite aimless. I frequently asked the cosmos: "Why am I alive? Why can't I find any meaningful thread that weaves its way through my life?" One day I was out walking, pondering my lack of overarching purpose, when suddenly I saw a shiny five cent coin on the ground. I smiled, picked it up and put it in my pocket, and then forgot about it. A few weeks later, an almost identical scenario played out. Once again I was on a walk, feeling the lack of direction in my life, when in front of me lay another five cent coin. Again I picked it up.

When I got home, I found the original coin and then placed them both beside me on my book shelves. And so started a pattern that continued on for a couple of years.

I liked to think of those coins as little gifts that did indeed seem to provide me with a thread: as long as I kept finding the coins I knew that there must be a reason I was still alive. It was magical thinking perhaps, but when I no longer needed their assurance, those shiny little gifts stopped. But as I type these words they still sit in a pile beside me.

***

nourishment

We need to be fed, to be filled. We need nourishment when we're suffering, when we're unsure, when we're questioning, when we're sitting ... our bodies need it, our minds, our emotions, our souls, our Spirit.

Nourishment is vital and yet amidst the turmoil, the angst, the busy-ness, the societal and therapeutic imperatives, in its utter simplicity it can all too easily be overlooked.

From the moment we are born, look into our mother's eyes and suckle on her breast we are nourished and we grow. We take in, we absorb, we drink, we eat. We long for it. We reach for it. We feel the emptiness in our bellies or hearts if it is denied us. We eat fresh healthy food and we feel invigorated and energized. We read books, and our minds are stimulated. In relationship our emotions are fed and held and reflected. Our soul expands and flourishes in the beauty and simplicity of nature; we drink in a sunset, feel ourselves embraced in the wooded groves of a forest, warmed by the vivid yellow of daisies. Our Spirit deepens and broadens in intimate discourse with Spirit as it is lived in others. There is constant movement: give and take, in and out. And always, *always*, there is the potential for nourishment. In the absence of nourishment we would naturally empty out, wither and then die

In times when I have been unwell or suffering, I always take great care to nourish myself. I slow my life down. I move very gently through the day. I make a piece of toast, I tidy some papers, I eat a banana. No big plans, no demands. I look out the window and watch the rain. There is simply what I am doing moment by moment. My thoughts slow down. My movements slow down. Even the slow movements of cleaning a benchtop or printing out a document, can become nourishing and somewhat delicious.

But our suffering can in itself be our nourishment and our food; it can nourish our renewal, our understanding and our deepening into soul and Spirit.

As my journey deepened, I increasingly found that it was Spirit that was the source of my deepest Nourishment. It was only in Spirit that I eventually found the all-encompassing satisfaction and contentment that I was yearning for. It was in Spirit that I felt wholly nourished, fed and utterly replete. In Spirit I don't want for more.

After awakening I knew myself as Nourishment itself; we *are* that rich, warm, encompassing, sustaining, nourishing essential lifeblood. We are not separate from it in any way. We never were.

***

humility

When I was going through difficult times, it was all too easy to think, "Oh no, something is going wrong! Everything has fallen in a heap again!" However, inevitably when I looked back over my life I could see that 'something' had been charting a course far better than anything I could ever have worked out for myself. It requires humility to realize that we are not the ones in control and that something far bigger is at play. It requires humility to step back and admit that sometimes we don't have a clue what is going on.

There is also an innate humility in the ordinariness of being. We sit on a park bench, we sip a cup of tea, or we watch the birds and we allow ourselves to simply *be*. We feel no need to be other than what we *are* in that moment; there is a deliciousness in not feeling separate from the life and the movement around us.

The everyday self, however, thrives on separation and specialness. It puffs itself up with false pride: "Look at me. Look at how busy I am. Look at how important I am. Listen to this amazing spiritual experience I've had." But when we open out into the simplicity of being, that need to impress and to look good naturally falls away. We relax into an ordinariness and with that inevitably comes exquisite relief and peace. As we move deeper, that need for reinforcement and for specialness falls away altogether. We awaken to the absolute ordinariness of our True Nature. It is an extraordinary ordinariness, but it is an ordinariness all the same.

Humility is also profoundly important in the process of awakening. Our Essential Self can only ever be approached with humility; it is not something that can ever be conceived, grasped or owned by the mind or everyday self.

I recall a time not so long after I awoke to Consciousness. I was in the middle of a meditation retreat and without realizing it, I had started to grasp at the awakened state. When I first awakened, the difference between everyday life and the awakened state was extraordinary; here was a peace, an ease and a sense of Home I had never thought possible. But as I sat meditating, the refrain in my mind was, "I must make sure I *never* lose this state." But in that refrain there was a grasping, and a desire for ownership and control. As I was going to bed that night, all of a sudden I contracted back into everyday limited consciousness; I 'lost' the awakening and it was awful.

Having seen what was possible I knew that it would be unbearable to live within that partial view. I could feel panic rising. I paced around the room, "How can I get 'it' back? What should I do?"

Then without any precipitating thought whatsoever, I went down on my hands and knees on the floor. I bent forward, put my forehead on the carpet, and stretched my arms and hands out in front of me. I bowed down as low as I could go. I prostrated myself. I bowed down and bowed down. I admitted my utter defeat in the face of All That Is. I knew I was powerless and I was literally driven to my knees. I wasn't pretending. I wasn't half-hearted. I wasn't doing it for any gain. There was only humility. I completely humbled myself, both outwardly and inwardly. I surrendered. I totally gave myself up to God.

And then, as I arose, I realized I had opened back out into the awakened state. And in the face of the That, I remain humble. Always.

***

dedication

A frequent question in spiritual circles is: "Do you really want it?" Do you *really* want it?

I learnt about dedication when I was studying to become a professional musician. There were very few positions in Australia for professional flute players, so I knew the odds were greatly stacked against me. People suggested I choose something easier: why not become a flute teacher, a school music teacher? But I wanted to play in an orchestra and that's what I was determined to achieve.

My commitment to that goal became my focus. It was a single-pointed and single-minded aspiration that did not waver. I tried to study with good teachers, I did as many 'gigs' as my schedule allowed and at times practiced up to 6 hours a day. And I *loved* what I was doing; it fired me like nothing else. I *knew* that this was what I wanted to do with my life. And by the time I reached my mid-20s, I got the job I wanted. And I know without a doubt that it was my whole-hearted dedication to that goal that made it happen.

And the journey out of suffering is a bit like that, except there is no fancy job and no kudos at the end of it. Most likely nobody will even notice that anything has happened. There is simply the quiet and unremarkable presence of Home waiting for you. But you ache for it, and you can't push the aching away. And you can't forget about it, even if sometimes you would prefer that you did. It is your passion. It is your 'thing'. You *want* to know the truth of your suffering and you *want* to know who you most truly *are*. You read books, you meditate, you ask questions, you sit in silence, you seek out a therapist if you feel the need, you look for a teacher, you go to lectures and meetings, you join groups. There can't be anything wishy-washy in your motivations. It can't be something you only think about when you have nothing better to do.

You want it. You *really* want it. And you're prepared to wholly dedicate yourself to that wanting.

***

faith

For me, the word 'faith' is tainted to some degree, because all too often in the past I heard it preached from a pulpit or from power. This sort of 'faith' means doing or believing something when there is no valid reason to do so. It means following someone else's ideas about how life should go. Blind faith.

But the faith of which I am writing here, is an acknowledgement of what I already know inside. It is a faith in what I sense in my intuition, in my deepest Knowing. It is a faith that there is a wisdom far greater than anything I could ever construct in my mind. It is a faith to follow my individuality and my authenticity. Faith that I can stand up straight on my own two legs. Faith that I will come through even the deepest of suffering. Faith in my courage. Faith in my calling to know the Truth. Faith that there is a fundamental goodness and wholeness of which I am unquestionably a part.

***

leaving positivity behind

I first came across positive affirmations in a book called *You can Heal Your Life* by Louise Hay; it was the mid-1980s and my life was definitely in need of healing.

I started to read the book. I underlined the sections that spoke of my life, I penciled my reflections in the margins, and found some positive affirmations that seemed relevant: "I am thin", "I am filled with love", "I am perfect and whole", "I choose to make changes". As I repeated them to myself, I experienced an immediate rush of well-being and positivity. I wondered if perhaps I was onto something.

However, as I made my way through the book, I felt a simmering irritation beneath the optimism. I tried to push it away by reciting more affirmations – "I am calm and peaceful", "I am whole and complete" – but the irritation grew into a blustery anger. Half way through the book, the neat underlining dwindled away and in its place came ferocious scrawls: *"I don't want to bloody change!"*, *"I don't want to be fucking calm!"*

As I look at that book now, I can see that it certainly contains some truth: we are indeed Love, we are indeed Perfect and Whole, we are indeed Peace. But these are qualities of our True Nature and we are gifted them by grace as we awaken to the reality of what we are. The everyday self can approximate these qualities, imagine them, but it cannot will itself into them by simply repeating over and over its desire to do so.[3] Doing so can only lead to frustration, a sense of failure and the telling of some serious untruths. The fact was, I *wasn't* calm and peaceful, I wasn't filled with love and I wasn't thin.

But on top of that, I also came to realize that there was a bigger issue. The Truth if we are ever to find it, is never anywhere else other than *here;* the Truth is what we have right in front of us. Now. Any attempt to try to escape that Truth leads to confusion.

While I was trying to tell myself that I was filled with love and that I was perfect, I was neglecting the reality of my life in that very moment: I didn't feel loving or calm. Our pain and suffering, in this very moment, is our doorway to Truth, and any attempt to bypass that by telling ourselves that our reality is different from the one we see in front of us, can only ever be a shallow or temporary measure. It is only by moving *into* our suffering, getting to know it in our bodies and understanding it,

---

3. For a further description see the chapter *The Child and the Fundamental Abandonment* and most particularly the footnotes that describe the The Diamond Approach of AH Almaas.

that it transforms and allows us to move more fully into the depths of what we are. How can we truly come to love, if we cannot know our capacity to be unloving? How can we truly know wholeness, if we cannot see how scattered we are? How can we know our fullness, if we cannot also know our emptiness?

Also, positive affirmations did no justice to my immense desire to know the Truth and did not give acknowledgement to the circumstances of my life that had brought me to such suffering. I didn't want to sweep the reality of the child I was, and the adult she became, underneath the proverbial carpet. It would have denied not only the far-reaching devastation caused by childhood trauma, but also the intelligence, courage, capability, resilience and utter dedication that had brought me through those times.

In addition, an active and intentional negativity carries an enormous power. It is only by truly saying "no" to something, that we are able to give our unequivocal "yes". If I am unable to say, "No I do not wish to be treated in this way", how would I ever be able to affirm how it is that I *do* wish to be treated? If I am unable to say, "No, I don't wish to socialize today", how would I be able to figure out what it is that I truly *do* wish to do?

***

understanding spiritual materialism

Many years ago I read a book by Buddhist teacher Chogyam Trungpa called *Cutting through Spiritual Materialism*. It was a powerful book and gave me insights into the living of spirituality which to this day I value immensely.

When I first heard about 'spirituality' I didn't really understand what it was, but after I read Trungpa's book I did, to some degree, understand what it *wasn't*.

When we begin our search into the 'spiritual' realms, we can all too easily transplant the requirements, experiences, actions and thoughts of the everyday materialistic (acquisitive) world, onto the inner world. We *use* spirituality in the same way we might use 'things': 'spirituality' can become some*thing* that we are trying to do, or some*thing* that we claim ownership of. We might use spirituality to reassure ourselves that we are good and virtuous and that our lives are worthwhile, we might use it as a new or 'nobler' identity, we might use it as an entertainment or a hobby, we might collect 'spiritual experiences' and then parade them in front of our friends, we might preach or flaunt our vast knowledge and learning on the subject. The list goes on.

But spirituality is none of these 'things'. Spirituality is about who/what we are without reference to *things*: without reference to thoughts, emotions, reflections on thoughts or emotions, actions, experiences (including spiritual ones), sensations, urges, impulses, other people, names, job, work persona, family persona, how we think of ourselves, who we think ourselves to be. Spirituality is about who/what we *are* in this very moment. It is about our direct experience of ourselves … *now*. Anything else totally misses the point. I certainly didn't fully understand this at the time I read the book, but I *did* understand that it didn't make any sense to turn spirituality into a materialistic endeavor.

If I found myself acting towards spirituality as I might when I wanted to show off a new car or when I wanted to impress someone, I would tell myself, "No, that's not where it's at." It wasn't that I implemented a strict regime of behavior management on myself, I simply inquired after my true motivation. I noticed: Was I puffing myself up? Was I feeling special because I was having 'amazing' spiritual experiences, insights or dreams? It was a gentle but very potent guide on the journey.

***

hope's false promise

You can always hope that things will get better.
   I can no longer hope.
That sounds so hopeless. Cheer up, we always have hope. Hope springs eternal!
   No, that sounds like a lovely sentiment, but that sentiment is killing me.

Hope is a bit like a positive affirmation: hope is always somewhere else. If I'm always hoping things will be different, then I'll never see how things actually *are*. When we live forever in hope, we are not living our lives in the present.

People might assume that without hope there is only hopelessness, but that is not the case. As with all polarities, hope and hopelessness exist together; they come as a package. If we cling to hope, then we're living in fear of its opposite: hopelessness. With hope we are inevitably bracing ourselves for disappointment.

Beyond hope and hopelessness, I live with what is here. What is here may be difficult, it may painful, but I don't resent or suffer it, by hoping for something different. Movement, growth and transformation don't happen because I am hoping for something else, they happen simply because change is in the very nature of Life. There is a natural flow of Life that can't be mediated and prodded and pushed. We *are* that Life and we can align ourselves with it. Life isn't something we make up in our minds prior to it happening. It is what we already *are*.

***

listening

Beyond the clamor of our phones and televisions,
Beyond the chattering of our minds,
Beyond the insistence of our ideas and beliefs,
The Truth is always whispering its presence to us.
It is reminding us, reminding us,
Reminding us of what we already are.
Only through listening will we hear its voice.

Listening paves the path on which we find our way Home.

***

"just shut up and listen!"

In everyday life the spoken word runs the show. Self-expression, articulateness, assertiveness, persuasiveness, making-a-statement, proving-a-point and having an opinion, are all highly valued.

Journalists, radio personalities, politicians, preachers, rappers, movie stars, teachers and chat groups. Everyone is talking.

In social gatherings with family and friends the talking continues: we talk about our problems, we talk about what happened last week or what we plan to do next week, we discuss the weather, we complain about our boss or our husband or our children, we tell jokes, we tell stories.

If we stop and sit in silence, the talking now comes from the mind. We are seemingly at the mercy of an incessant stream of inner chattering that tells us what we should or shouldn't do, justifies what we have already done or makes up conversations we will never have.

But with all this talking, few people seem all that interested in *listening*. We don't like to listen; we're uncomfortable with it.

Although we might stand around nodding and smiling when other people are talking, in reality we're just wishing they would shut up so that *we* can talk; *we* want to be the one in the spotlight doing all the talking. We might listen half-heartedly to a few words, but before long we're already planning what to say in return. We can't wait to interrupt: "Oh that happened to me too!" At other times, instead of listening fully, we might gradually tune out and become preoccupied with our inner chatter: "What will I cook for dinner tonight? Wow, her hair's going grey!"

Even in the 'healing' professions there are many for whom listening is merely a technical skill that allows them to hear what they want to hear and ignore that which they don't.[1]

And yet despite this tremendous shortfall in listening, it seems that we *all* want to be listened to; we even crave it at times.

On some level, we know that when we are truly and deeply listened to, something powerful happens. Whether in a therapeutic setting, in the kitchen when we're doing the washing up with our partner, or sitting on a park bench with a person we hardly know, true and deep listening is a very potent activity.

***

deep listening

When we listen deeply to another person we listen with *all* of who we are.

At first we may listen only with our physical ears to the actual sound of someone's voice or even simply to the fact that they are speaking.

Then we listen with our minds to grasp the content of their words.

As we listen a little more fully, our hearts come into play. We lean in with interest and curiosity, resonating with the emotions, values and meaning communicated *through* the words. We begin to care. We give the other person our time and our attention. And we also give them our silence.

---

1. For a discussion of listening in the therapeutic or teaching setting, see the section *Listening Deeply* in the chapter *Therapists and Teachers* and also the section *The Stories that Encircle* in the chapter *Stories*.

But we can also reach between, behind, and beneath the words to reach for the person who is speaking them. Just as with our arms we might reach for them in a physical way, so we can reach for and embrace them with our listening. We *sense* the other in our body, in our openness and in our presence. Listening in this way, we have no expectation that they be other than the way *are*; all judgements, preferences, agendas and evaluations that come from the mind are suspended. We listen deeply into their soul and perhaps also listen ourselves into intimate connection with them as Spirit.

And in doing so, the other will feel held, validated and accepted. They will feel loved.

But more than this, they will feel that our listening gives them a path by which *all* of who they are is given life in this world. Nothing need be left out, pushed away, or deemed 'unacceptable'. It can *all* be brought to light and to consciousness, and if needed, to resolution and healing. *Listening* in this way, is an extraordinary gift.

But this sort of deep listening is not just for others.

Whether in the silence of meditation, in contemplation and inquiry, or simply as we walk the pathways of our everyday lives, we can also gift this listening to ourselves.

We can listen beyond the voice in our head, beyond our beliefs and stories, beyond our judgements and imaginings and beyond our automatic interpretations. We can stop, and with inner ears, reach for what's *really* going on inside. We can give ourselves the time, the space and the silence to listen for and embrace what is truly *there* in our direct experience.[2]

It is with listening that we can move ever deeper into the Truth of what we are.

The writing of this book, too, is very much a product of moving into my depths with a profound listening.

As I write, I *listen* for what is actually *there* before any story or interpretation, and it is this that I am then putting into words. Listening *precedes* my words. For instance, in this chapter, I am listening for what listening actually *is*. I ask the question, "What is it that I do when I listen deeply?" I then feel 'listening' in my body. This process is deeply *experienced and felt*, and is not in any

---

2. For a more complete discussion of embracing direct experience, see the chapters *Beyond the Battle* and *Life*.

way the result of intellectualization. I do use the mind, but only as a tool, for organization, grammar, sentence construction and syntax, and also for checking that the meanings my writing conveys, are accurate.[3]

***

listening to myself, an invitation

Listening.

What is it to listen to myself? Really listen?

I stop.
Dispense with words. Dispense with busy-ness and noise.
Listen ... just listen within ... listen ...
I sink beyond the surface. Beyond my skin. Beyond my mind.
I slip into silence ... listen ...

Listening is a silence that knows nothing.

Here I find a deep subtlety and sensitivity ...
This listening ... it is beautiful. It is compassionate. Open.
This listening ... it makes no choice about what it will listen to.

Listening is a waiting,

It is a quiet questing.
A questioning: what is here?

I reach with inner hands.
Deeper. Deeper.
What is it I touch? What is it I hold?
I listen with inner ears.
I am curious. I want to know.
I listen with my body. My heart. My being.
What is here? What is within?

I listen to murmurings and hints
Of small still-wordless voices.

---

3. Also see the chapter *Creativity* for the process of writing.

To inklings and intuitions,
That speak their knowing into my bones.
I listen to a joy, a thought, a radiance, a shadow, a knot, a grief ...

I listen deeper into my soul.
Into Being.
I listen into the space beyond preference,
Beyond stories and beyond time.

I listen.
I listen to the place where I have always been
What I already am.

And through listening I will know that I am Home.

And then I listen for the movement of wisdom when it comes.
And for the movement of love.

***

listening to my inner voice or intuition, a process

The following process took place as I was writing this book.

> For days I have been restless. Unable to settle. I've just finished a major piece of writing for my book, and although I'm full of new ideas and directions, I'm unable to settle.
>
> I sit down at my computer, reply to emails, and complete an online order for dog treats. I look at the writing I've just completed. I find some small sections that need further editing. I open another piece of writing that is almost complete. I glance through. I hear a voice:
>
> > *No this is wrong.*
>
> I look out the window. I feel such a pressure to be productive. I glance through the piece again, but I feel no inspiration. I decide to open a blank page and start a new chapter. The voice repeats:
>
> > *No this is wrong.*

I try to push through. I sprinkle a few words down on the page. Once the words are there, they might offer a point from which I can work. But these words offer me nothing. They are motionless. The voice is insistent:

No this is wrong.

I ask the voice: "What do you want?" I listen inside. There is no answer and yet in the silence I sense a resolve.

I ask the question again: "What do you want?" I decide to let the question dwell within.

I get up from my computer. I put on the washing and go out into the garden. "What do you want?" The dogs run up to me, tails wagging. I pat the dogs. I watch them play; they are glorious happy souls. I start to weed. Clear the edges. "What do you want?" I hear that the washing has finished. I fill a basket with wet clothes and hang them on the line. I ask the question again: "What do you want?"

And suddenly as I'm standing with pegs in hand at the clothesline, the answer is there:

> *I want to sit in stillness. Complete peace. No pushing to move or do or be busy. Deepest peace. This is what I want.*

I realize that I resist meditation. Meditation is difficult with this constant movement.[4] I prefer to meditate as I walk. But it's not enough this time. I can feel myself pulled down into stillness. I cannot resist it now. Dogs and gardens will be there later. My writing will be there later.

The voice is right in its insistence and I know I must follow it.

I sit. The voice says:

Yes.

And I know without a doubt that this is exactly the right thing for me to do.

---

4. The inner movement of Disembarkment Syndrome. For a description of Disembarkment Syndrome see the preface.

I realize that all too often I disregard that little voice of intuition or inner knowing; I ignore its sense of undeniable truth, clarity and inner certainty. I push through and think I have a better idea about how life should go. But I wonder if this is at my peril. I wonder if in doing so I am denying that this voice might possess a deeper Knowing than that of my everyday self.

Whether it speaks to us about a relationship ending or beginning, about watching our step as we cross the road, about contacting a friend, about a major career change, or about sitting still rather than working, where are we led if we listen to the wisdom of that small inner voice?

God always lets us know what to do next.

Listen.

***

therapists and teachers

We can't do this journey on our own.

It is in the mirror of another's gaze that we are invited to see all that is still unconscious, unknown and unnamed. It is through the embrace of another's heart that we learn to hold our torment and anguish, allow it and then set it free.

This chapter contains some reflections on therapists and teachers, after having been a client and a student for many years. I hope it will offer insight, clarity and considerations, but also some cautions.[1]

***

what do you want?

When you seek out someone to accompany you on this journey, what do you want from them? What do you want help with? What are you looking for?

Each time I sought out healing or therapy, it was because I was suffering in some way and was unable to find a way through it on my own.

I certainly wanted relief from my suffering, but more than that, I wanted to *understand* it. I wanted to know *why* I was suffering and I wanted to know what that suffering *was*. It did not make sense to try to rid myself of something when I didn't even know what that 'something' actually was. Without that understanding how would I ever find *true* 'relief' and freedom?

---

1. I have written about various aspects of therapy and teaching in a number of chapters throughout this book; the material in this chapter is further to that. Although I have tried to cover most points that were relevant to me, I am aware that within the confines of this book, this material is in no way comprehensive. Added to this, although traditionally therapy and teaching were seen as quite distinct paths, and it was generally assumed that teaching commences once therapy has finished, I have found the two to be inextricably linked. My questions as to the nature of Truth could not, in any way, be separated from my desire to understand, move into and transform my suffering.

When I first sought help, it confused me that frontline healing professions weren't all that interested in questions about the nature of suffering. In the mainstream medical world, the primary goal seemed to be symptom relief and camouflage. The human being was seen as a biological machine that could be tweaked and 'oiled' with medications in order to keep it in a semblance of working order. In mainstream psychological practice the approach wasn't much different. In place of medication there was a technique, the implementation of which would help me to 'function better in the world'. There was no room for meaning or understanding, no room for questions or depth, no room for the vast interiority of my humanity.

And so, I learnt what I *didn't* want.

I didn't want bandaids. I didn't want a biological or psychological technician trying to 'fix' me. I didn't want to fit into 'normality' at the expense of my depth. I didn't want an 'expert' who believed they knew me better than I could know myself. I didn't want to be infantilized or patronized. I didn't want to be traumatized by needless procedures, both physical and psychological, the sole aim of which was to fit me into the particular 'worldview' of which the practitioner was an exponent. I didn't want to be stigmatized or have my life defined by a diagnosis or label. I didn't want my torment reduced to meaninglessness, or my questions or emotions relegated to the symptomology of an arbitrary 'illness' or 'dysfunction' as classified by a wealthy psychiatrist sitting in an office in the US somewhere.[2]

And so, once I knew what I *didn't* want, I could also begin to work out what it was that I *did* want.

I wanted someone to walk by my side. I wanted someone to help me explore and question and discover. I wanted someone who could help me tie my shoelaces when needed, but also show me how to unfurl my wings and stretch them into flight. I wanted someone who could tolerate ambiguity and muddiness. I wanted someone who could engage with me in the breadth of my humanity. I wanted to be held and embraced. I wanted someone to guide me ever deeper into truth and understanding. I wanted to be met with honesty, intelligence, compassion, breadth, and clarity. I wanted to be valued and believed, and have the profound knowing, meaning and validity I carry within, acknowledged and met.

What do you want?

***

---

2. I am referring here to the Diagnostic and Statistical Manual of Mental Disorders (DSM) published by the American Psychiatric Association, that increasingly seeks to pathologize so much of human expression and suffering.

choosing a therapist or teacher

I searched for therapists in a variety of ways: word of mouth, recommendations from friends or from other therapists, Yellow Pages, an Internet search of relevant words (e.g. 'therapy', 'trauma', 'anxiety', 'spirituality' and the name of the city in which I live) or a search through the listings of therapeutic umbrella organizations or associations. At one time I approached health centers and asked if they might know of someone.

Once I had a person in mind I did some further research. What was their qualification? What was their experience? What was their area of expertise? What techniques did they use? What was their background? What was my gut sense about them?

I then made contact and set up an initial appointment. However, I always made an internal agreement with myself *never* to commit to a particular therapist or course of therapy, until I had undertaken four sessions with them. Four sessions were *always* enough to know whether I could work with a therapist or not. Usually it was only one or two that were needed, but I never made the leap of commitment, until the four sessions were over. By this time, the therapist knew me to some extent, they had relaxed and shown me their mettle as a therapist *and* as a human being, they were no longer trying to impress me, I knew whether I liked them or not, and I knew whether I found my interaction with them stimulating and interesting, I knew whether there was a connection between us, I knew whether I felt completely safe[3], and I knew how they worked and could gauge how that work impacted on my life.

I never told any therapist that they were 'on probation' until after the trial period was over. In doing so, I was able maintain my integrity and safety; if the therapist stuffed up or acted inappropriately I felt 'protected', because I had already given myself permission to walk away. I maintained control and I also remained the authority in my own life.

After the trial was over, I then made a decision about how I would proceed. I recall that for one counsellor that decision was to continue for a few more sessions, get help with the issue at hand, and then walk away. However, once I made a commitment to a particular therapist, I truly *did* commit. I let

---

3. The issue of safety is an important one. It includes many of the points that are discussed in this chapter: ethical considerations such as confidentiality and boundaries, the capacity to be wrong, self-awareness, honesty, acceptance, embodiment of qualities such as compassion and care etc.

the therapy run its course through both the 'good' times and those that were difficult. I never walked away because the going got tough; it was during these tough times that the greatest healing often took place. I also trusted that I would know when the therapy was 'over'.

It is worth noting that although for the purposes of this chapter I have separated discussion of 'therapists' from that of 'spiritual teachers', it was therapists who were my greatest all-round teachers.[4] Therapists may not have had the depth of realization of spiritual teachers, but in terms of their professional knowledge, their personal insight and their capacity to engage in the cut-and-thrust of deep, intimate, intelligent and conscious interaction, they were exemplary life teachers and mentors.

I believe that it was through the initial process of determining exactly what I wanted from therapy and from a therapist, that I found those who were able to be teachers in this way. Many therapists and counsellors would not have the experience, depth or breadth to be able to do so.

With regard to spiritual teachers, although there were times I actively sought out a teacher it was never with the same systematic approach as I sought out therapists. Rather, it was as though teachers appeared to me in the course of my life or I felt a particular 'pull' to contact them; there were times it seemed as though there was a deeper and often quite puzzling or difficult-to-live current at play, which, when felt and followed, led me to a teacher.

Also, because of the significant scarcity of advanced spiritual teachers in my general vicinity, there were times I worked with a teacher only because I could find nobody else. I generally felt it was better to have access to *some* face-to-face spiritual work, rather than be too picky and have access to none at all.

Generally I went into these relationships with an attitude of learning as much as I could, but also discarding that which did not resonate with me. However, at times this was a difficult path to walk and I often had to consider very carefully whether a situation with my teacher was uncomfortable because I had something to learn from it or uncomfortable because the teaching presented was somehow false, skewed or irrelevant. I never approached a teacher from whom I felt I would have nothing to learn.

---

4. I think here of two therapists I saw for quite extended periods, one at the beginning of my journey for five years, to whom I have given the name Mollie for this book, and one towards the 'end' for three, to whom I have given the name Colette. In the many years between, I did access or try out 'therapies' for short periods of time when I couldn't find my way through an issue on my own.

In recent years, the increasing use of Skype by teachers has provided a world-wide base from which to choose. Although there is a substantial amount of spiritual 'teaching' available on-line in the form of written material and videos, and there can certainly be much to learn from this, I have always found the immediacy and 'realness' of person-to-person interaction vital if real progress is to be made. We simply *cannot* be our own mirror.

***

qualifications, credentials and experience

The people from whom I sought help had a wide variety of qualifications: psychiatry, psychoanalysis, psychotherapy, psychology, counselling, body work and social work. Although, in my initial search for a therapist, I took these into account, it was never the qualification that made for a good therapist. Other factors were far more important and will be discussed below.

After initial experiences with psychiatrists I realized that in general they do not have further training in talking therapies. Although there are some exceptions, psychiatrists generally just prescribe medication and talk is generally limited to discussion of dosage, side effects and effectiveness.

It is also worth noting that the training to become a 'counsellor' is far less rigorous and substantial than in other fields. Although I have no doubt there are some counsellors who are highly experienced and effective, a counselling diploma (as opposed to a degree) requires less supervised practice and there is no requirement to have undergone therapy or counselling of one's own. Also, in Australia, there is no restriction on counsellors calling themselves 'therapists' or 'psychotherapists' even though they have no further training or experience specific to these fields.

Beyond academic background, however, it is always valuable to do some additional research on a therapist. A simple Internet search can reveal a great deal: licensing status; further training; years of experience; participation in or running of relevant support groups, organizations, foundations or charities; specific areas of professional interest such as trauma, bereavement, addiction or abuse; commitment to their own spiritual and personal growth; other interests such as yoga or meditation, hiking or photography; relevant details about their personal life.[5] This sort of

---

5. For instance, because I was in a long-term relationship, I would not have wanted to work with someone who did not know what it was to be in a long-term relationship. There are understandings that can only be gained by the living of them. For others it might be important that the therapist also be a parent, that the therapist is either male or female etc.

information can often provide an overall picture of the person themselves and whether they are someone with whom you wish to connect. I also tried to find out the age of a therapist; I generally preferred someone older than me, in the hope that the years had brought a wealth of life experience and wisdom.

Although not a conscious decision in my journey, I see in retrospect that it was enormously valuable that each therapist I worked with focused on the human being from a different perspective. For instance, by doing body psychotherapy I was able to move deeply into the present moment and 'now-ness' of all experience in a way that would have been impossible through a talking therapy alone.[6] And through a 'talking' therapy I gained valuable skills in analysis, reflection, dialogue, discernment and reasoning I would not have gained just through body work.

Most spiritual teachers I came into contact with, although they had some sort of qualification in psychology or counselling in their background, were typically self-styled without any qualification specific to their teaching. Generally their 'qualification' was experience within a spiritual tradition, the archive of their written work or their level of spiritual realization.

In looking for a spiritual teacher I think it is important to recognize that many are not capable of handling deeper psychological issues with the skill and insight of a therapist. There were times I found their 'teaching' on this level, although well-intentioned, to be uninformed, unhelpful and even damaging.

There are also some teachers with very little psychological understanding, who seek to bypass suffering as 'unspiritual', 'of the ego' or as 'illusion'[7]. There are, however, exceptions. For example *The Diamond Approach* of AH Almaas, is a process of self-realization that includes a systematic inquiry into all levels of our human experience: body, personality, mind, emotions, soul and Spirit. I have also increasingly come across teachers who have done significant exploration in both psychological and spiritual realms and have devised a teaching practice that effectively combines both. For these teachers suffering is the gateway into knowing oneself, and psychological and spiritual development are seen as inseparable aspects of that process.

---

6. Radix body-centered psychotherapy is discussed more fully in the chapter *The Body*.
7. 'Spiritual bypassing' is a term coined by psychologist John Welwood in 1984, to describe the practice of using spiritual beliefs or techniques to avoid our messy humanness. This can be done in any number of ways, some of which I discuss in this book: relentless positivity, ignoring our darkness or depth, moving away from any uncomfortable feelings through meditation or prayer, focussing only on light and love, proclaiming that because only Awareness is real all else (including suffering) is therefore an illusion etc.

Although I cannot comment on the use of the word 'guru' in Eastern traditions and lineages, I did come across teachers in the West who wished to give their teaching an aura of validity or 'specialness' by calling themselves such. It is worth taking pause and trusting one's intuition in this regard before accepting such self-appellations as legitimate.

A true teacher has no need for robes, special names or other fancy frills. The truth and clarity of their presence and depth of their realization is unmistakable, utterly extraordinary and in no need of embellishment whatsoever.

***

techniques and methods

Therapists use many different techniques or methods: Cognitive Behavior Therapy, Desensitization Therapy, Narrative Therapy, Hypnotherapy, Art Therapy, Neo-Reichian body psychotherapy etc. Some of these techniques are designed to address relatively superficial issues over a short period of time while others enable a deeper and deeper inquiry over many years. It is worth doing an Internet search to ascertain what a particular technique entails and also whether it feels 'right' or not.

I never pursued any therapy with a practitioner whose sole 'method' was the implementation of their particular technique. I found this sort of therapy tremendously restrictive and it did nothing to acknowledge the profound healing power of genuine relationship. I recall a time I inwardly cringed as I watched a therapist enthusiastically lay out my life and my suffering on a whiteboard diagram. I stayed for a few sessions, learnt what I could, but moved on.

Some therapists can however use their technique wisely, never allowing it to suffice for a depth of relating and relationship. The technique used in this way, provides the framework within which the qualities and activities of true healing can be expressed: compassion, acceptance, kindness, deep listening, resonance, care, genuine connection.

Spiritual teachers also use different techniques or methods: meditation, inquiry/questioning and dialectic. Generally, a combination of these worked well for me. There were times when discussion was appropriate, times when sitting in stillness or meditation felt right and times when inquiry into a situation, into written material or into a path of inner exploration was valuable.

For a time I went to a meditation teacher who generally frowned on any sort of discussion because he believed it was all "of the ego". Although meditation is enormously valuable I found his blanket rejection of "all talk", unnecessarily limiting and narrow. In spiritual teaching, as in therapy, one shoe simply cannot fit all feet at all times. Good teachers were generally quite capable of flexibility.

It is worth making the note that a primary difference between therapy and spiritual teaching is that the therapy is led by the client, whereas in teaching it is usually (but not always), led by the teacher; the therapist uses their techniques to respond to and follow what the client presents and in teaching the student generally follows the techniques, instruction or material offered by the teacher.

***

ethical considerations

There are three areas in which a therapist might cross legal or ethical boundaries: having sex with a client[8], breaking the confidentiality of the therapy room, or having a dual relationship with a client. I have found that therapists who are qualified and licensed are acutely aware of these boundaries and never cross them. Therapists I have worked with have also cared very deeply about their clients and would never knowingly have jeopardized the therapeutic relationship nor their professional standing.

Spiritual teachers, however, are not subject to any such legal or ethical requirements, and although I have known teachers with impeccable standards, some I have come across, have at times shocked me by their behavior.

I recall one time disclosing to my teacher that during a week-long retreat I had experienced very intense sexual energy coursing through my body and that afterwards I had rushed home to have sex with my partner. At the next meditation sitting, as people smiled at me 'knowingly', I realized with horror that this information had been shared amongst the group.

Countless stories abound of spiritual teachers for whom there are no boundaries with regard to sex or extracurricular relationships. Regardless of the fact that the student may be a consenting adult, there is always an implicit power imbalance

---

8. This also includes making sexually charged comments or even just sending out sexual vibes. In the section below on *Listen to your gut/intuition,* in which I describe a trial session with a therapist, I felt a very confused sexual energy in the room. If there had not also been a number of other things of concern I might all too easily have disregarded this sexual energy as something I was 'making up' or something of little consequence.

between teacher and student. A number of times I have experienced how very hard it is to say 'no' to a teacher even about quite simple matters, because in doing so I would have risked their goodwill, and as such, also access to their teaching. It is always worth taking great care not to be swayed by the aura of charm and authority that can surround the 'guru' persona.

Many years ago, my partner and I attended a meditation and yoga venue. The teacher, who was quite charismatic, often asked us to stay back for a chat after class. We felt quite flattered by his attention and assumed that he wished to foster our spiritual development beyond what he could offer us in the group setting. It was not until he suggested a *ménage à trois* that we realized that his interest in us was definitely not of a spiritual nature. We felt saddened not only that we would lose our teacher and the meditation group of which we were a part, but also that we had been duped by his charm and his interest in us.

***

connection

The most healing attribute of any successful therapy is the depth and quality of the connection.

In counselling jargon and clinical studies the connection between client and therapist is frequently termed 'rapport'. This 'rapport' refers to a relatively superficial affinity or understanding that can be encouraged by the use of therapeutic skills such as listening, empathy, humor and physical mirroring. I have no doubt that there are some things the practitioner can *do* to promote 'rapport' or conversely hinder it, but I believe that as is the case in any relationship, the alchemy of two people liking one another and feeling a deep connection and resonance, cannot be manufactured or reduced to that which it gives rise to. In my experience, it either happens or it doesn't.

For me, it was this connection on which all else was based. It was the ocean in which the therapy took place. Although many other things came to swim in that ocean, ultimately it was the quality and depth of the waters that determined the power and profundity of the healing that took place.

There are many very simple ways in which such a connection might be expressed: You can laugh together and you can cry together. You can have a gentle chat about vegetable gardening or animals before getting down to the work of therapy. You can agree on some basic ways of looking at the world, for instance, care for the environment or healthy eating. The therapist respects your capacities, your strengths and your adulthood. The therapist allows you to see a little of their life beyond the therapy room. The therapist allows the relationship to develop and gives the relationship importance beyond their particular technique or agenda. The therapist is available for crises or questions outside the allotted session times. The therapist does not portray themselves as an expert, above it all or somehow 'special', but rather as a 'real' person with the same fears, pains and life difficulties as everyone else.[9]

Ultimately also, in the two most profoundly healing therapeutic relationships I undertook[10], I felt loved. I did not doubt that I was deeply, deeply cared for and that this care was not in any way a contrived therapeutic 'skill'.

Although many of the above points with regard to connection also apply to teaching relationships, I have generally found that teaching involves a much lesser degree of 'ego' connection or attachment than that needed for a successful therapy. There can however be a very profound and conscious meeting between teacher and student on the transpersonal or spiritual dimension. It is on this level that we move ever more into the Ultimate Intimacy. It is here that there is no separation and one quite simply senses that one is meeting oneself.

∗∗∗

is the therapist/teacher committed to their own personal or spiritual work?

I have been very puzzled that some therapists and counsellors (and also teachers) have not undergone their own therapy or counselling, even beyond that which may have been a training requirement.

For me, a *major* determinant of whether a therapy or teaching was successful or not, was whether the practitioner was committed to their own personal or spiritual process. Rather than an 'expert' on how other people should live life, such a therapist/teacher was a fellow traveler, one who was perhaps walking a few steps ahead, and who possessed an insight, compassion and humility into the process of inner exploration that simply could not be acquired in any other way.

---

9. Although I have always found it valuable if the therapist can be 'real', this does not mean that the therapist should share their own process with the client or should talk at length about themselves. This would entail a breach of therapeutic boundaries. It is simply an acknowledgement by the therapist of our common lived humanity: "Yes, I too have felt this pain, this insecurity … "
10. With the therapists I have called 'Mollie' and 'Colette' in this book.

In addition, I believe that many of the qualities of successful therapy discussed in this chapter were a direct result of the work that the therapist had done on themselves.

I found that therapists who had not done this sort of inner work had an edge of impatience and of 'pushing through and getting the job done' that showed little true understanding of the nature and 'tempo' of inner processes. How could a therapist embrace my most vulnerable and damaged parts if they themselves had not known what it is to meet and embrace their own? Such a therapist, I believe, could be little more than a technician.

I once heard the wonderful story of a gastroenterologist who underwent a colonoscopy (an unnecessary one) so that he would know from his *own* experience, what he was putting his patients through. He said that by doing so, he gained a very profound insight that could not but be reflected in his practice. What had previously seemed like 'unnecessary' and annoying complaints, he now realized, were entirely justified. He was even astonished that so many of his patients had not complained *more*.

Many teachers I have known, although they may have done significant *spiritual* work and have substantial spiritual realization, had done very little personal or psychological work. I wonder whether it was their lack of insight on this level that resulted in the shortfall of ethical, honest and open relating that at times I witnessed. As with therapists, however, it was those who were committed to their own lives as an ongoing and indeed never-ending process of unfoldment and deepening who offered the most grounded, wise and beautiful teaching.

***

listening deeply[11]

It may seem to be stating the obvious, that listening is important in therapy (and in teaching) but I have found that very few therapists (or teachers) are able to listen *deeply*.

So often therapists and counsellors use listening merely as a precursor to a verbal response, whether that be a reflection, a paraphrase, a question, further discussion, problem-solving or the implementation of their particular

---

11. For more material on listening see chapter *Listening*.

technique or strategy. Many times they listen only for whatever it is they are already looking for.[12]

But listening in its own right is a deep and potent activity. It has been profoundly powerful for me as a client (and a student and a human being) to feel *deeply* listened to, just as it has felt profoundly damning *not* to be listened to.

I recall going to a preliminary meeting with a spiritual teacher, and being shocked at his incapacity to truly listen. Although he asked me about my life, he frequently interrupted my answer in order to finish my sentence with his assumption about what I intended to say. All 'communication' that followed was merely a response to his assumptions; I was left to either agree with him or try to correct him. Needless to say, I felt frustrated and any true meeting of souls, hearts or even of minds, was impossible.

In deep listening the therapist (or anyone for that matter) listens not only with their ears or with a preconceived idea in mind, they listen from the deep inner silence and open receptivity of their entire being. It is from this space that they can attune to the deeper meanings and resonances of *all* that the client communicates. It is a deeply *felt* or *bodily* listening that can encompass the whole expanse of our humanness, from the personal to the vastness of the All: What is the client communicating through their words? What is this tightness in their body conveying? What is it that lies in the cracks of their torment? What is in the client's soul/heart? What is this extraordinary depth?

To be heard and received in this inner way is the beginning of a true healing and *always* communicates to a client. A client will *know* when they are embraced in the openness of a therapist's listening space. Not only will they feel 'met', cared for, accepted, valued and heard, they will feel quite literally 'listened into existence'.

It is only once this attunement has been made, that a therapist can 'listen' within themselves for a response that is *truly* appropriate, whether that be in words, with a look, with an action or with silence.

The therapist's deep listening will also provide an invitation for the client to begin to listen to themselves and look within with an ever-deepening curiosity and compassion.

---

12. This is also discussed in the section *The Stories that Encircle* in the chapter *Stories*.

***

the capacity to be wrong

I found one of the most important attributes of both therapists and teachers was their capacity to be wrong. Could they make a mistake and apologize for it? Could the therapist or teacher embody the same authenticity and 'telling the truth' that they demanded of their clients or students?

The two therapists with whom I had the most healing relationships were able to say, "I stuffed up and I'm so sorry." At all times I felt honored, valued and also inspired by their honesty. There were times their apology was about a simple mix-up over payment or session times, but at other times it was a very significant admission that, on reflection, the handling of a particular issue or situation was inappropriate or even injurious.

Nobody can be right *all* the time. We are *all* human and we *all* have blind spots. Admitting you are wrong, rather than a sign of weakness, is actually a sign of integrity and strength that builds tremendous trust in any relationship. If a person can be wrong, then you know that their opinion or their feedback can be relied on. There is little reason to trust someone who is always right, because realistically *some* of their 'right' *has* to be wrong. As in everyday life, having a relationship with someone who always has to be right, is difficult: there is little scope for healthy discussion or give-and-take.

It was particularly in spiritual teachers and practitioners who were self-styled and had done little work on themselves, that I encountered the need to be right. At one time, in front of a group of about forty people, a teacher accused me of something I did not do. Later the person who had been responsible for the 'misdeed', told the teacher that she was at fault and not me. Shortly after, the teacher came up to me and said, "I won't apologize to you, because there will undoubtedly be something in this for you to learn." I was stunned by his comment but also at his inability to show humility. I did indeed learn something however: that although teachers may be enlightened in some areas of their lives, there may be other areas in which the light has yet to shine.

Such teachers and professionals were also unable to tolerate questions concerning their conduct or contradictions in their practice. Disagreement of any sort was generally not welcome. I recall a time when a disagreement with a psychiatrist brought the threat of further diagnosis and medication, and similarly, a disagreement with a teacher brought a dissection of my faults and the warning that I must never again question his authority if I wished to remain as a student.

It is in being cast adrift from who/what we most truly *are*, our Essential Self, that so much of our suffering takes root. If along the way, someone to whom we have gone for teaching or healing, demands that we keep silent and take their authority over our own, then in essence they are asking that we give that Self up. In any arena whatsoever, that price is far too high.

***

the capacity to say "I don't know"

I witnessed many occasions when teachers had to be right on topics on which they had no expertise, qualification or experience whatsoever. I recall sitting open-mouthed in disbelief as a teacher spoke of sexual abuse in such a way that showed absolutely no understanding of the depths of traumatization nor the far-reaching impact it can have on people's lives. Students came to him with a wide variety of issues so it may well have been easy for him to generalize his proficiency and yet there were many times when a simple "I don't know" would have been far more appropriate.

I did not necessarily walk away from such teachers; there were still things of value I could learn. I simply remained wary, and used my judgement about what was of value and what I would discard. I ate from the table of their offerings with great care and discernment.

Experienced therapists or those who had done work on themselves, generally had no hesitation in saying, "I don't know". As with the capacity to apologize, the capacity to say, "I don't know", builds trust and safety in any relationship.

***

listen to your gut/intuition

At all times with both therapists and spiritual teachers, it is important to listen to your gut, to your body, to your intuition. What is your instinct? What is your sense? What is the undeniable truth that you know in your bones? What is your instant internal response? What is that little niggling voice in the back of your mind muttering about?

I once went for a trial session with a therapist, and from the moment I stepped in his room I felt uncomfortable. The room was dark, he was trying too hard, he talked too much, he continually leant towards me, and the session went far longer than the allotted time. I felt a gnawing discomfort in my belly and every bone in my body spoke an unequivocal "No!" Needless to say, I did not go back.

***

acceptance

It is on the issue of acceptance that I feel there is quite a significant and indeed, at times, necessary divergence between what is appropriate in therapy and what is appropriate in spiritual teaching.

In therapy it is vital that as a client you feel that *all* of who you are is welcome; you must feel *completely* accepted and safe. The therapist must be utterly worthy of your trust and never be judgmental or disapproving.

Therapy works best when you feel that there is nothing whatsoever that you cannot share with your therapist: your 'ugliest' feelings, your most keenly-felt vulnerability, your most excruciatingly painful memories, your most embarrassing moments, your silliest fantasies, the fears of the child you once were, the capabilities of the adult you now are, your joy, your anguish. The person at your side must not only be very skilled and experienced, they must be able to welcome and hold *all* of who you are, with care, empathy, interest, compassion, acceptance, understanding, congruence and sensitivity. There must be no barriers to complete openness and 'telling the truth'; there must be room for you to move ever more fully into a ruthless authenticity.

It is only when we can inhabit this present moment fully *as* ourselves that change and growth can begin to happen.

Many years ago, I saw a therapist for a short time, with whom I did not trust particular material. I could sense that he was uncomfortable with the issues involved and also wanted to push me into a line of action that at that time did not feel right. This therapist certainly sensed that there was something on which I was holding back and without knowing the real reason why I was doing so, assumed that my evasion was because I was not telling the truth. It put me in an extraordinarily difficult and uncomfortable position. There were times he eyed me with distrust and hinted sarcastically at my 'dishonesty'. It was only many years later that

I was able to heal this material with a therapist I deeply trusted.

In spiritual teaching, I believe there are occasions when it is necessary for the teacher to challenge, confront and question students in a way that would be inappropriate in the therapeutic setting.[13] There may still be encouragement and validation, but there are also times to be pushed, times to be held to account, and times for a reality check. A teacher can be supportive and gentle, but also tough and provocative. A good teacher knows what is needed and when it is needed.[14]

In some spiritual circles there can be a certain attachment to light, love, angels, rainbows and feel-good experiences. But the spiritual path isn't like that at all. It isn't a pastel-colored hobby we pursue only on a Sunday afternoon or when we feel bored. It can be very *real*, uncomfortable, unflattering, and very threatening and destructive to the 'ego'. The spiritual path will bring us to our knees, it will bring us to surrender, and that can never happen quietly or easily. A good teacher is not there to sanitize and sweeten life for us. Spiritual teachers are there to help us get real and wake up.

However, I think it is in this realm of confrontation and challenge that some spiritual teachers can run amok. It seems to me that unethical, selfish, bullying or just plain childish behavior can all too easily be excused under the umbrella of 'enlightenment'. And because the students who gather around are 'not enlightened', it is often deemed by the teacher that there is no one who is qualified enough to call their motives or actions into question: How can mere mortals possibly understand *their* lofty purposes? It seems that all too easily such teachers can do whatever they want with little or no accountability or appropriate boundaries. This, I believe, produces teachers who are indulged and worshipped, not enlightened.

It is essential that spiritual teachers remain ethical and honest, open to all scrutiny and embody the Essential Truth to which their teaching is pointing. Truth *always* embodies Essential qualities, such as Love, Compassion, Clarity, Joy and Peace. Is the spiritual teacher in front of you walking their talk?

---

13. A therapist may also challenge or confront a client, but the manner in which this is done is entirely different. For instance, a therapist might gently challenge a client's belief that she was hit as a child because she was 'bad' and therefore 'deserved it'.

14. I am writing here also with my experience as a flute student and flute teacher in mind. In the musical world in which I grew up, I learnt not to take criticism or confrontation 'personally', but rather as a valuable and necessary way of encouraging strength, toughness and self-belief as a performer. With my own students I was always acutely aware when gentleness and encouragement were needed, or when it was time for a little 'tough love'.

Do Love and Peace speak as effortlessly through them as a breeze blowing through the leaves of a tree? And if not, why not?

***

the perfect therapist? the perfect teacher?

I know of someone who sees herself as a counsellor and a guide for others, and yet she has never opened her own life to therapy, counselling, or learning from a teacher. Her rationale is that she has never found anyone who is good enough; she doesn't want to run the risk of being upset or hurt.

And in a certain sense she is right. Regardless of everything I have written in this chapter, there is *no* perfect therapist and *no* perfect teacher. And there is never ever any guarantee that we won't end up getting hurt or upset, even with the most professional, kindest, caring and empathic of practitioners. Therapists and teachers are just people. They can be fallible. They can sometimes say the wrong thing. They can sometimes be tired. I have been upset with them, I have been annoyed, I have been puzzled, I have realized in retrospect that the way they treated me wasn't great. But does that mean that I would never go to one?

Absolutely not.

We truly cannot be a mirror unto ourselves. Sometimes the mirror that is a therapist or teacher has some blemishes or cracks in it, but that just shows that it's real and it's been through some tough times of its own. It is still quite capable of reflecting an adequate likeness back to ourselves.

As in any relationship, you're going to idealize and you're going to feel let down. You're going to love and you're going to be disappointed. That's how it is.

Anything else is a fantasy story.

In the end, regardless of what happened, whether in therapy or in teaching (or in life), there was nothing from which I did not learn even if it was only to learn what I *didn't* want. I used *everything* to bring greater and greater insight and awareness into my life. I let it *all* be my teacher.

As an example, there were many occasions when therapists forgot something[15];

---

15. All therapists have been 'guilty' of this at times, although some more than others.

at times it was only a simple oversight with regard to payment, but at others it was something of considerable intimacy or importance. In everyday life people forget things all the time and it is something we have *all* undoubtedly been guilty of. However, in the confidence of the therapy room and in a situation in which the therapist is paid for their professionalism, their attention and their time, this forgetfulness, although often understandable, can be a very difficult thing for a client. Numerous times I have felt quite annoyed or saddened.

Throughout my life I have found it extremely difficult to be assertive and point out when I feel hurt by someone's actions, so within the 'safety' of the therapeutic relationship (but without necessarily telling the therapist what I was doing), I used this 'forgetting' as an opportunity for learning. How do I feel when I try to ignore the therapist's forgetfulness and don't say anything? What happens if I gently point out that we have already discussed something? What if I precede a disclosure with the question: "Do you remember that I told you ...?"? What if I say to the therapist, "It brings up enormous feelings of anger/abandonment/confusion that you have forgotten to tell me you are going away on holidays."?

As I experimented with taking control of such situations in a quietly assertive way, I no longer descended into despair or victimhood as I may have done in the past. I came to allow the therapist (and also other people in my life) their imperfection and humanity while still voicing my disappointment or my hurt. I came to acknowledge that anger and disappointment, and love and trust could all co-exist in *any* relationship, whether it be a therapeutic one or not. The therapist/other people didn't need to be perfect, for the therapy/relationship to be powerful and for me to still feel cared for or loved.

***

moving beyond "life is my teacher"

In some spiritual circles it is common to hear the phrase, "Life is my teacher".

Of course, life is our teacher. There is no moment in life, no place in life, no person in life, that does not offer us a sacred teaching.

A sore knee. My partner's stubbornness. The old woman down the road who always forgets to put in her hearing aids. The man in the supermarket who stares unashamedly at my breasts. Desperate grief. A rainy day. A child's joyous laughter. The voices from the past that leave me feeling ruined in their wake. The echoes of a complicated family history.

It is *all* Divinity. If we resist it, if we fight it, if we grab hold and refuse to let go ... then what do we have to learn? What is it that still pushes our buttons? Where, in our inner world, do we still contract and harden? Where do we still claim a separate stance?

And yet, there are those among us who have gone before. And they will know where the pitfalls lie, they will know when we want to tell ourselves a fairy story, they will know when our motivation is less than honest or when we want to puff ourselves up with our specialness, they will see what we can't yet see, they will know the questions we did not think to ask, they will help to move us forward when we are stuck ... and they will ask that not only do we realize the Truth, they will ask that we be committed to the Truth in *every* moment ... not just when the going is good, or when we choose to, or when it suits us ...

Yes life is a teacher, but if we are serious about the Truth there will also come times, both before and after awakening, when we *must* seek out a flesh-and-bones teacher and with complete openness, honesty and vulnerability, put *all* of our cards out on the table in front of us. Anything less can all too easily become a game.

***

limitations of therapy and teaching – a cautionary note

I feel that it is worth noting that there are limitations to all paths, approaches and methods of healing.

In my therapy work, particularly after awakening, it became apparent to me that there was a very real danger that I might stay forever mired in 'therapizing' every contraction or discomfort that arose, however minor. Once my deep woundings had been faced and transformed, there came a point at which I knew that a lot of this material was merely habitual or 'comfortable', and rather than needing deeper work, could simply be surrendered into Spirit.

Conversely, in spiritual work and spiritual communities it had always concerned me that it seemed to be all too easy for people to bypass or skip over their very necessary psychological healing with intensive meditation practices, attachment to 'spiritual experiences' or a 'guru', clever words, or surrender. Although this was never the case in my own life, it did give me an insight into the necessity for balance.

As indispensable as they may be for our journey, any method, any technique, any teaching, any therapy, can, in certain circumstances, also become our prison. Ultimately the vastness and majesty of our humanity cannot be circumscribed or contained in any way and the goal of any true healing path will ultimately be to strip from us the veils that blind us to that knowing.

***

beyond the battle

It goes against the grain to move in close; it goes against so much we believe, so much we've ever learnt.

And yet if we move in close, really close ... we realize this is where the battle ceases. This is where our suffering can come to an end.

***

chased by a woolly mammoth

Eons ago our bodies were hard-wired to avoid discomfort and suffering at all costs.

And frankly, it made sense; our lives depended on it. If a woolly mammoth was chasing us, it would have been foolish not to run away as fast as we possibly could, or, if we had the strength, turn around to fight it. Similarly, in a modern-day equivalent, if we're alone in a car park late at night and a strange guy is checking us out a little too closely, it's probably a very good idea to get away as fast as we can or call the police.

However, somewhere along the line we've decided that this scenario also applies to large swathes of our inner lives:

> If we feel fear, we try to run away from it or tell ourselves to stop being so scared.
> If we have an uneasy feeling in our gut, we try to distract ourselves or take an antacid.
> If we feel angry with our partner, we disappear into the garden to avoid them or yell at them about their annoying habits.
> If we catch sight of ourselves in a mirror in the supermarket and are horrified at how fat (or ugly, old, wide-hipped) we look, we try to avoid all mirrors from then on or soothe ourselves by eating a choc-chip muffin or two.

When there's something in our experience we don't like our immediate reaction is to try to remove ourselves from it or do battle with it.[1] We try to create as much distance between ourselves and this 'something' as we can, or otherwise we fight it until we can 'kill' it. We believe that without this 'something' in our lives we'll be happier, freer or safer. And we won't suffer so much.

And we may certainly have times when things are going well and we think we've finally conquered all those bad and uncomfortable things. However, something else invariably comes along. There is always one more woolly mammoth, one more guy in a car park, one more annoying feeling, one more painful memory. We are in an interminable battle against life, but what else can we do?

Many of my early journals are filled with this fight against myself: I must try doing a little exercise every day, I mustn't eat so much sugar, I mustn't care what other people think, I must try to follow my own rhythms, I must try to accept everything, I must relax, I mustn't get so upset by things people say.

Many ego-based therapies also talk of fighting ourselves: one bit of ego has to fight another bit of ego. And so we talk of fighting depression, fighting anxiety, fighting our self-criticism, fighting our anger. We also use medications to fight our various emotional states: anti-depressants, anti-anxiety medications.

This 'fighting' is assumed; we take it for granted.

I can't remember the occasion, but I recall a day many years ago when I suddenly realized how very tired I was of this relentless battle with myself. I realized, that if *I* was going to be the 'winner' in that battle then of course I would also be the 'loser'.

I had to find another way.

***

who would be the loser?

Which bit of yourself will you fight?
Which bit of yourself will you run from?
Which piece were you planning to take with you?
Which piece were you planning to leave behind?

---

1. This is generally called the 'fight-or-flight' response.

Splitting yourself in two, or three, or six.
Who would be the loser?

And how can you be so certain
that the bit you're leaving behind
isn't the bit in which the healing takes place?

You can't run from this piece of yourself.
It's not the enemy.
Life has no enemies.

***

closing in on panic attacks

For a number of years I suffered from panic attacks. Panic attacks are episodes of sudden, intense and debilitating terror. With every panic attack, I truly believed I was going to die: my eyes lost focus, I struggled to breathe, I shook violently, my chest tightened, I felt faint and the world receded.

Although initially panic attacks may come about for no apparent reason, they subsequently become associated with the situation in which they originally occurred: a shopping center, a bank, the hallway, a closed space, an open space. A cycle of escalating avoidance then ensues.

I tried many different things to overcome the attacks: I went to a group for people with panic disorder, I read books about anxiety, I took prescription meds, I tried hypnotherapy, I slowed my breathing, I tried to desensitize myself by going into the very places I feared. But none of these approaches had any significant or lasting impact. In fact, the harder I 'fought' to eliminate the panic attacks, the deeper they became entrenched. Over time I became desperately unwell and there was even a period I was unable to venture outside the house.

Eventually I began seeing a Radix body-centered psychotherapist, Mollie, who thankfully lived only a couple of streets away.[2] Although it had appeared on the surface that it was particular situations that triggered the attacks, as we worked it became apparent that it was actually my fear of being trapped and controlled by 'other people' that was at issue. Queues and crowds were difficult, but any one-on-one conversation with another person was nightmarish: a neighbor, a shop owner, the teller at the bank.

---

2. For further discussion on Radix body-centered psychotherapy see the chapter *The Body*.

Once I committed to a conversation the panic began to rise, but I would still force myself to stay glued to the spot, fighting desperately to smile, chat, make eye contact and act like a 'socially acceptable and normal person'. Above all I did not want to let on that I was disintegrating into panic. I did not want to risk being judged, mocked or laughed at. I *had* to look like everybody else. The effort required for even one short exchange, exhausted me for hours or even days afterwards.

There were certainly many deep-seated issues at play that would take many more years to understand and work through, but at that time there was one thing that significantly reduced the severity and frequency of the panic attacks. Although simple, it was a very profound and far-reaching way of approaching not just fear, but all of life.

Rather than focus on controlling the physical symptoms of the panic attacks, or making a deliberate attempt to expose myself to the situations I had come to fear, Mollie suggested that I begin to take people *in*, truly *see* them and get *close* to them.

Together we went to the local shopping precinct. At first we went for only ten minutes, but then for increasing lengths of time.

I recall quite clearly the first time we walked into the supermarket together. From a distance we saw an elderly woman standing at the deli counter. Mollie invited me to truly *see* her, to allow myself to move inwardly close to her and deeply take her in. What did I see? Here was a wrinkled face, knotted knuckles struggling with the supermarket trolley, head craned up high to talk over the counter. Mollie then invited me to look at her eyes, to see what was actually there beyond my fears, or my projections. What was it? It was a lifetime of memories, of pain, of hardships, of joys, of kindness.

And then we moved slowly on, taking our time, Mollie reassuring me that if necessary we could leave at a moment's notice.

Here was a mother with a toddler. What was in *her* eyes? It was impatience and anxiety. What was in the toddler's eyes? It was tiredness and boredom.

Here was an old man comparing the prices of cat food. Life was tired on his face, in his movements, in his clothes. He seemed sad. Had his wife just passed away? Was he ill?

These were just people. I could see that. They had their fears, their love, their grief, their sadness. They weren't scary ogres, and they weren't on the lookout to laugh at me or judge me because I suffered from panic attacks. Quite frankly, they hardly even noticed me.

After a time I was able to carry out small purchases and have brief conversations on my own. If I felt fear building I deliberately moved *closer* to the people around me, eye-to-eye, soul-to-soul. Often I asked silent questions of them: What is it that I see in your face? What is this sadness? What is your life like? Who are you? Frequently I saw self-absorption, sometimes it was friendliness, sometimes kindness. Sometimes arrogance too. Brusqueness. Agitation. But all of them were humanity. People just like me. No different. No better. No worse.

There were times I still panicked and there were times I still pushed myself too hard and dropped into exhaustion afterwards. But slowly, slowly, the distance between me and others diminished, as did my fear.

I recall one day I was standing in a queue at the checkout of a large and busy supermarket; it felt like a triumph of sorts to be standing alone in such a public place. All of a sudden I felt panic rising. Rather than desperately fighting to regain some inner control or dumping my shopping and running away as I might have done in the past, I turned to the kind-looking woman next to me and I said, "I suffer from panic attacks. I'm about to panic. Could you please help me? I want to try to get through the checkout." And she took my arm and said, "You're doing really, really well. I've got your arm. You'll be okay and I won't let you go." With her help I was able to complete my transaction. I realized that people were more than willing to help and to care and to love. But to come to that realization, it was first necessary for me to make that move closer to *them*, to openly share with them my vulnerability, my difficulties and also my courage. They couldn't read my mind.

Prior to awakening I had heard the phrase 'there is no separate self'. It had certainly sounded like a profound spiritual truth, but I had no idea what it meant. After I awoke, I saw that 'no separate self' is simply how Truth is. Our True Nature is one indivisible whole and there is no separate entity or personal self that is in some way split off from that.

In retrospect, I see that the process of 'getting close' to people when I suffered from panic attacks, 'worked' for me, because in essence it was a more-inclusive and as such 'truer' way of experiencing life than going into battle with it. By including other people, moving closer to them, seeing them as they are, I had begun to make the very first movements into an alignment with the

Oneness that is our True Nature. It was many years later, in fully moving into that Truth that my suffering would come to an end.

Have you ever truly *seen* someone?
Without the lens of judgement,
of history or of fear?

A stranger?
A person you have never met before
And are never likely to see again?

Here in the supermarket.
Here on the street corner.

Have you ever seen
An old woman?
Wrinkled hands
Pushing a supermarket trolley.
Faraway eyes that have seen many days.
Many losses. Many joys.

Have you ever seen
A man in dirty clothes

Sitting on the pavement?
Head bent over his guitar
Strumming over and over
The only three chords he knows.

Don't move away.
Come closer, come closer.
Here is Perfection in each expression of Spirit

***

what we fight grows stronger ...

There was a time when a small group of my friends were lesbian separatists; their political choice was to associate only with lesbians or other women. As much as possible they removed themselves from what they saw as a male-dominated society and from interactions with men.

The movement of lesbian separatism did not appeal to me in any way. I wasn't a person whose primary motivation was political, and frankly two of my oldest and very dearest friends were men. I had also worked with men, my music teachers had been men, my brother was a man. I had had very positive interactions with men, as well as some that were extremely negative. The same could have been said of my interactions with women.

But there was something else that disturbed me: these women were openly and unashamedly aggressive, vicious, hateful and belittling towards men. And in the light of what they saw as countless years of male-dominance, injustice, global gender imbalance and male-on-female violence, they felt that this position was entirely justified.

However, it seemed to me that not only were they mimicking the very behaviors they so reviled in men (and so setting up a circle of aggression that could never be 'won'), they were also bestowing upon men a power that was far beyond the reality of what actually took place in their everyday lives. The men in their lives apparently had the ability to take away their identity, their livelihood and their freedom. I may have been politically naïve, but the men in my own life simply did not have such a power. I felt that in this present moment, my identity, my livelihood and my freedom were entirely mine to decide and to live.

It was an interesting lesson for me. I could see so clearly that when we fight something, whether it be men, anxiety, depression, sadness or anger, it is given an 'otherness', a conceptual existence and a life, a supposed domain of action and power, an imagined weight and influence, that it simply *does not have*. And in the face of that, we do indeed become powerless, because we ignore the actual ontological reality or *direct experience* that this 'thing we are fighting' has in our lives. We become unable to clearly see that 'thing' as it actually *is* and so we can never get close to it, understand it or see its Truth. We remain blind and blinded.

And we remain at war.

***

the battle of 'acceptance'

There is a teaching in some spiritual circles called 'acceptance': it's just a matter of 'accepting everything' or 'allowing everything to be as it is'.

If only it were that easy.

Such teachings can usurp deep spiritual truths or the depths of awakened reality and turn them into 'something the ego has to do'. This Truth can then all too easily become a platitude with which the ego can placate itself; the ego can feel okay about itself because it believes that it is doing 'something spiritual'.

Although 'acceptance' is undoubtedly a worthy ideal, the reality is that the everyday self or ego cannot *do* this thing called 'acceptance'.

The everyday self can certainly try to *approximate* acceptance, but for me this approximation all too easily became another battle, another fight with myself and with life, another 'thing I should be doing', that only served to separate me against 'that thing I should accept'. So often I steeled myself so that I could 'accept' the unacceptable, I berated myself to relax in the face of the unbearable or the unworkable. But all the while I was ignoring the voice inside that said "something feels wrong with all of this acceptance business".

True Acceptance is an aspect of our True Nature; it is what we *are*. We simply cannot make it happen, we cannot manufacture it, we cannot will it into existence. When Acceptance comes, it will wash in with the tides of our Essential Nature.

Although the ego can't 'do' this thing called 'acceptance', the ego *can*, however, move in closer and closer to the Truth *of this very moment*.

It can align itself deeper and deeper with the reality of what is here. It can be *present*.

What is here in my experience right now? What is here in this body? What is this sensation? What does it feel like? What does it do? Is it sharp, dull, prickly, soft? Is it heavy or is it light? Does it move to the left, to the right, or go around and up? Does it tremble, throb, or quiver? Does it come and go? What is moving, what is changing, what is dancing?

And as the ego develops a greater and greater capacity to move in close, it is able to be present for more and more difficult experiences; it can more easily embody them. We begin to shine a light in the places we thought would forever remain hidden. And as we do, we find that the pain, the difficulty and the suffering is gradually given its freedom.

Can I align myself with what is actually *here*?

***

moving in close through therapy

I found therapy a profoundly important medium for 'moving in close'.[3]

Did the therapist open a space from which I could align myself deeper and deeper with the reality of what is *here*? Was it a space in which I could be present with and curious about my all my experience? Was there room to move in close to my anger, my desperation, my neediness, my desire to be liked, my hatred, my fear as well as my health, my intelligence, my humor, my sexual feelings and my depth? Was there room to explore every bodily sensation, every discomfort, every contraction? To *really* feel it? Its sharpness, its dullness, its softness, its prickliness, its lightness, its heaviness? Could my body, my mind, my emotions and my spirituality all be acknowledged? All be explored? Could it *all* be held?

It was in therapeutic relationships in which *nothing* was taboo and *all* my experience could be approached, that the most profound healing took place. As I shone a light into the places I thought would forever remain hidden, my suffering was little by little given its freedom.

If I sensed that there were bits of my life and experience that were not welcome, that had to be 'fought', or were an 'issue' for the therapist, then I knew instinctively that it could not work.

Early on, I saw a talking psychiatrist who 'forbade' me from seeking out any sort of 'mothering' from her. Even though at that time I had no awareness whatsoever of the aspects of my behavior she was referring to, I now wonder what it was that I was supposed to do with the very young parts that in their desperation so much needed acknowledgement, holding and nourishment. How were they to heal if their needs were 'forbidden territory'? Perhaps she hoped that by fighting or ignoring them, they would magically disappear.[4]

***

moving in close through art[5]

There were many times when my inner world was complicated, extraordinarily

---

3. I discuss therapy more fully in the chapter *Therapists and Teachers*,
4. I was only able to fully resolve my 'need' for mothering many years later. See chapter, *The Child and the Fundamental Abandonment*.
5. Also see the chapter *Creativity*.

painful, and difficult to put into words. Painting and drawing gave me a medium for moving in close to this complexity, exploring it, and becoming aligned with it rather than pushing it away.

As an example, there was a time when my body felt extraordinarily fragile; it seemed almost incomprehensible to me that my body would survive much longer. My back was painful, I struggled to walk, and there were days and weeks I suffered excruciating neck pain. At night my dreams were filled with images of splintered and shattered glass; there was often broken glass lying on the ground which I had to carefully avoid. At other times I dreamt of being forced to eat glass against my will and as much as I tried, could not spit out the shards. I often woke up in desperate fear, only to realize a few moments later that I didn't have glass in my mouth after all.

In the painting below[6] I was able to approach this disturbing mix of dreams, feelings and sensations, and then bear witness to them in the completed work. Through the broken glass of the window behind me, the screws and nails skewered into my spine, and the angularity and anguish of my painted body, I was able to truly *experience* how very precarious my life felt.

Afterwards the dreams about glass eased, although the bodily fragility remained. Even now, the power of this painting takes my breath away, and recalls to me one of the most suffered times of my life.

***

6. I feel it is worth noting that this painting is very large and as such, quite confronting.

moving in close through journaling

From my early 20s I wrote in journals. At first my journals were merely receptacles for my anguish, but over time they also became avenues through which I could move closer to my suffering and pain, explore it, question it and come to clarity and understanding.

Although many of the processes I followed in my journaling were informed by therapy, over time I was able to instigate and move through such processes on my own. Below is an example of stream-of-consciousness writing. I found this technique very useful in following and deepening into my experience, and as such, transforming it. Such a process could take minutes, hours, days or weeks.

> This afternoon I am once again pushing myself. I feel I must push myself to be in the world. I have been pushing myself my whole life.
>
> I feel the fragility of my body - physically I feel on a knife edge. I am so tired.
>
> I lie down in bed. I feel the pushing. I move in close to the pushing. I see that the world pushes: rushing around, talking, constant busy-ness. All action in the world seems like pushing.
>
> I believe that to move in the world, I must push. Is this true?
>
> I ask myself what is at the core of this belief. What am I most truly, when I am not pushing? What is it that I am protecting with my pushing? I stay with those questions ...
>
> And then the answer comes in my body ... I open out into the most exquisite softness. I am softness. Softer than softness. I have always been this incredibly fine open innocent softness.
>
> Is this True Nature? Or is this the child I was? It feels as though this is what I am in some fundamental way. Perhaps this is my Essence as it is bodying as Marianne. Perhaps what I am as I come into this body is softness. Are we all this softness? I wish to dwell as this softness forever. The ego's actions and strivings, seem so angular and coarse in comparison. The hardness in my chest protects this softness. As a child this is how I protected the softness.

***

moving in close through simple sitting

What is to sit? It is not something we do a lot of. We flit from busy-ness to busy-ness, Facebook post to Facebook post, work to home to television to sleep to work, shopping to a football match. When do we simply sit? This 'sitting' can be in the form of meditation, it can be simply sitting in the backyard, it can be a sitting in a comfortable chair, sitting on the beach …

Frequently when I am out walking I sit for a while on a bench at the local oval and take the time to come close to everything that is there, regardless of what it is. I don't fight it, I don't run away. It is all welcome. In that closeness, in that non-separation, is the Truth of direct experience, of Now.

> my concern about the pain in my neck
> my tiredness from a restless night's sleep
> the delicious smells of freshly-mown grass
> a gentle warm breeze on my skin
> my breath as it moves in and out of my lungs
> the hum of the cars on the road nearby
> a conversation with a friend who joins me

***

ultimate reality is the ultimate closeness

Our True Nature is nowhere other than here.

We go off looking for it everywhere, on top of high mountains, in spiritual fantasy stories, sitting with a guru or in experiences of extraordinary bliss or unity, without realizing that it is closer than close. What we are looking for is right under our very noses … and yet it is even closer than that …

When we come to see the Truth of our Essential Oneness, the ramifications of that are extraordinary. There aren't bits and pieces that come together to create a coherent whole. There isn't something that needs to be defeated, dismissed or overcome so that we can finally be whole. No, **there simply is only One**. And the reality is that because there is only One, we can never be apart from that, not even for one moment. It is quite literally impossible.

However, when we are suffering we believe we must be a long way away from this Truth. And so we begin to do battle with ourselves, believing that if we just fight all our troublesome bits and make them go away, we might move ourselves closer to our Truth and closer to Home. But *this* bit of pain, *this* suffering, is as close as we'll ever get to the Truth. Here. Here.

I understand that this might sound completely absurd to someone who is in the midst of a torturous pain; to the everyday mind what I have written here sounds like complete and utter nonsense. I know that. In the midst of my own pain, it would not have helped me one iota to hear about Oneness and Truth. I would simply have wanted to find a way to make my pain go away as soon as possible. Pain, after all, is pain.

However, I do hope, that in writing this I might open a door, even if only a crack.

When we do battle with ourselves, we our fighting what is true. When we pitch one piece of ourselves against another piece, we are fighting a pointless war. Truth is not to be found in the spoils of a battle. Truth is to be found in what we already *are*. It is in the coming-in-close, whether that be to our pain, our anxiety, our turmoil, our grief, our love, the spring sunshine or a violent storm, that we are aligning ourselves with Reality.[7]

Right now, as I am sitting here writing, I have a substantial pain in my neck and I've been up since 4.30am. I'm tired and the day hasn't yet begun. This is what my life is right now.

The everyday mind would wish to fight this reality. It would wish to tell me that this neck pain is not okay and that because I'm up early my day will now be difficult. If I listen to this story before long I would feel anxious, miserable and perhaps even fearful of the day to come. I would start to 'suffer' the pain in my neck.

But, rather than fight it, I can also simply *feel* the neck pain and the tiredness. I can become intimately *conscious* of everything that is in my direct experience right now ... I can literally bring my everyday consciousness towards everything, around everything, and *into* everything ... the pain, the constriction, my concern, my weariness ... and if I continue to move in closer and closer I will find there is a profound peace with it all that is very much the natural state of affairs ... and as I move in even closer I may feel myself spread out and deepen into the vast field of the Totality, the Consciousness that all at once *is* everything and holds everything (including this pain). I might still consider going to the osteopath later in the day so she can work on my neck

---

7. Of course we may need an experienced therapist by our side when we 'come in close' to deep wounding or pain.

and I might still go and have a nap later, but that does not alter or judge what is here right *now*.

One of my meditation teachers used to suggest a simple practice of becoming aware of the body. She guided meditators progressively through the body, from the top of the head down to the toes, suggesting they bring awareness to each part as it is named. Beyond the grounding that this brings, I used to think that this was all a bit of a waste of time: "Come on, let's do something a bit more spiritual!" But I now realize that it is in our capacity to be utterly present that we find our True Self. We don't find it over there somewhere on an out-of-body excursion through the cosmos. No, we find our True Nature on an in-body experience in our very ordinary and yet oh-such extraordinary lives.

What we are looking for is here, here, here. Closer than here.

***

soul

Soul has been an oh-so-rich stepping stone on my journey out of suffering.

In soul is the beginning of our movement into depth ...

***

what is soul?

For a long time I wondered what the words 'soul' and 'spirit' actually meant. What was it in my experience that those words referred to?

I read a lot of books, listened to talks and chatted with people. It was clear that 'soul' was used in a variety of ways to describe a variety of experiences.

Some seemed to think that 'soul' and 'spirit' were pretty much synonymous, and yet others clearly weren't so sure. Many people I spoke with would have referred to themselves as 'spiritual' and yet I doubt very much they would have also referred to themselves as 'soulful'. Wherever I looked there was vagueness and ambiguity.

So what is soul?

> Soul is not our physical inwardness: our blood, bones, kidneys, lungs.
> It is not our emotional inwardness: sadness, happiness, anger. It is not our psychology.
> It is not the circularity of the mind: thoughts, beliefs, deductions, aversions, desires.
> It is not the inwardness of dreams, imagination and metaphor.
> It is not the inwardness of New Age spiritual experiences: light, crystal healing, angels.
> It is not the boundlessness of Consciousness, Emptiness or Spirit.

Amongst all these, soul can be so easily overlooked.

So what is soul? What is my direct experience of soul?

> I go inside.
> I feel the inwardness of my body.
> Here is a space that can so quickly be dismissed as mere emptiness or irrelevant blankness.
> But in this space we have infinite movement and infinite sensing. Here is richness and sensuality. Here we hold beauty, darkness and fertility.
> In this space our language is of exquisite qualitative subtlety, depth and meaning. Here are the movements, shapes, textures, temperatures and colors that characterize our soul body.
> It is here that we can roam and flourish, without the ownership or demands of 'ego' and yet still with a sense of ourselves and our inner world that is deeply personal and deeply felt.
> It is here that we can expand into our capacity to be moved and changed and touched by the world around us.
> It is in this space that I am uplifted by a sunset, flow with a breeze, expand with love, greened by the leaves of a tree, or filled with wonder at a newborn baby.
> It is in this space that I might feel the claggy and weighted threads of depression pulling me down.
> It is here that I feel the sharp edges of my fragility or the movements of my fluidity.
> It is in this space I come inwardly close to my lover, or contract away in the heat of an argument.[1]

So what's so significant about soul?

It is through soul, that I have understood my life in this world as one of depth and meaning.

It is through soul, that I have understood my deep sensitivity and been given a context for expressing it in this world.

---

1. I acknowledge here the influence of British independent philosophical thinker Peter Wilberg, most particularly his book The *Qualia Revolution*. Although my current understanding and terminology differ somewhat from Wilberg, what I describe in this paragraph as the movements, qualities, textures and colors of soul, Wilberg calls 'qualia' or qualitative units of awareness. I also describe Wilberg and his work in the chapters *Depression* and *Descent* and *The Body*.

It is with awareness of soul that I have understood why even as a child I found significance, consolation and refuge in nature, beauty, solitude and music.

It is with the awareness of soul that I have understood the deep sensitivity of the child I was, and the reasons why her subtle perceptions and insight were so often misunderstood and also punished.

It is in the embrace of soul, that my inner woundings have found nourishment and healing.

It is in understanding soul as a profound medium of attunement and relationality, that my connection with the world, with nature and with others has been immeasurably enriched.

It is in acknowledgement of soul that I have understood my inner nature as innately musical, and have been given a powerful insight into the significance of my career as a musician.

Soul is the vital, energetic and qualitative inwardness through which I inhabit and enrich my everyday life.

In many ways I see 'soul' as an intermediary between the world of Spirit and my everyday life.

Soul is my *inner* world as it is individuated by 'me', my soul is *mine* alone but without the ownership or circular purposes of mind we call 'ego'.

Spirit on the other hand I understand as the indivisible Oneness or Consciousness with no separate self or 'me'. In Spirit all polarization ceases. Spirit is All That Is.

***

no further than my own backyard

During the very suffered times of my life, my world contracted. As I journeyed into my tormented interior, my outer world diminished in size. It had to. The brashness and busy-ness of what other people call their 'lives' would have overwhelmed me.

The consensus world can so easily dismiss lives of suffering, as 'unimportant', 'withdrawn' or 'self-obsessed'. People are never comfortable with what they don't understand or would prefer to ignore in themselves. And society as a whole can never be comfortable with a suffering that can all too easily bring its very foundations into question.

But as my outer world narrowed, I was given a gift. While others might have needed the thrill of exotic overseas holidays or the rush of skydiving to give their life meaning, immediacy or dynamism, I found that the minutiae of my backyard took on an intense vitality and preciousness; every tiny bit of creation had wisdom to offer, depths to explore, and a soul world to inhabit and learn about.

During this time I spoke with a friend about my difficulties. He said, "I suppose the main thing is not to lose touch with people and with the world." At first I felt an anguished self-doubt at his comment; I *was* losing touch with people, I *was* losing touch with almost every aspect of the world 'out there'. But then I started to wonder: "What is it to be *truly* in touch? With people, with myself, with the world?" For him, drinking with his mates, partying and going on holidays, was 'keeping in touch'. And yet, on what level was that touch? I certainly would have liked to be a person who was seen to be 'in touch' with lots of people; I would have liked to look popular and outgoing. But for me this 'touch' would only ever have been superficial and pressured.

I had to ask myself, "On what level do I choose to live? On what level do I find the aliveness and intimacy that is meaningful for *me*?"

I realized that it is the *depths* of soul that allow true touch; that allow one soul to truly touch another soul, whether that be of another person or a flower or a rock. And it is this depth that gives my life its meaning, not because there is something called 'meaning' at that depth, but because at that level, meaning is its very medium.

And I knew that this depth was everywhere, including in the small space that was my backyard. Tropical hideaways or remote wilderness might be great fun for some, but in order to live a meaningful life, I really didn't need to travel anywhere but to where I was.

People won't notice a rich inner life.

The delicacy of a white and pink of blossom in early spring.
The solidity of rock.
Dark storm clouds brewing their promise of rain.

The deep and simple peace of sitting.
The grounding joy of a wriggling puppy.
The ceaseless and ordered movement of a winding ant trail.
Stifling summer heat.
The stark stillness of a dead goldfish.
The quiet damp cloak of a morning fog.

People won't notice a rich inner life.

***

texture

I touch the roughness of tree bark and run my fingers across its jagged and irregular outlines. I place my hand on the solidity of the trunk and feel the intricacies of its outer face on my palm.

The 'fingers' of my soul body too reach out, touch and take in the bark. I allow myself to be changed and informed by the angularity of its patterns, by the sharpness of its edges. I allow myself to inhabit more fully my own textures and my own edges: the jolted abruptness of a sudden movement, the edges where I dare not go, the layers of each moment and each day, the surface smoothness that belies the furrows, the pits and the chasms held within.

Can I participate fully in all the intricate textures of my being?

***

shape

I hold the delicious and rounded perfection of a lemon in my hand, the promise of its fruit held within.

I open readily to the roundness and fullness within my soul. My soul is curved and contained and contented. My soul is a womb that holds and gives fruit. I softly curl, bend and meander. Here is my rounded gentleness and the embrace of all I hold within. I am at home in the delicious curves of gentle words and of breasts and buttocks and beauty. And silence. I am spoken to of the roundness of my days and the rounded completion of this moment. Of the rounded eyes of my lover as they mirror her soul and meet mine. I am spoken to of the stars and the sun and the moon.

***

color

From the time we are very young we learn that color is a secondary attribute of an object: a yellow flower, a pink dress, a blue sky. But on its own, color is extraordinarily dynamic and powerful. If we lean into a color, allow ourselves to become that color, we can feel our souls changed by it. We are challenged or calmed or lifted or informed or touched or expanded.

I am redness.
Flushed hot in the sun. Blushing with embarrassment.

I want to burst. I am angry. Pissed.
Blood-engorged vibrant sensuality.
Body, breath, heart and pulse.
Uncompromising solidity and strength.
A red t-shirt standing out in a crowd.
I am redness.

Beautiful woman, painting detail, acrylic.

***

fluidity

Just as a small stream forever moves and flows, so does our soul. Our soul is never static; *we* are never static. Every moment is change. We are forever swept forward by the stream that is life.

Can I flow into the words that I am writing here? Can I feel the resonances of meaning pouring into my sentences? Can I flow into my depths and then let those depths flow back into my words? Can I feel myself flowing into this day, carried along, moving, bubbling, rolling? Can I flow into the beauty of this flower? Or into the eyes of a child? Or flow with my pain and grief?

***

the musical soul of inclusion

For many years I was a professional musician. As a musician I was given an insight into soul expression and communication that at that time I probably took somewhat for granted.

Music is a part of our lives in so many ways: clichéd music in an elevator, stage musicals, rock, three-hour long symphonies, a child learning to play violin, singing in the shower.

Music affects and informs us on many different levels or depths. On a surface level we hear music much as we might noise: with indifference or annoyance, or as a background companion. On a slightly deeper level, music affects our emotions.[2] But beyond our emotional experience, music offers us a path into the world of soul.

Music is humanity's language of soul. Its notes and harmonies are the 'letters and words' that allow us to step beyond the everyday world, and express the *felt* meanings of our inner soul world.

As a musician, in order to fully perform or 'language' a piece of music, I first had to form or shape the particular soul state or quality intended by the composer, in my inner body. Just as one might hear of an actress inhabiting her character in a movie, so a musician inhabits the character (or soul) of a piece of music. Just as we *know* when an actor in a movie or on stage is fully inhabiting their role or their character, so we *know* when a performance is truly being 'languaged' by the performer.

For instance, if I wanted to convey the music flowing forward, I first leant into that flow in my soul body. If I wanted to convey the heaviness of the music, I first felt that heaviness within my inner body. If the music was warm I felt that

---

2. For further discussion of emotions and music see the section *Music informs Life* in the chapter *Life*.

warmth. For intensity, I would form intensity. That shaping of my soul body could be of the finest intricacy, as in a single note that may slowly yearn its way into the one that is to follow. There could be ever more subtle gradations: shades within shades (gentle pastel versus lifeless pastel), colors within colors (bright blackness versus a somber blackness), textures within textures (delicate sparseness versus an austere sparseness). I learnt that our soul is an infinitely malleable, suggestive, open and flowing field that we all carry within.

But beyond my experience as a performer, I know that when I listen to music something happens that is beyond nameable emotions. I sense flows, weights, temperatures, colorings, shades, nuances, shapings, textures and intensities. We generally take these movements and qualities very much for granted or believe them to be merely metaphoric descriptions or emotional states. But it is these movements and qualities of soul that allow us to be 'spoken to' through the music. We feel ourselves smoothed, jolted, we rise, we fall, we flow, we feel small and delicate, large and expansive, we feel warmed or we feel cooled.

However, as we 'listen' to the 'music' of our everyday lives, we rarely allow ourselves to be altered, informed or moved in the way we would with music. We don't allow the events of our lives to 'play us'. In fact, we frequently resist this at all costs.

In particular, movements of soul such as contraction, descent and fragility, although valued and 'felt' in music, are often seen as threatening to our fixed sense of self and its functioning within the busy-ness of this world. We imagine that if we descend we might never rise up again, if we contract we might never expand again, if we flow into our fragility we might never again feel strong. We imagine ourselves as rigid and hard objects that need to be defended and fortified.

And yet, what would happen if we were to flow with life as we flow with a piece of music? What if the darker shades of life were welcomed just as fully as the brighter shades? What if we felt our uncertainty and hesitancy just as much as the uplifting and inspirational moments? What if we flowed into our heartache and allowed it to transform us in its own rhythm and time? What if we were to explore the infinite subtleties of life and their capacity to mold and move us?

I have no illusion that we can live our lives with the intensity of a performing musician or even with the intensity with which we might listen to a piece of music. Nor am I ignorant of the fact that some feeling and soul states can be acutely painful to open to or re-experience. And yet, in my own life, I know that the awareness of my capacity for soul expression, soul shaping and soul inclusion, was an extraordinarily potent invitation to engage more fully with the vast richness, breadth, vitality, meaning and radiance bursting forth in each moment of life.

For instance, I can 'feel' the 'yellowness' of a daisy and allow my soul body to take on its particular shining brightness. I can feel the texture of a rocky path beneath my feet and allow it to inform my capacity for roughness or jaggedness. I can feel the qualitative difference between old mossy brickwork and new sterile brickwork. The difference between olive green and lime green. I can feel the cool blueing of my body as I take in the sky. I can feel my soul body blown with the wind as I stand on a beach on a gusty day. I can feel the softness of a single delicate butterfly mirroring my own softer moments.

But beyond this, I can sense the soul qualities of the people around me. I can feel another person's warmth or coolness. I can feel their expansion or contraction. I can feel their prickliness or softness. And I can also feel when I resist particular soul qualities and when I don't. And so I ask myself questions: What is it in this person's iciness that scares me? What is it in this expansion that makes me feel my own capacity for expansion? What is it in this gentle delicateness that opens my heart?

After awakening into Spirit, I realized in retrospect, that the ground for that awakening was in part nurtured by this deepening into the world of soul. It seemed that the further I had moved within and the more of the life of soul and the depths and beauty of *this* world I understood and lived, the 'bigger and bigger' I had become, until ultimately all boundaries were dissolved into Spirit as the all-encompassing reality.

We have such a tremendous potential in our depth and yet so often we hover with fear or with unknowing only on the surface of life.

The experience of music has a profound gift to offer. It can not only inform us *about* life, it can deepen us immeasurably *into* life. At heart we are musical beings.

We are fluid and flowing beings.

***

words fail

The poem that follows was written on a wintry day. I had stepped briefly outside and as I looked skyward, two galahs[3] were swept up by the wind. I felt my soul swept along with them.

In that very simple occurrence was so much subtlety and nuance, so many ways in which my body and soul were moved and affected. I felt how very limited our language is when we seek to express those exquisite depths of sensitivity and sensing.

This poem is an homage to soul. And it is an invitation ...

> We are sensitive
> Sensuous
> Sensing
> Beings.
>
> As I open to myself,
> To the world around me,
> To every nuance,
> Every qualitative subtlety,
> Every blessing,
> Every movement and every moment,
> Words fall by the wayside,
> Only dim reflections of the glory of manifestation.
>
> How many words could convey
> A wintry and wind-filled sky?
> Hues of grey,
> And scudding clouds.
> Two galahs thrown up by a gust.
> My soul tossed with them in flight,
> And then let go.
> My body greyed and pinked and windswept,
> And filled with a humble joy.
>
> How many words could adequately describe
> A dog's soft muzzle?

---

3. The galah is an Australian cockatoo/parrot with pink and grey plumage.

The hint of bristled, whisker hairs,
And a wisp
Of eager, warm breath on my hand.
Wet-rubber nose.
And the delicious sensing in my body of
Such simple and unabashed dog-ness.

How many words could ever give form to
The space where my soul meets another?
A touchless touch
That holds and invites.
A weaving. And a questing.
Eyes that smile and see,
As my body plays
And loves.

And how many words could have ever sufficed for
Those troubled and suffered times?
The inconvenient pain and hidden wounds
Of a bewildered and tremulous soul.
An innocent heart
Too-soon broken and raw,
And my body
Held fearful and hard.

We are sensitive
Sensuous
Sensing
Beings.

***

edges

Why would I invite you to explore the edges? Why would I invite you to wander here on such treacherous ground?

Because here, here, here, is the frontier between what you are and what you will become ...

***

only those who have gone over an edge ...

It is only those who have gone over an edge, who know all about them.

The rest of the population lives only in fear of them. It is the place they dare not name, the place they dare not look, the place they dare not go.

On occasion they may have felt themselves pushed towards an edge, propelled towards an edge. They may have been shocked to suddenly find themselves balancing precariously on an edge staring down at a gaping abyss below ...

But at the last minute they have pulled back, they have resisted, they have fought mightily to get away. They have distracted themselves or medicated themselves. They have built their fortifications and walled off their fragile havens of safety. They have defined and limited their worlds with words and smiles, or bitterness and confusion.

These edges, they are the stuff with which some people fill their worst nightmares and they will do anything, *anything*, to escape them.

But the edges will always remain out there, somewhere. The edges don't go away.

Fortunately.

It is only those have gone over an edge, who know all about them.

***

the edge, pencil sketch

***

on the edge

Many times life has presented me with an edge: between what I am and what I will become, between what I know and what I don't yet know, between what is familiar and what I must still give birth to.

That edge is never comfortable. I have never found myself willingly balancing on that edge, patting myself smugly on the back at how clever I am.

No, when I'm on that edge I'm in turmoil. I'm dazed. Shocked. Struggling. Pissed off. I feel pushed beyond my limits. There is nowhere else to go. Nothing else to do. Everything feels unsolvable and unfixable. I'm at a dead end. I've run out of options. I am terrified. I am certain I will die.

In front of me looms only the emptiness of my worst fears. An ominous oblivion. I can distinguish no bottom and no horizon, no promise of foothold or embrace. There is only indeterminacy and endlessness. Dare I risk myself to this unknowing or should I clamber and claw my way back onto unstable ground, a ground that is, at this very moment, giving way beneath my feet. Crumbling. Caving in. A ground that no longer sustains me. A ground that betrays the trust I had placed in it.

What should I do? I have nowhere to go.

Am I prepared to risk everything? To fail? To fall? To drop down? Dare I give up all that I believe and all that I know? Dare I let go of the old and stale pathways, the creaking and rusty gates, and the monotonous and worn-out movements? Dare I plunge into this hole before me?

But then, then ... when I feel least ready, least prepared ... just as my resolve is wavering and I am considering a line of retreat ... of avoidance ... of distraction ...

I find myself pushed ...

It is life that pushes me, or pain that pushes me, or a friend, or a lover. Or the crumbling ground beneath my feet finally gives way, divesting me of any choices I felt I might have had. There is nothing I can do now. I am in freefall. Nothing. Nothing.

And then. Then. As I hand myself over. As I let go. As I surrender. As I release myself. I realize I have wings that I did not know I had. I am flying. I am at home in a world that I could never have imagined, never have problem-solved my way to, never have constructed or planned.

Here now, I am soaring. I am loving. Blessed life! I am moving in new ways and with new understandings. Here, now, I see only possibility. New paths. Undreamt-of potential.

Why did I fear? Why did panic freeze my limbs? Why did I not trust that I would be held? Why, why, *why* did I not let go willingly?

This is the lesson of edges and of falling and of flying ...

It is letting go that is the hardest ...

***

risking it all

> Can I hazard myself?
> Can I risk everything I would still secretly call 'myself'
> for this beckoning edge that might set me free?
> For this intimate danger that feels so very right?
> Can I reach for this new ground regardless?

For this unknown origin that is
always calling me Home?
Ultimately, are we not here in this world
to risk it all?

***

on our own terms

We live in a world in which there is very little languaging, context or understanding of inner experiences like 'edges'.

Edges don't fit into normality, into happiness, or into our comfortable, step-by-step lives. Edges don't fit into the world of espressos and idle chatter. And so edges are usually problematized or medicalized; they are relegated to the something-wrong basket. In our society angst, uncertainty and torment are generally considered to be an aberration, a deviation.

And so, when we feel our lives balanced on an edge we're probably not sure what words to use.

We might tell people we're in crisis, we might say we can see no way forward, we might talk about plunging into a terrifying nothingness, we might scream that we're about to be drowned by an internal tsunami, or we might we tell our friends and family that we've fucked up our lives and that we want to kill ourselves.

And naturally enough, our friends and family will try to fix us, manage us, contain us, help us and heal us. They'll take us to the doctor, to the hospital, to a psychologist. They'll tell us not to be so self-absorbed, so selfish. They'll tell us that if only we'd keep busy, sit in the garden and have a cup of tea like everyone else, we'd probably feel a whole lot better. They may even retreat from us because they're so fearful of their own edges or their own precarious hold on existence.

And we can't blame them. What else can they do? They have no context or language for understanding these edges either ...

In our society we don't talk a whole lot about the edges that are lived between the norms and maps of our everyday world and the mysteries we might sense within. We don't talk about our True Nature or the processes that might plunge us into depth. We don't speak of the extraordinary potentials inherent in our human existence.

And if we do mention that our desperation might also be our turning point, if we declare that our crumbling life is a godsend, if we suggest that risking ourselves into the unknown might turn out to be our savior, well then … then people will think we're crazy. Mad.

And so I'm writing this chapter (and to some extent this book), because it is hard to be out there on your own, standing on an edge. It's hard to live in a world in which there is so little understanding or vocabulary for processes that are spiritually profound or spiritually meant.

And it's even harder to trust that when you let go of the edge, you will have wings that will spread you into flight.

The true measure and expanse of Life is forever calling us Home.

***

notes from an edge[1]

The piece that follows was written only relatively recently.

After developing Disembarkment Syndrome (MdDS)[2], there were times I felt an immense physical fragility and extreme tiredness. My body which had previously been strong and well, was now no longer wholly mine.

My tendency throughout my life had been to push relentlessly forward, always willing myself on. I now believe that one of the reasons I developed MdDS was that I pushed my body too hard for too long, and it was quite simply unable to cope.

With MdDS I had no choice but to stop pushing myself and physically rest, but the internal dialogue that pressured me ever onward remained intact to some degree. Over and over, in countless different ways I had come to the edge of 'stopping' and although I might have surrendered into it for a brief moment or even for an hour, I had resisted a true leap.

---

1. Although here I describe the edge in my life between pushing myself relentlessly forward and finally 'letting go' into a true 'stopping', edges can present themselves in infinite ways from relatively minor edges to those that change the course of a life. As examples: an edge between always saying "yes" to family members and finally saying "no", an edge between closing off from extreme pain (physical or emotional) and open-heartedly surrendering oneself into it, an edge between always arguing the point with people and simply allowing people to have their opinions, an edge between keeping one's heart closed and opening to someone with genuine intimacy.
2. See preface for a description of MdDS.

The 'stopping' and the 'not pushing' was my abyss. It was my 'unknown'. It felt dangerous and uncomfortable because I didn't know what I would find there. I could not in any way conceptualize or imagine how I might live my life without pushing through it. I certainly could never have 'thought' my way to the soft, gentle holding I found on the other side.

Although the reading of the piece below might take only a couple of minutes, it took place over a few hours. It was not in any way a mental process. Rather, it was a process of deep feeling.

Vulnerability. I feel so vulnerable. Physically vulnerable.

My body isn't wholly mine any more. I am so weak, so tired.
I rock and sway inside endlessly. Endlessly. Day in and day out.

I am so tired.

I move in closer.

Here in my body. My body that isn't wholly mine. I am achingly tired. I can't go on. I really can't go on like this.

I move closer again.

I always try to make myself feel better. Stronger. I try to will myself on. And yet that only accentuates this yawning vulnerability. This desperate tiredness.

Move even closer.

I stand at the edges of this tiredness. Here is such exhaustion. I have nothing left. Nothing to spare. Nowhere to go. I am completely spent. I have no energy for struggle any more.

Here I am, standing at the edge of this gaping hole. No choice. Nowhere. Nowhere. Please God, help me. God help me!

I know that I have no option but to risk myself to annihilation and take a step into this open air, into a place I have never been before, into a space I do not know. I let go.

Suddenly there is an opening inside that I had not seen, that I did not know was there. I look around. Here is a chasm, and yet rather than the emptiness and destruction that I had imagined, its edges are now hands that are holding me. It is a supremely soft and open embrace. The chasm no longer gapes its threat. It is a chasm of openness. Of gentleness. Of support. A place of rest.

I am held! I am always held! There is no longer any need to push. I am held. I always have been.

I have stopped. I breathe.
I can rest.

***

emptiness and holes

Is emptiness the wasteland of our annihilation or is it a womb for our renewal?

Dare we venture forth into the unknown?

From the very mundane to the Infinite, an embrace of emptiness and holes was vital in my movement out of suffering.

***

into the hole

Our minds thrive on 'knowing' and certainty. We feel comfortable when our lives are neatly mapped out around us. We feel secure and at ease when we know what's going on.

But of course 'something' inevitably comes along to disrupt our tidy little worlds: our children move out of home, a dinner date falls through, our computer won't turn on, a friend dies, we finish writing a book, we don't get accepted into university ...

When something disappears out of our lives we literally feel 'at a loss'. Where previously something was, there is now a hole, an emptiness, a vacuum. What am I going to do without access to the Internet? Who am I when I no longer have my children to take care of? What will I do now my book is finished? To whom will I talk about my problems now my friend is no longer here? What will I do about my future?

The mind doesn't know what to do with uncertainty and not-knowing. The mind's job is to 'know', and without 'knowing' the mind can only see its own non-existence. And so the mind believes that something is wrong. And for the mind there *is* indeed something wrong. The mind has come up against its own limitations; the mind has come up against the place where it cannot go.

Absence, mystery, holes and emptiness are not the mind's domain.

And so the mind will always scurry around, searching frantically for something with which to fill a hole: shopping, problem-solving, positive affirmations, watching television, buying a new computer, putting on a happy face … anything, *anything*, feels better than emptiness.

And yet, we rarely consider what it would be like to actually tolerate a hole. Or *live* with a hole.

What if we don't try to escape the discomfort or fight that empty space? What if we don't rush to fill the emptiness as soon as we possibly can? What if we ignore the familial or societal imperatives to keep busy? What if we ignore the voices around and within us that with the best of intentions tell us how to manage or problem-solve that hole away?

What if we truly *felt* that emptiness and *allowed* that emptiness? What if we were curious about that hole and asked questions of it: "What is the experience of a hole *actually* like? What is essentially *there* if I move in close and take a good look?"

We're not accustomed to just *feeling* emptiness; we're not accustomed to feeling the space from which 'something' has disappeared. But if we don't pull back, it really is just empty space. Nothing is there. It might feel unnerving or unsettlingly, but in and of itself it is actually not scary. It's not painful. It doesn't have 'evil' intentions. We might even be surprised that we can actually do something like 'feel a hole'. We might realize that the 'nothing' that seemed so daunting or overwhelming is in fact, just an empty hole. We might even feel some relief that finally we can *feel* a hole, *as it is*.

And then we wait. We just feel the hole and let it be there. It is a hole. We don't listen to the panicked voices of our mind as it tries to tell us that this hole is a 'bad thing'. We don't rush to fill it. We don't feel the hole for ten minutes and then get impatient and give up. Certainly at some stage 'something' will happen, but we can't pre-empt when that will be. We can't force or hurry it. We can't think we know how things will turn out. Holes don't conform to our demands or to our time-driven schedules. Holes only function according to *their* timetable, not ours.

Often it is only when we look back over our lives that we realize that it is through holes and emptiness that transformation, deepening, insight or understanding have taken place. Holes and emptiness are the space out of which something fresh and new can be born.

Out of the emptiness of a womb a new life is born. Into the emptiness of our stomach we take in food and so feel nourished and replete. We plant a young sapling in a hole and watch it grow into a tree. From the emptiness of losing a dear friend, there is a new appreciation of the beauty of simply being alive. From the emptiness of our children moving out of home, we rekindle our love of art. Out of the emptiness of having no Internet, there is the peace and contentment of sitting a long time over a cup of tea. Out of the emptiness we feel within our everyday lives we might begin to inquire more deeply into the meaning of life. Out of allowing ourselves to feel an unnerving emptiness deep in our soul, there may now be room to listen for our deepest Truth.

In writing about holes, my intention is not in any way to minimize or downplay the circumstances that may bring holes into our lives. Life can be extraordinarily difficult and painful. Nor am I intending, in any way, to hint at the awful inanities some people parade out when they see that from your adversity or loss, something powerful has grown: "Everything happens for a reason", or "You must have brought this into your life so that you can grow."

When we experience and *feel* a hole, we may still worry, we may still be very scared or grief stricken, but we may also feel the soft invitation into insight and understanding. And we may gently open our ears to listen for the first tentative whispers of new life.

When we experience a hole in our lives, something meaningful is going on, but it is a 'something' that the mind can never encompass or pre-empt.

The mind can only allow.

***

a holiday with holes

Holes happen all the time. Sometimes we hardly notice them.

As I was writing this chapter, I went on a short holiday to a beachside town about two hours' drive away. We rented a dog-friendly holiday house and spent our days relaxing, walking, sitting by the sea, swimming, sleeping and eating.

And yet, despite the simplicity and calm, in the first couple of days I was aware of a discomfort, an emptiness. Although I relished being away from home for a week, all the usual pathways of my life didn't apply and so I felt a little bewildered, a little uncomfortable. "What will I do in the morning if I don't write for a couple of hours? What will I do if I don't go for my usual walk after breakfast? What if Internet access is sporadic and I can't check my emails? Where did I put the tea bags? How do I operate the taps in the shower?" I *liked* these changes and indeed *welcomed* them but I still felt a hole. It wasn't a big hole, it wasn't a hole that came from a loss or crisis. It was simply the hole of a little holiday, but it was a hole nonetheless.

And because it wasn't an earth-shattering hole, it was easy to allow the emptiness and the feeling of 'not-knowing'. I didn't rush to fill it. I didn't worry about it. Then slowly, over a couple of days, the hole filled. There were new ways of acting and being. I sat for a long time watching the changing light over the water. I watched a small boat slowly making its way out to sea. I breathed in the soft ocean breezes. I moved more slowly. I made a cup of tea and did a crossword. I went for a walk. Where previously there was a hole, something quite delicious and refreshing had grown.

And then a week later I was home, and once again there was a little hole. It was a hole where the gentle simplicity of the holiday had been. I resented having to reply to emails. I felt a little irked at having to meet deadlines and go to appointments. The lawn needed mowing. I had to make time for my writing. This 'usual life' now felt a little hollow and empty.

But then after a couple of days, the hole where the holiday was, had filled. I once again loved my garden and the challenges of my writing. Life once again felt comfortable.

And that's how holes are. We've all experienced them.

***

the death of 'the pusher'

Holes also function on deeper levels.

Many of us have parts within that in our childhoods were vital for our emotional, physical or spiritual wellbeing or survival. These parts sought to protect us from the very painful feelings that may have resulted from circumstances such as abuse, rejection, trauma, humiliation or abandonment.

However, in adulthood, these parts may continue to function as they have always done. Their intention is still to protect us, but because our circumstances have changed their patterns of operation now bring suffering and inner conflict, and prevent us from leading a full and free life.

Each time I brought to consciousness, worked through and healed such a part, I experienced a hole or a sense of emptiness where that part had previously been. It was in this hole that a new way of being in the world could grow.

One such part in my life, I came to call 'The Pusher'.[1] The Pusher was essential for the child I had been: it pushed me ever forward, allowing me to act in the world despite a tremendous underlying sense of confusion and fear. I was able to do well in school, maintain friendships, become a professional musician, and project a reasonable countenance into the world even through periods of internal upheaval and suffering.

However, the cost was immense. I had very little sense of a true self from which I was able to act and I felt I had no 'right' to my feelings: my anger, grief, terror, shame, but also my love and joy. As a young adult trying to take my place in the world, I suffered from extreme anxiety, panic attacks and depression. I wasn't able to function like everyone else, and I didn't know why.

I sought help, but because 'pushing forward' is generally perceived to be a positive attribute, The Pusher was seen as an indication of my immense capability and resilience, and so it remained essentially invisible. As my life crumbled around me, The Pusher only intensified its 'protective' pushing. Even when I was desperately suffering, I continued to push myself to look 'well', to pursue therapy, to be a good client, a good partner, a good daughter, a good friend. I tried to be a sociable, active, responsible, hardworking person even when my inner world was tortured and difficult.

The following poem was written about the dissolution of The Pusher. At that time, although I could no longer push, I had no idea whatsoever how to act in the world. My primary way of functioning had collapsed and I experienced a very big hole and a very daunting sense of nothingness. It felt like oblivion. But as the poem makes clear, I knew full well that I was going through a process through which I would eventually move and that in due course something new would take root and then grow.

---

1. I also discuss The Pusher in the chapter *The Child and the Fundamental Abandonment*.

After writing the poem, that hole has indeed been filled: with the natural, unmediated and quite delicious flow of Life/Consciousness as it is moves through me. But that could not have happened if in the first place there had not been a 'death'.

oblivion

Why is it that I think of oblivion
when there is absence
when there is a hole?

Why can I not remember
what it was that I was filling that hole with?
Why can I not remember
two days ago? three days ago?
Why can I not remember
years upon years of my life?

Who was I?
Who did I think I was?
Who am I now?

The mind cannot define itself by absence.
It can only use words like
emptiness
desolation
worthlessness.

But I have been in these places before.
I know the superficiality and limits
of the mind's language and imaginings.
I know the mind's desperate desire
to set life into concrete.
I know that the mind's desire to moan and lament,
is like dry tinder to a spark.

We are far deeper, far more complex
mysterious
beautiful
than the mind could ever conceive.
We are fluid and flowing beings.

We are made to move and bend like the seasons,
like branches in the wind.

There will be times of strangeness,
and of winter and death,
times seemingly without purpose or sanity.

But there are also times
of growth, healing and new understandings.
Of wellness and a living fullness.

I know that what is asked of me here
is not to remove myself from
this chasm,
this hole,
this emptiness,
nor to trap myself
in the prisons and alarm of the mind.

I must simply bear this,
allow it,
feel it in my body,
tiptoe gently to its edges,
have the courage
to follow what needs to be followed,
sit, breathe, cry,
understand the wisdom of withdrawal
and gestation,
understand that holes and emptiness
are the opening that
will allow the light of my True Self
to shine through.

Movement and rebirth
will come by grace in their own time.

***

the 'emptiness' of the interior

It was many years ago, long before my spiritual journey had become conscious, that someone first suggested that I look within to find out who I truly was.

I took their suggestion and did indeed look within. And I came to the rather panicked conclusion that there was absolutely nothing there. As far as I could see it was just one big fat gaping hole. And so I quickly discarded that line of inquiry and decided that the person who had made the suggestion was probably woefully misguided in some way.

And yet, many years later, I came to the realization that it is this hole, this emptiness within, that is the key to everything ...

... for it is this emptiness that we fill when we awaken.

Over the years I have read countless books about adventurers who have trudged across vast unexplored deserts, labored through impenetrable rainforests or set out on a lone journey across ice or sea. And many times I have thought, "Yes, your story is exciting and inspiring and extraordinarily interesting, but here, here, here, closer than here, each of us have within us, a vast realm of unexplored territory that is just ripe for discovery."

Our inner world really *is* the empty continent or the vast unexplored ocean that lies behind the all-too-comfortable shores of our civilization, and as we do the shopping or as we sit around flicking through our emails, it is always there, beckoning and begging us to explore.

And when we *do* have the courage to travel within, set up camp for a while, claim that desert as our own, and then return into our everyday lives, we most probably won't get a write-up in National Geographic, nor will we get a knighthood to show off to our family and friends[2]. But as we take our place in this world, knowing ourselves as the Emptiness that is never empty, as a body that is not a body, as a Self that is not a self ... we will almost certainly have on our faces an uncaused, unabashed and utterly contented grin that not only stretches from ear to ear, but extends back back back into the enormity of All that we are.

It is not possible for it to be otherwise. For we are Home.

---

2. I think here of Robyn Davidson's book *Tracks*, and Sir Ernest Shackleton's extraordinary journey of survival to South Georgia after his ship *Endurance* was trapped in pack ice in Antarctica and then sank.

And there will be times when others look across at us and in the narrowing of their eyes we will see that they are wondering, "Where have you been that I haven't? What do you know that I don't?"

***

depression and descent

When we feel depressed we fear something is terribly wrong. And yet ...

... what if our depression or sadness is an invitation to connect in deeper and deeper ways with all that we are?

And what if we ignore it?

Understanding and embracing depression and the movement of descent has been pivotal in my journey out of suffering.

***

the meaning of depression

There are experiences in our lives that define us. Or at least, set a course that seemingly for years and even decades, informs not only the path we take, but also the path we choose *not* to take.

For me, one such experience was my first encounter with a psychiatrist. At the time I was suffering greatly and had just begun to look for help. I had little knowledge of the healing professions and so assumed that the best place to start was with the mainstream medical world of doctors and psychiatrists. In the chapter *Stories*[1] I describe this encounter and the sense of crushing invalidation when my suffering was reduced to a "chemical imbalance in the brain called depression" and the cure touted as anti-depressants.

Over the years, that diagnosis and its 'cure' was paraded out on numerous other occasions. Even if I went to my doctor for a quite unrelated health matter, the fact that I was "having therapy" or "wasn't working full-time" or

---

1. In the section *The Stories that Encircle*.

"seemed a bit down" was all the reason she needed to look at me with concern and ask, "Do you want to try the latest anti-depressants? They might help you live your life like everyone else."

But the fact was, I didn't want to live my life "like everyone else". Even at that time, I found it bizarre and blindly superficial, that an always-smiling and always-active 'normality' was put forward as healthy, and depression, withdrawal, inactivity, contemplation or inquiry were relegated to the domain of aberration, abnormality and illness.

If depression was merely the result of a chemical imbalance in my brain, then what did that say about my humanity, my history and my suffering? Was my most human of responses merely the meaningless by-product of a chemical dysfunction? And could a 'good life' *really* be lived by trying to banish all the difficult bits with a neat diagnosis and a prescription for pills? Surely I was *so* much more than this.

Although there were times I doubted myself and acquiesced briefly to medical 'treatments', I knew that depression was *meaningful*, and that *all* suffering, including that of sadness, despair and anguish, was *just* as much part of life and part of the Truth, as joy, freedom, contentment and peace. Truth would never leave out one whole side of human expression, and only embrace that which was deemed by the medical profession to be acceptable.

From that time forward, I began to search for a view of reality in which depression or sadness, and indeed *any* human expression, could not only be included, but could also be understood and wholeheartedly embraced.

In 2001 I was introduced to the writing of British independent philosophical thinker, Peter Wilberg.[2] In it I found a deeper context for the suffering of depression.

The basic premise of Wilberg's writing is that 'depression' is not a 'disease' or 'illness' of some sort, but rather a natural deepening process by which we sink beyond the surface of life and reconnect with the solidity of our inner being. It is from our inner being that we can truly heed, listen to and digest the stresses and questions posed to us by our everyday lives and then incubate new and deeper ways of thinking, acting and being in the world. Wilberg believed that chronic or acute depressive states result when we fight, flee or 'freeze' this depressive process.

---

2. I have also written about Wilberg's work in the chapter, *The Body*.

Although the material on depression in this chapter has its foundation in Wilberg's writing, in the years since, my understanding has somewhat diverged from it. However, at that time it had a profound impact on me, on my movement into depth, and also on the course my life subsequently took, and for that I will always be very grateful.

In 2004, as Wilberg's writing moved into other arenas, I published a website[3] to showcase his writing on depression. My wish was that it inform the lives of others as it had mine. To this day, I continue to receive responses to it from around the world, most of which describe a lifetime of depression and the relief of knowing, that rather than a malfunction, it is a process that has profound meaning.

***

we call this depression

We call this depression,
this lowering
this beckoning down
this deepening
this movement away.
Away from the world
and the mind
and the circling
and the frenzied grasping.
The grasping for more,
for better,
for bigger.
We call this depression.
And yet ... and yet ...
looking closer ... sensing closer ...
What is it that is here in my body?
There is a lowering
a beckoning down
a deepening.
To where? To where am I summoned?
Could it be to Myself?

---

3. www.meaningofdepression.com. It has since been updated to include my current understandings and life.

***

the profound gift of sadness and depression

We are beings of infinite vastness and depth. As I sit writing this now, I know myself as that depth. It is Truth. It is Peace. It is Home.

However, the spotlight of everyday life increasingly illuminates only the tiniest speck within that enormity; it focusses almost exclusively on the ego or everyday self and its interaction with the material world. A 'good life' is equated with a busier and busier movement of this 'self' across the visible surfaces of life: a horizontal gathering of faster, bigger, more exciting, more entertaining and also more horrific experiences. We go shopping, we travel, we buy the latest mobile phone, we look for spiritual highs or we sit transfixed with fear as the latest environmental or political crisis plays out on our television screens.

This mainstream world does not value depth and indeed has very little understanding or languaging of depth. And so how is depth supposed to make its presence felt in these frantic surface lives?

If depression strikes us, inviting us to stop and move more deeply within, we recoil. We fear that something is dreadfully wrong. And so we try to get rid of depression. We go to the doctor, the psychiatrist, the psychologist. We take up jogging or positive thinking. We do anything to cling to our shiny surface norm.

But what if depression, as the bodily feeling of movement downwards and within, is simply showing us the way into depth? What if depression is an indication that the life we are living no longer holds sustenance or meaning for us? What if depression is pulling us into a depth from which we might be birthed into a new understanding, solidity or breadth? What if it is in these depths we will eventually find peace or even the Truth of what we *are*?

And what if the alarming increase in depressive illness around the world today is a reflection of the fact that we are living our lives cast adrift from our True Nature?

ooo

Even in the simple feeling of sadness, the movement or process of 'depression' is evident.

Quite recently I felt sad for a few days.

A dear friend had moved overseas several months prior. I had come to terms with her physical absence, but after a couple of conversations on Skype I could sense she was also moving away internally. I had tried to meet her in depth as I had always done, but she was not there to meet me in return.

I understood my friend's need to engage with her new country, new people and new life. I understood that friendships, people and circumstances, fluctuate and change, even from moment to moment. I understood that she probably doesn't have the energy for our friendship at the moment. I knew all this and accepted all this.

And yet I was sad. I missed my friend very much. I missed our laughter and I missed our connection.

We generally accept that there will be times in our lives when we feel sad. We don't *like* feeling sad, we even avoid sadness if we can, but we know that sadness is a normal response when there is a loss or an unforeseen and unwelcome change in our lives. We feel sad when we lose friends, sad when a beloved pet dies, sad when we are sick, sad when someone is unkind to us, sad when we see ignorance or deceit played out on the international stage.

Understandably we see these occurrences as upsetting and as such, the cause of our sadness.

But what actually *is* sadness? What is actually happening to me when I use the words, "I am sad that my friend has moved overseas."? What am I *actually feeling* in my body? What is the raw experience before I interpret or judge it?

The first thing I feel is a movement down inside myself. I feel my awareness retreating a little. I feel a contraction away from the everyday world and away from that part of me that is upbeat, energetic, sociable and busy. My customary way of being in the world has quite literally been 'upset' and I feel at a loss. Uncomfortable. At odds. It feels as though I don't quite know what to do with myself any more. I don't quite know what to think, how to act, what to say. It is as though am literally weighed down or burdened by the questions that life has presented me with. It is as though my life as it was, is being brought into question by the absence of my friend. How do I live without my friend in my life?

This movement within, both in the case of sadness and depression, is not in any way mediated by the mind. It is nothing I control, contrive or think about. It is nothing I plan. It is not a technique I impose on my life as an exercise or practice. Nor is it something that I simply undergo once or twice and then *recover* from. Just like tiredness or the desire to sneeze, it is a natural response to life, but in this case one that takes the *whole* human being into account.

We don't 'do' depression, rather depression 'does' us. All we can do is *allow*.

And so I allow myself to stay down, down, down in my sadness. I allow the waves of sadness as they come and go. I do the shopping with that sadness. I sit quietly in the garden with that sadness. I have a cup a tea. I go to bed for a little while in the afternoon. I cry a little. Reminisce. Cook dinner.

And as I am doing so, I know that I am being pulled into a depth that is alive, intelligent, and very real. And it is within the holding of that innate intelligence that a process of transformation and growth is literally *done* to me. I move into the very place in which I can incubate a new way of being in the world. It is as though in my depths, in the womb of my soul, an alchemy of sorts, a metamorphosis takes place that will eventually allow me to walk with solidity and meaning in a life that no longer includes my friend.

And then after a time, a few days in this instance, I am driving home from the shops, when suddenly I realize that the sadness has lifted. I am no longer sad. I have somehow been reborn. I sense a new strength within, a new opening, a new clarity, a connection to a new depth, a new bearing in my soul.

And even though I have undergone such a process countless times before, I am surprised by what has happened. I am astonished that unwilled I am smiling as I catch a glimpse of the sunlight shining through the rain clouds. I check inside, feeling for the absence of my friend, and where previously there was sadness and emptiness, there is now acceptance, a new solidity and a love for life as it has now become.

My sadness has at the same time been both the response and the solution to losing touch with my friend.

Although sadness does not carry the intensity, charge or associations of depression, in a very basic way the process I have outlined above is *identical* to the process that takes place when we are depressed.

However, the depth to which we descend is often directly proportional to the 'weightiness' or intensity of the feelings or life questions by which we feel questioned or burdened.

In the case of sadness, we may descend only a short distance and in a few hours or days quickly grow into a new bearing or new solidity. However, when we feel questioned by our lives in very deep and powerful ways, such as by the death of a loved one, the loss of our livelihood, the loss of our health or a lack of deep meaning, we can often feel *profoundly* depressed. And it is in the intensity of those feelings that we are then swept a long long way down, often into the most remote and hidden valleys of our being.

Such a process of descent can often be very lengthy and intense, but I have found that this intensity, although extraordinarily difficult to live, often attests to the fact that there is a significant belief system or indeed an entire perspective or orientation to life that is being radically shifted or transformed.

When we fall in the physical world, we know we will hurt ourselves: scrape our knee, break an arm. In our internal world too, we fear that when we fall, there will surely be injury or death; we cringe and splutter with fear at the tenuous hold we feel we have on life. And in a certain sense that fear is completely warranted: there will indeed be a death, but it is a death of all that is stagnant, crumbling, worn out or no longer of use.

It is in moving through these most difficult of times that I have come out the other side and opened into profound spiritual understandings, expanded consciousness, deeper insights into my True Nature, or new and different ways of living or understanding my life.[4] Although this process is never ever comfortable I do know that the more I have befriended it, understood it, and embraced it in the gaze of Truth, Love and adulthood, the easier it has become.[5]

I now understand that *all* movements of descent, whether associated with depression or not, have allowed me to connect on deeper and deeper, vaster and vaster levels with all that I am. It is in opening to that ever-deepening movement that I have been brought to the realization of the extraordinary and overflowing immensity of what we truly are.

It is when we fight the natural movement of descent and label it as an illness

---

4. I also discuss depression in the section *Darkness, darkness and darkness: the problem with words*, in the chapter *Darkness*.

5. In writing about the healing power inherent in the movement of depression, one of the most common misconceptions is that 'depression' can now become an easy and 'happy' process. Depression is never easy. It is never comfortable. If it were, then it simply wouldn't be 'depression'. When major changes are occurring in our inner world, there is *always* discomfort. However, with the realization that this process is profoundly meaningful, there is no longer the burden of illness, aberration and suffering, and the process itself is much less complicated and fought.

or as 'something that shouldn't be happening', that we stay locked into an interminable battle with ourselves and as such, deny ourselves the opening into depth that will bring about the very healing we so crave.

God was never born through the will or maneuverings of the mind.

***

descending into Home

One of the first times I felt the extraordinary power of descent was very early in my spiritual journey.

It was at a time when I felt desperately depressed. Day after day I was in wretched emotional and physical pain; I suffered greatly and my life as a whole was devoid of meaning or hope; I was unable to envisage a way forward. All around me lay desolation. I couldn't imagine a future in which I might live with even the smallest degree of peace or happiness. I felt I had nowhere else to go, nothing else to do. I believed I had come to the end of my life.

I remember walking up to my small art studio out in the backyard, fully intending to come up with a plan for ending my life.[6] What follows are my journal entries from that day:

journal entry

This is utter despair. I feel truly hopeless. I shake with the fear of knowing that this is my life and I am not doing anything with it. Why can't I move?? Why do I keep getting up in the morning? Why don't I just suicide like so many others? Why do I keep on going? I have no hope left. I can't function in this big world. Voices from my past continually leave me ruined. They toss me around. Fucking up my life.

Later: *I can't go on ... I cannot go any lower ... and yet that seems the only direction I can go. I FEEL so desperate. I begin to FEEL how low I can go. I FEEL it. In every ounce of me. In every bit. How low can one human being go? How low? I keep going down. I have nowhere else left to go. I don't care if I die doing it ... I will just keep going down until I die. Fuck everyone ...*

---

6. Also see chapter on *Suicide*.

Later: *And then suddenly I literally SEE the absolute connection of everything. I SEE it. There are no doubts. I am not imagining it. It is utterly real. It is as though there is some sort of vital substance that connects everything and yet IS everything – the trees, me, my feelings, the clouds. Everything belongs. Everything is absolutely as it should be. On the one hand I am astounded but on another it seems so completely obvious. It so much more ordinary, and yet extraordinary than anything I have ever experienced. I try to find the right words, but the coming of this experience is beyond that. It was just 'with' me. How, when, why – I can't seem to pin down. And it doesn't seem to matter. It is timeless – there is just this eternal present filled with infinite hope and possibility.*

Later: *From the point of utter despair, when I shook simply from the fear of being alive, I have arrived at this point. It seems miraculous. Perhaps I have been given a short glimpse of something that is attainable. Perhaps now I know what it is that I am working towards.*

After the experience I walked back down to the house in complete awe of the world around me. Where before there had only been desperation and hopelessness, there was now intrinsic meaningfulness, supreme beauty, connection and perfection.

I wasn't in an altered state of consciousness of any sort, I wasn't in an angelic nirvana of heavenly light and bliss, but rather, I was witnessing the very fundamental nature of Reality. I could literally *see* the 'stuff' that formed everything, and I could see that it was the same, regardless of whether it was the 'stuff' that formed the most beautiful flower or the 'stuff' that formed the most tortured pain. It was all One. There was only *one* thing happening. I knew this as the Ultimate Truth and I knew that there could never be anything that was apart from it. Everything belonged, *I* belonged.

Over the next few hours the experience slowly faded and yet I remained awestruck. The ramifications of what I had just witnessed were immense and the questions it raised stayed with me over decades. The experience did not magically wipe away my suffering and nor did I yet have an overarching context within which to understand it, but it did give me a profound presentiment of all that can be lived and known through this human body. I also came to understand that it was in 'letting go' into the 'lowness', surrendering to it, moving down *into* the chasm of my despair and being wholly prepared to risk my very life, that I was gifted such an extraordinary glimpse of Truth.

Encounters and experiences of depression can also be much gentler and less intense than the one described here, and they can also lead to vastly different insights, openings or renewal. However, each and every time, there is always the accompanying sense of amazement and surprise that somehow out of the rubble of our torment and distress we have been literally 'born again'.

As a postscript, my journey has once again brought me to that Oneness, but now as the lived reality of my life.

***

darkness

Come, embrace the beautiful and bountiful darkness.

***

clarity

How do we find that cloudless sky?

The mind will contrive,
and puzzle and plot,
believing in its own power and its own fairy story.
But the mind can never know
the patterns and formings
of reality.

A true clarity
comes only from stepping fully into the darkness.

Beyond the easy light
There is a much greater wisdom.

***

darkness, darkness and darkness: the problem with words

There is a problem with the word 'darkness'.

When I recently mentioned to an acquaintance that I was writing on darkness, I saw shock in her eyes, and then a look of more pressing concern: "You have to be *very* careful! Isn't it better not to think about such things?" I wondered what unspeakable things she thought I was writing about. I wondered what it was that she so feared.

When I was a child I was fascinated by the fact that the Inuit have a multitude of words for ice. Their lives are lived on and around ice, and so they need innumerable words to convey its changing conditions. I recently looked up a Greenlandic dictionary: siku (sea ice), aakkarneq (freshly formed sea ice), quililiaq (sea ice with no snow on it), sikuliaq (thin sea ice), tuaaq (sea ice connected to the land) …

But in English we have very few words for darkness: dark, darkness, black, blackness, night. Dimness, shade, shadows, murkiness, gloom and obscurity, hint only at the edges of darkness.

And yet there are *so* many darknesses.

There is interior darkness and exterior darkness, expansive darkness or constricted darkness, cold darkness and warm darkness, rich darkness and fallow darkness … and within those darknesses there are countless meanings and forms, countless nuances … but also countless assumptions, fears and projections.

ooo

In my childhood, darkness was a place of delicious aloneness, in which I sheltered my soul and my beauty safely away from the world. In darkness my soft knitted toys came to life and spoke with sweet little rhymes and happy voices. In darkness there was the freedom to dream and flourish and dance. In darkness I stood at the window and expanded into the silent night sky.

As a child, I also knew that in darkness trust could be betrayed and silences set into stone. In darkness there were nightmares, monsters and creaking floorboards. In darkness, the certainty of my body slipped away from me, only to be found again in the light of day.

As my suffering uncoiled, I learnt very quickly that there was a vast and unexplored terrain of darkness within, in which lay all that was yet unclaimed and unknown. A psychoanalyst told me that such darkness was called the Unconscious. In the Unconscious my beautiful flute was a silver dagger with which I wished to stab those around me. In the Unconscious there were sexual drives and errant forces that I did not know I possessed. I read up on Jung and

Freud, and try as I might, could not find this Unconscious within. It was only in the love and safety of a more compassionate therapy that I opened into the hidden places inside. If indeed this was a darkness, it was a darkness that contained the oh-so-justified responses of a small and innocent child.

In my search for healing, I learnt that my desperate pain and torment was also called a darkness. And yet although I never entered that darkness willingly, in the passage of time I found its harvest to be unfailingly rich and profound. Everything I have ever learnt that was truly worth knowing I found by moving into the valleys of my anguish, and shining the light of awareness into its darkest recesses. The secrets to life and to myself were never found in the easy sunlight. It was in darkness that sanity, peace, compassion, love and wisdom could be born. It was in darkness that I found everything that would eventually make me whole.

There were times I lay in bed no longer able to move my body and mind to the pace and bright lights of the everyday world. This, I was told was depression, and depression too was termed darkness: a black dog, a dark cloud. And yet, although these periods were extraordinarily challenging to live, somewhere in the use of the word 'dark', this process was given a meaning that it did not have for me. It was not evil, not a threat, not a disease, not perilous. In fact, I came to realize it was a 'darkness' that this world needed *more* of. In the darkness of 'depression' I was given the very necessary time and space to descend and to deepen away from the brittle surfaces of the mind and the everyday world. Here I could rest, contemplate, re-evaluate. Here I could allow the death of all that was old and worn-out, and feel the birth of the new. If depression was a darkness, it was the darkness of a rich humus-laden earth that lay fallow only because the seeds of the coming season had yet to be planted and the rains had yet to come.[1]

I also came across the phrase, 'dark night of the soul'. In that phrase I was given a validity for those times when that the movement down and within had seemingly dropped me into a pit of utter despair, and the collapse of all meaning and all mind. And yet it was when I lived myself fully into those days and weeks of dying, walked that dying, allowed that dying, valued that dying, that inevitably there came a moment of grace when as if by the hand of God, I was plucked up and somehow birthed into a new and profound consciousness.

There were certainly periods in my life, particularly early on, when rather

---

1. Also see chapter *Depression and Descent*.

than dark or black, I would have used the descriptors, gray or shadowy, murky or mucusy. But almost without exception these were times I resisted or fought that natural movement into depth and into 'dying' and so felt myself caught in a claggy viscosity, that like quicksand, tightened its grip the harder I fought.

There were also people in my life who with narrowed eyes, warned me of the darkness of evil spirits and 'the other side'. There were times I lay in bed desperately trying to surround myself with a protective coating of 'white or angelic light' in order to escape these malign energies, but eventually I concluded that the only darkness of which I might have to be afraid lay in the very fear that these fantasy stories created.

I also see so clearly that our everyday self or 'ego', given even the tiniest inkling that there is indeed a looming emptiness or blackness within that will spell the end of its fragile reign, can come to believe that all that resides in un-knowing and un-creation is threatening. It can make up endless stories of 'darkness' and lurking danger. However, it is only the 'ego' or mind that can 'think' in this way. On deepening into these spaces and filling them with the 'light' of Consciousness, there truly is only ever the knowing, "I am Home". In darkness is forever waiting the truer Self we have yet to know.

But the ego, can also project this darkness onto others. Darkness is what we assign to other people when we do not understand their intent or like their behavior. Darkness is for those whose God is not our own. Darkness is for the fringes, for finger-pointing and for the places we refuse to own in ourselves.

But I am also very much alive in the physical realm and cannot but notice the very pressing difficulties of our time, the so-called 'darkness' of our present-day world. Undoubtedly in every age, there is 'darkness'; war, famine, disease, violence, abuse, greed, divisiveness, intolerance, bigotry and injustice weren't just invented in the last decade or two.

I see a climate in crisis and the utter blindness of some in power. But I also see the indifference of people around me who litter, who pour chemicals down the drain, and who seem not to care about the degradation of the very ground on which they live. Is this darkness? Perhaps. But I also prefer to name what I see, which in this case is arrogance or ignorance or laziness. If we knew our true Oneness with all life, we would treasure our planet, each other and ourselves, in even the very smallest of ways.

I hear and read of those who perpetrate or condone wanton acts of violence, who join militant groups and who have a blatant disregard for the sanctity of *all* human life. Is this darkness? Again, I prefer to name what I see. In a soulless and superficial society cut off from the deeper currents of our being, how are people to express their frustration, their anger, and their dissatisfaction? How are they to cope with their very real fragility, fear, vulnerability, and pain? How are they to cope in a world that reduces their human form to little more than that of a machine? Without any deeper meaning or understanding of humanity, is it any surprise they are drawn to aggression, division, greed, fanaticism or the numbing effects of drugs and alcohol? Without any awareness or languaging of our True Nature, is it any wonder that they treat themselves and others as objects of disdain?

I see and read of the utter horrors and senselessness of war, and in my own life, far from any present-day war zones, I know that I have weathered my own small zone of conflict. And I have no doubt that this zone of conflict was in part the result of the generational reverberations of a bigger war, a World War. Is this darkness? Or is this a terror, a horror, a grief, a brokenness, that unspoken and unacknowledged has festered and so passed on its legacy into countless more innocent lives and quiet suburban homes?

My invitation here, is to question the sweeping use of this word 'darkness'. It is of great concern to me that wanton acts of violence, abuse, war, hatred, fantasies and fears, are by virtue of a linguistic habit or shortfall, relegated to the same place as the dark, rich and fertile world we have within.

Words have such a power to either limit or to liberate. Darkness isn't just darkness.

***

darkness and the Incan constellations

A few years ago, a friend went on a holiday to South America.

When she returned she shared with me a little about the astronomy of the Incas. Rather than constellations which are defined by the patterns made by the dots of light that we call stars, some of their constellations were defined by the vast dark spaces *between* the stars. These spaces were considered to be living forms such as a mother and baby llama, a partridge, a toad and a fox.

I found this fascinating. So often our world is defined by what we can physically see or what we are taught to see. We ignore the negative spaces between objects whether they be stars or human beings. In relationship we assume that we are simply two little pinpricks of fleshly matter talking to one another; one talking head and another talking head looking at each other through empty space.

But what if that 'empty space' is actually a glorious constellation that defines our connection with one another?

What if that empty space is the dancing floor of our souls entwined as the grace of a butterfly, the shimmering beauty of a leafy canopy or as the glorious sensuality of a red red rose?

What if that 'empty space' is our true Home?

***

glorious kali

Many years ago I came across the Hindu goddess Kali, a female deity standing on the body of her consort Shiva, in all her unapologetic nakedness and black glory. Her tongue was outstretched, her hair wild, she wore a necklace of severed male heads and a waistband of arms. She was the opposite of the soft, delicate, acquiescing, pastel ideal of femininity that is often portrayed in Western culture as the norm. I thought she was wonderful!

There was something in her power and intensity that spoke to me deeply. I had felt within me that same dark power: the annihilating divine power that destroys the old, and in the dark and nurturing womb, paves the way for the birth of the new. It was destruction and creation as inseparable, but dynamic and vital opposites. She represented the process I had undergone countless times: going within, going 'under', allowing the death of old and stagnant parts, and feeling the birth of new and deeper ways of living in this world. That power is something we all possess and yet something which too often is misunderstood; in its intensity, wildness and in its tremendous fearlessness, this destructive side, this dark side, this side of death, is all too easily relegated to so-called 'evil', 'violent' or 'unconscious' impulses. The powerful dark female isn't in any way valued in our society.[2]

---

2. As I write this, I think of the negative comments I have heard from sports commentators and the media when referring to tennis players Serena and Venus Williams.

I recall sitting in a lounge at London's Heathrow airport, waiting for my flight back to Australia. Snow had wreaked havoc on the motorways, so I had made sure to arrive at the airport in plenty of time. Now, I had four hours to fill.

I slept for a little while and woke up thinking of the Goddess Kali. It was a time of tremendous change for me; I had only just begun to feel my own potential for power, action, freedom and fearlessness.

I sat slouched on the airport lounge, watching the snow falling onto the planes and the tarmac below, and thought back over passages from a book on Kali I had just been reading. Without realizing it, I started to feel a sense of Kali-ness in my body and in my eyes. I was asking myself a question: "What would it be like to allow myself to fully feel that dark power in my everyday life?"

Opposite me sat a group of older and traditionally-dressed people from India. I hadn't really paid them much attention, except to notice the beautiful saris of the women. Then suddenly I caught the eye of one of the older men, or perhaps it was the case that he caught mine. We held each other's gaze for a good deal longer than customary, and then he said straight into my eyes, "Kali". I was dumbstruck. I wondered if I had misheard him, but I could see by the intensity of his gaze that I hadn't. I didn't have a clue what to do, so I looked slowly away with something that I hoped looked like mature and calm indifference, but I did so with goosebumps on my arms. I wonder what it was that he had so clearly recognized.

Around this time I wrote a poem, no doubt inspired by my interest in Kali. It speaks of the power of destruction and my desire to embrace it, not as something evil or 'bad' but rather as something that is essential for the birth of the new:

> I have always made myself so small, so weak and so suitable;
> It is the only way I can live in this world, so tied as it is to hollow frameworks.
> All the while I only want to sweep it to the side with the brush of one hand and watch it burn in the fires of all hell.
> I want to destroy the comfortable and the nice.
> I want mayhem, lust, passion, not-nice. I want darkness and death.
> I do not wish to die peacefully, inwardly.
> I do not wish to be placated. Told to go quietly.
> Come dance with me in hell and rejoice with the flames and the bones.
> Loudly.

***

a light without darkness

I have loved the darkness. I have understood the darkness. But the question of what 'light' is, has puzzled me for many years.

Throughout much of my spiritual journey I frequently heard references to inner light: love and light, children of the light, light of God, angelic light, healing light, spiritual light.

But for all the talk of light, I had no clue what was meant. I wondered, "What is light? Do all these people actually know what light is? Why am I too stupid to grasp what they so readily seem to understand?" My questions weren't philosophical or scientific or esoteric. I simply wanted to know what was happening in their experience that they chose to signify with the word 'light'. Whatever it was, it wasn't happening for me.

It was only many years later that I realized why I had been so puzzled: the light they had spoken of made no reference whatsoever to darkness.

It was a light that hovered only in its own incandescence, somehow birthed from itself, light from light from light. It was a relentless loop that focused only on the visible surface of life, and chose to ignore the question of where that light was coming from.

It was a light that spoke of a spirituality that could only give birth to a monotonous positivity and blindness. It was a spirituality that tried to sidestep the grime, the tears, the suffering and the realities of everyday life, by masking them with a tale of nirvanic or magical bliss. It was a spirituality that was a product of the same wishful, shallow, and even desperate, thinking that I had seen around me all my life.

It was a light that spoke of a childhood in which my seriousness, thoughtfulness and questions were unwelcome: "Take that frown off your face", "Smile and be happy", "I don't want to see those tears in this house."

It was a light that spoke of a soulless and superficial society that does not value or understand depth and indeed has virtually no language for depth.

It was a light that spoke only of the visible and superficial surfaces of life – of acquisition, amusement and appearance – and our fruitless attempt to emulate the qualities of our Essential Nature – Meaning, Joy, Strength and Beauty – through them.

213

It was a light that spoke of a society that must increasingly diagnose, treat and medicate away its darker edges and quickly quieten those who might speak of mutiny.

It was a light that believed its narrow little flashlight beam could illuminate all of reality, without realizing that it was no more than the briefest of flickers in the immense expanse of our Infinity.

It was a light I have never been particularly interested in.

But as my journey into and through darkness was coming to an end, I knew I had to address light. Was there a light other than that of superficiality and soullessness?

Where is light? What is light?

I was very well aware of the accustomed answers to those questions: "God is Light" or "Consciousness is Light". But were these also *my* answers? My deeply-lived answers? I wasn't so sure. I spent many weeks and months on that inquiry. Was God *really* synonymous with light? What about Consciousness? Could a deeply embodied spirituality as it is lived in this world, be called 'light'?

But in my inquiry, I had somehow overlooked the darkness. I had forgotten to turn around and look back within and ask, "Where is the darkness?"

Over the years I had *so* loved the darkness. Darkness had been my home, my fertile ground, my warm womb, my deepest refuge. I had spent so many years uncovering all that lay in its depths that I didn't realize I had come to take it very much for granted: *of course* darkness was there. Darkness was a given. Wasn't it?

But now as I looked within I saw only vast openness, clarity and peace. I could not find the darkness. Darkness had dissolved. Without realizing it, the polarity of darkness and light had collapsed and now there was only Emptiness.

And yes, that Emptiness, Totality, that Truth, that Infinity, could perhaps be termed "Light" or "Radiance" ... but it was a Light or Radiance without opposite.

But 'Light', of course, is only a word.

***

creativity

We are Creation. In each moment we actually are Creation.

And Creation is forever moving, ebbing, flowing, streaming, bubbling, orgasming, bursting forth ... offering us its aliveness, its wholeness, its wildness ...

Dare we pick up our paints, our words, our bodies, our hearts and the hands of others and dance the dance of its unthought gifts and untaught freedom? Dare we be that bold, that passionate, that fierce?

Dare we be so fully ourselves?[1]

***

opening into creativity

I was never a creative child.

If I remember myself into that small body, I feel its restriction, its hesitancy. I feel my acute shyness. I feel the necessity of doing the 'right' thing. And of copying others.

When I was eight years old I wrote a poem called *Jocko the Monkey*:

Here Jocko with his little cup,
Runs to pick the pennies up.
Then he brings them to his master,
Back he runs even faster.

---

1. For further discussion of the creative processes of poetry, art, journaling and writing, and their impact on my suffering, see the chapter *Beyond the Battle – Moving in Close*. My art, journaling, writing and poetry are used throughout this book. I also make mention of the inherent creativity of the body, in the section *Homage to the Body* in the chapter, *The Body*.

> Jocko always does his best,
> But when he's tired he has a rest.

My father took the poem and without my permission made photocopies of it to hand out to family friends. I could never bring myself to admit that I had actually copied the first two lines out of a coloring-in book. I was ashamed by my deceit, but also by the knowledge that I could never have put words and ideas that were wholly mine onto a piece of paper. I did not know how.

I tore the page out of my book and threw it out so no-one would find it.

When I was eleven years old I was given a small leather-bound diary with a gold lock and key. I loved the smell of it and I loved the feel of it. I imagined that the words with which I would fill it would be magical and special. I pressed my pen hard into the paper and delighted in the slightly crumpled feel of the pages as I filled them:

> **Wednesday** In the afternoon at school we had to go out of our classroom because our desks had to be varnished. We did our Social Studies outside. Then we played softball. I was captain of one team.

> **Thursday** I walked to school. We didn't do much, but Mr. Ashford my teacher made us do Mathematics instead of art. I got 85 in Social Studies.

But when I read back over those entries, my heart sank. My words were bland and anonymous, and I had no clue how to bring them to life.

The world, I had learned, could not contain me. My very presence in it assumed my guilt. My face, body, actions, feelings and words were enough to move others to anger or to violence. My motives, I was told, were spiteful and nasty. I was a child whose will must be broken and whose voice must be silenced.

By denying me the right to say words like 'hate', 'angry' or 'sad' it was as though the feelings they gave name to magically ceased to exist. Just as with my vagina, clitoris and anus, there were entire areas of experience that disappeared from my conscious thoughts. As more and more of my life was relegated to the unutterable, the shameless or the meaningless, I gradually went missing. My body kept living in the world, but the 'I' that lived through it was gone.

I looked with envy at the people around me. They seemed to embody an ease that I could never hope to possess. They moved their bodies and their minds to their own rhythms, and that expression was inevitably fitting and apt. Just as I had copied the lines from a coloring-in book, so I tried to copy their freedom. But my attempts were only poor imitations, and in my awkwardness I was dismissed as rude or aloof, naïve or tactless. The taunting rhymes of my schoolmates reached me across the playground:

> "Hey Brick! What are you doing over there?
> All you do is sit and stare."

As I hunkered forward, bracing myself for their laughter, I knew I would be forever trapped. There would always be one more life circumstance for which I did not know the rules, one more situation in which I could not find the words.

As I grew into adulthood I filled countless journals and notebooks and systematically numbered and dated them. I imagined that their pages would one day recall me to a lifetime of questing and thought. But despite the fact that the descriptive narrative of my childhood had now grown to include all my doubts and personal angst, when I leafed back through them, my words were hollow and bare. It was only intermittently when I took on the language and authority of the various authors I read, that my writing came to life; it was only through someone else's voice that I felt capable or even justified, in using my own.

Even when I picked up pastels, paints and pens, the ideas and styles were those of someone else. I painted and drew subjects that were virtually irrelevant to my life: palm trees, bamboo, jungle scenes, tigers …

At other times, when my torment was acute, I attempted to calm or distract myself by spending hour-upon-hour, day-upon-day, methodically copying my photos of buildings or houses into watercolor or rendering nature scenes in intricately inked lines and patterns.

On occasion I even considered the comforts of autistic repetition as a viable option for disappearing from life altogether. In repetitive patterning I could lose myself, and for a short time at least, escape a world I found overwhelming.

But when, through therapy, I began the journey inwards to meet the child I had been, the intensity of my emotional pain could not be contained; a flood of raw memories screamed for release. As I sat at my desk bawling my agony, unprompted and unmediated, flood after flood of wild expression broke through.

I shredded and screwed up reams upon reams of paper. I took tubes of paint and squeezed out their entire contents on cardboard, on paper, on canvas or on wood. I smeared the thick wetness around with my hands. I scratched fiercely into the impasto with pencils and pens, I tore and gouged at it with my fingernails.

It felt like a wayward and forbidden destruction, but in actuality what was being destroyed were the shackles that for far too long had held me as their captive.

And as I sat back to survey what to others might have looked like utter artistic carnage, I felt only the swelling of greatest pride, accomplishment and blessed relief. The child-like messy pages in front of me were in actuality one of my greatest and most glorious triumphs. For the first time in my life, I felt the extraordinary power of the creative act.

What I saw on that paper in front of me, was ME!

I started to experiment. I learnt to give myself time to move more intentionally within, listening with ever-increasing subtlety to my body and to the places of meaning from which the images arose. I reached with inner ears and inner sensing into the depths of my pain and my past, and asked, asked, asked, "What is here? What is this that has yet to be known, felt, and understood? What is it that has been banished into obscurity but now longs to be birthed into this world?"

And then slowly, slowly, a form arose, a line, a color, a shape, a figure ... a truth. The 'artist' behind my life, began to 'speak'. I felt the beginnings of a potency and a freedom that I did not yet allow myself in any other arena of my life.

Over months and years my paintings and drawings got bigger and bigger. The edges more assured, the colors bolder and more intense. The meanings I sought to convey were increasingly unmistakable and powerful. My love of patterning remained, but rather than using it to numb or sedate, I now used it to communicate. [2]

---

2. In the first painting, *Patterns of Fear* I used the repetition of the spirals and crosses to convey the relentless and overwhelming nature of fearful thoughts and sensations. In the second oil pastel, *Pieces of Self*, I used the patterns of the faces and boxes to convey my different 'selves' which at that time felt quite unintegrated and scattered.

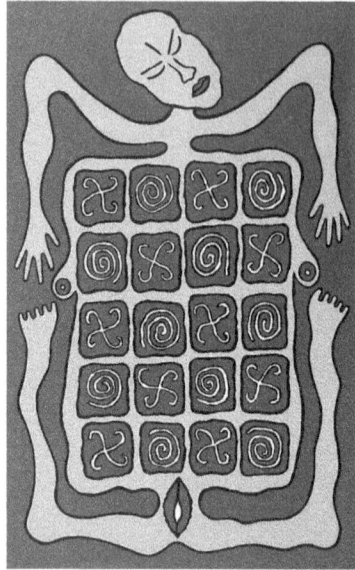

But I had never had any great yearning to be an artist or even to draw well. Rather, it had been to writing that over and over I had been called.[3]

Perhaps it was because I had never been able to speak or write words that were wholly mine, that it felt so necessary for me to find expression through words.

---

3. Also see the chapter *The Call*.

I began to read about writers, writing and the creative process. I found a book called *Writing for your Life: a guide and companion to the Inner Worlds* by Deena Metzger. It was as though the book was written just for me. It was beautiful, wise, and pragmatic. I had never much liked doing 'creative' exercises of any sort – they had always seemed like a contradiction in terms – but in linking the creative process back into the depths of the inner world, Metzger's book was my most wonderful writing medicine.

Early in the book there was an exercise that had a profound impact on me. It suggested making a list of random nouns, participles and verbs, arbitrarily pairing them, and then creating associations between those pairs.

I opened various unrelated books that I had at hand, and wrote down words to which I blindly pointed. Out of this came a poem. As I was writing it, I had assumed my words would be utter nonsense. However, on reading back over it, I was astounded and literally breathless at the layers of meaning and its unambiguous relevance to my life. My words spoke of what it was to live as a girl and a woman on this planet, they spoke of my relationship back into the suffered history of millennia and they spoke of that vital connection to the vastness of Spirit.

On reading that poem now, even though in light of its origin it is clearly strange and disjointed, its resonances are quite unmistakable.

Deserts of time

Deserts of time for the fathers of old,
Ringing the bells,
That herald the birth of daughters.
Sense the secrets of time immemorial:
A fragrant bough of a poison tree.

An arrogant bitch, the obsequious ones,
The lewd and lascivious creature of a Latin night,
Crooning over lost memories and mummies,
Soiled in the cocoon of a raping fantasy.

The planets tell otherwise.
Catching the light of invisible kindness,
Tenderness of the watchful mother,
Well play on, sad Yorick
The bells are now ringing for us.

And so I began to allow myself the freedom to write nonsense or make mistakes, to create strange bed-fellow metaphors if I wanted, to experiment, to be curious, to discard whatever I didn't like, to trust my intuition and inner voice, to give myself time and then more time, to listen for waves of meaning and the qualities of soul, to know what is true and what isn't, to welcome the darkness, and to tiptoe to the very edges of that immense realm of potentiality we all have within and claim everything that I might rightfully know as 'mine'. For me, it was the beginning of a liberation.

And so I began to write.[4]

***

the creative process in action

How do I write?

> *I sit here. This, here, now, is the creative process. It is taking place in this moment. It is taking place as I am writing on the creative process.*
>
> *I have just come home from a walk and feel a strong desire to write. It is an urgency, a burgeoning necessity, an intense and undeniable need for something within to be given voice through writing. I have been unsure how to proceed with this chapter, but now I sense a way forward. It is yet beyond the edges of my mind, beyond the edges of what I know. And still it is there, insisting its entry into life.*
>
> *I sit at the computer, but feel uncomfortable and edgy. There is a part of me that doesn't want to write. It never wants to write.*

This is a part I know very well. It is the 'everyday self'. This 'everyday self' comprises the psychological construct that is generally called 'ego' but also includes that part of me that loves having a body, relating to people and interacting with the physical world. This everyday self prefers the outer arena of action and 'doing', to the inner arena of 'being' and the movement into depth that is required for the creative process.

---

4. I would like to make a comment here about my life as a professional musician. Although in some ways music might be seen as a 'creative' outlet, I never saw music as inherently creative. I felt my role as a performing musician was more as a 'translator'. I was certainly able to 'put myself' into the music, but that expression, although of soul, was limited by the composer's notes on the page, the style, the conductor, the audience, and my fellow musicians. In the light of what I have written about creativity in this chapter, it is interesting to note that as a musician I was very good at playing in the styles required by Classical music, but very poor at the free and 'creative' improvisation characteristic of Jazz.

I look out the window, away from the keyboard, away from the computer screen, away from this chapter. I want to water the plants, sweep the paths, go to the library, have a cup of tea. I want to go outside and feel the warmth of the sun on my skin. I want to do anything but write.

The desire to get up is very strong. My legs are jiggling up and down and I am wringing my hands. I get up. "Just for a little while," I tell myself. I walk around the house and then the garden, but I am meandering aimlessly. The urge to write is still there. I go back to my chair, back to the keyboard.

The everyday self must relent a little in order to create. And so I always make a small contract with the everyday self that recognizes its desire for activity and engagement, while still allowing me the space to go within.

The best way I have found of doing this, is to read back over some of my writing from the previous day and edit it a little along the way. The everyday self likes being occupied with this sort of practical editing activity and without realizing it, will slowly step aside.

I open the file for this chapter. I scroll down and glance back over my writing. A paragraph in red lets me know the section over which I struggled yesterday. I read it out aloud to check for readability and flow. I realize there is a sentence that brings unnecessary complexity where none is needed. I cut and paste the sentence to the end of the chapter, just in case it is needed later on. I move another sentence, add some adjectives and punctuation. I reread the section. The meaning is clearer now. Still, I leave the paragraph as a whole in red so that I can check it through again tomorrow.

I continue to read. I feel myself slowly drawn into the writing. I become immersed in it. My eyes narrow. I lean forward. I have moved into a deeper self. A soul self. A listening self. A self that delights in an unswerving authenticity. A self that experiences the inner reality without the constructs of the mind. A self that is inherently creative. I have begun to write.

Then all of a sudden the dogs are barking. The neighbor is knocking at the back door. I am pulled abruptly away from my writing and back into the everyday world. I feel a sharp sting of resentment but get up. The neighbor wants to pick some mint from the garden. It is a short conversation and I quickly get back to my writing.

This is a lesson I have learnt all too often, but which, from time to time, I still fail to heed. I must make sure the creative self is given its due respect and time. I must remember to give the dogs their bones so they are busy for a couple of hours, I must remember to close the back door to let the neighbor know that I am working, I must turn down the phones. It is vital that I give myself the space to create. Creation doesn't happen in random five-minute slots crammed into the busy-ness of a day.

> *I have settled again. I have settled into my depths and the pathway within is open. I feel connected. Whole. Centered. Happy. There is a slight smile on my lips and a thrilling of bliss moving through my body. It is joyous to sit here. This is who I am: Creation itself. I wonder briefly why there is always such resistance, such difficulty, before I can get to this point.*

The everyday self will never like the fact that it isn't needed for the creative process; it will never like the fact that there is an activity in which it is almost entirely defunct.

> *I have my writing in front of me. There is the edge between what I have written and what I have yet to write.*

> *I am silent. Very silent. I reach within. Feel within. Listen within. I heed all that is there: the patterns and textures of felt sense and meaning, the overarching subject matter on which I'm focusing. Wave upon wave of whispers caress the edges of my mind.*

This is the realm of potentiality. It is the place before words. Everything that has yet to come into form is swimming in this vast ocean of possibility. I too am a part of that ocean, but I am also here to translate it into the physical world, through my words.

> *I continue to listen and to sense. There is an edge of anxiety as I wait. But I feel that a birth of words is imminent. I am leaning into it, bending into its weight and feeling its growing form. I don't hurry. I don't push. I just allow. And then wondrously, magically almost, it starts to shift, to coalesce, to transform. And then the words are there. And I am typing them onto the page. I feel a delicious flow of rightness, of joy, of expression, of inspiration and of energy.*

> *And as I read and reread my words, I know by the life that speaks through them, that they are gloriously true. And gloriously mine.*

There are times when this process of bringing potentiality into form is relatively easy, but there are also times when, as with any birthing process, it is arduous and difficult. On those occasions I find it helpful to simply write down a few words or a few sentences. They may not yet be quite right, and indeed they may later be proved to be completely wrong, but once there is a starting point, it is as though the world of 'created reality' has now changed a little, so that my entry point back into potentiality too has changed. Sometimes, even that small shift is enough for me to make a start.

It is interesting to note that although in writing this chapter, and indeed this book, I am choosing to engage with the creative process, and am relishing that engagement, as I have deepened further and further into knowing myself as True Nature itself, there has been less and less of a pressing need to be creative as a writer or as an artist.

Rather, I now know myself as not separate from Creation itself. Every moment, every movement, every uttering, every tree, every leaf, every gesture, and certainly every book and word, is Creation.

All of Life as it is lived, has become my ultimate creative act. And that is Joy.

***

the body

We live in a body.

We mightn't like our body a whole lot, we might force our body to get us through the day, we might feed our body a diet of coffee and junk food or tofu and broccoli, we might spend a lot of time dreaming that we're somewhere else other than in our bodies, we might forget we have a body when we're playing computer games … but when we're finished with all of that, the body is still there. We have to take it to the toilet, brush its teeth and tuck it up in bed at night. We can't get rid of the body. At least not until we die.

But what is the body? What is this 'thing' in which we are living? And what is the relationship between the body and our journey out of suffering? What is the relationship between the body and Spirit?

***

the journey of Spirit is a journey *into* the body

From my earliest years, I learnt that life in the body was painful and difficult.

I still clearly recall the shock and utter incomprehension as my very small body was grabbed up and beaten for the very first time. I recall the distress as I was yanked off a chair and dragged down the hallway. I recall the disbelief when I was hit for crying too much. I recall the sadness of having my body mocked because my legs were too big and my stomach poked out. I recall the shame of having dirty places I should never touch or speak of. I recall being warned that my body carried a guilt simply by virtue of being a little girl. I recall my fear. My silenced outrage. My growing distrust.

At school my experiences of the body were much the same. In kindergarten I was humiliated in front of the class for wetting my pants, in second grade I had to stand in a corner for an hour when I spoke out of place and in fifth grade I was caned on my hands for writing on a classmate's pencil case. In physical education, trying to force my hard-held body to run and jump and roll with the same ease as everyone else, reinforced the fact that life in the body was never going to be much fun. My body, I learnt, had to be ignored, denied, pushed, pulled and resisted.

And so I slowly moved away from the bodily surfaces of life and from the tight knots that held my pain and confusion. I was no longer fully in the flesh. No longer fully alive. I became numb, aloof and rigid; remote from others, and from myself.

As I became aware of different religions and spiritual practices it didn't seem all that strange to me that the body had to be subjected to harsh practices: sexual abstinence, penances, fasting, beatings, painful postures and severe austerity. The body I was told, was evil, a breeding ground for sin, a hindrance that had to be overcome. The body was a barrier to goodness, to purity and to godliness.

As my spiritual journey became conscious, the belief that my body was an obstruction, was further confirmed. Everywhere I looked, spirituality seemed to be about being somewhere *other* than in the body, somewhere *other* than here. And frankly as I increasingly suffered it gave me hope that if I could leave the body behind somehow, my life would be a whole lot happier.

I recall being on an orchestral tour through the country regions; we travelled by bus from town to town, performed concerts in the evening, and stayed in motels overnight. One of the members of the orchestra spent most his time on the bus sitting bolt upright, eyes closed and an expression of deep absorption on his face. Eventually someone asked him what he was doing. He proclaimed loudly that he was 'astral travelling'; although his body remained on the bus, apparently some part of his inner world was capable of infinite movement.

I was a little skeptical, but intrigued nonetheless. It was very early in my spiritual journey, and if astral travelling was possible, it seemed like a wonderful thing to be able to do. And so, day after day, without really knowing what I was doing, I tried to astral-travel to the Egyptian pyramids. I have no idea why I chose Egypt as my preferred destination, but irrespective of that fact, I never arrived. My backside stayed quite firmly on my seat in the bus.

I read countless books about inner journeys beyond the body; of bright points of light, of past lives, of mind-blowing LSD trips, of disembodied teachers, angels and interplanetary beings.

After reading one book I spent many weeks trying to visualize a point of light in my forehead, hoping that as the author had done, I might disappear into a rainbow world of darting and brilliant lights. On another occasion I tried to imagine that I might have a guardian angel standing by my side in whose other-worldly arms I might be enveloped. Then I read the channeled words of Seth and Edgar Cayce, most of which I found extraordinarily sage and informative. I wondered if I too might be capable of channeling such wisdom. I meditated and tried to open myself to anyone who might wish to speak through me, but I only heard the incessant chattering of my mind.

But there *were* some small glimpses that one day I might be privy to a life beyond the body. One summer evening at dusk I saw extraordinary auras around people as I sat on the beach. Another time I saw apparitions of people, that seemed quite real, but then disappeared abruptly from view as I came closer. For hours I chanted Hindu words that I didn't understand and yet for a time felt my consciousness powerfully expand beyond my skin. And so I kept hoping.

And then I started therapy. My body still walked in the world, but its terrain was not my own. My muscles and bones were held taut with pain, my anxiety was extreme and my day-to-day life was falling apart. I had been to doctors and psychiatrists, but their pronouncement that my suffering was little more than the static from an imbalanced brain had only added to my despair. Many nights I lay in bed terrified as I felt my body slipping away, a strange taut hair-like strand all that connected me back into the physicality of the consensus world. I pushed steadily on, trying to hold myself together but without any notion of what that 'self' might actually be, my task was a fruitless one.

My first therapy was with Charlotte[1], a psychiatrist who practiced psychoanalysis. I learnt a lot in the year I saw her[2] and I have no doubt she believed she was helping me, but as I reread my journals from that time I feel anger, and also horror, at the degree to which her practice reinforced the sense that my body was a problem and indeed that *I* was a problem.

Within my body it seemed there was a cesspool of unconscious desires, fantasies, fears and 'sins' that may well have been beaten *into* me, but now, apparently, had to be beaten *out*. In the same way as I had been prodded

---

1. All single first names in this chapter are pseudonyms.
2. I learnt how to inquire and reflect with intelligence and with insight, but I also started to read Jung, Freud, Gurdjieff among others. It was the beginning of my lifelong interest in the workings of the inner world, both psychological and spiritual.

and poked as a child, Charlotte now prodded and poked me with the clever words and maneuverings of the mind. At that time, I was naïve and completely ignorant of all that therapy should entail, and because her actions corresponded to the verbal and physical beatings of my childhood, I accepted that what she was doing was 'good for me'.[3]

There were countless occasions when I felt deep humiliation and distress that I was unable to bring about the changes she demanded of me. In one session she mocked the skirt I had worn as "something only a silly child would wear". Perhaps her intent was to shake me out of my childlike naiveté, but my lack of sophistication remained and any sense of bodyhood or self-worth I may have had, retreated even further away. I never wore the skirt again and to this day I have no idea what it was that she so took issue with.

As I look back now over that entire therapy, there is one moment that invited me *into* my body more than all her words and haranguing ever could. In deep distress at my inability to move forward in my life, I looked across at Charlotte and pleaded, "Please help me. *Please* help me." At that point she stood up, walked over, sat next to me, and took my hand in hers. In that simple touch was a validation of my body and my humanity that I still feel today. At that time, however, I was so ill-at-ease in my body and so unable to truly *inhabit* it, that I physically froze. However, in my heart the resonances were powerfully felt.

Eventually Charlotte decided that my problems were "deeper" than she could "deal with", and suggested a form of body-centered psychotherapy called Radix. For the next five years Radix was my life, but those five years of Radix with Mollie also *saved* my life.[4]

The definition of the word 'radix', is 'root' or 'source' and it is used by Radix therapy to denote a 'life force' or 'life energy' that underlies and unites body,

---

3. Also see the section *But it's good for me* in the chapter *What if there's nothing wrong with me?*
4. Radix was founded by Charles Kelley in the 1960s and was based in part on Wilhelm Reich's principles of bodywork: that the body and mind are actually one, and that the body is a 'frozen history' of our lives. Prior to this time the body was given little relevance beyond that of 'illness' and was generally seen as quite separate from anything that might have been termed 'mind' or 'spirit'.
The goal of Radix work is to help people become more alive and authentic. Although Radix work is unique for each client, common themes are mind/body integration, grounding, centering, establishment of effective and flexible boundaries, developing the ability to contain and express feelings, ego strengthening, and increasing the capacity for intimacy, pleasure and awareness. Methods may include movement, physical and visual exercises, verbal dialogue, feeling work and intentional touch. Rather than therapies founded on the medical model, Radix does not pathologize clients or see them as 'ill', but rather works with each as a unique person with their own unique issues and history. Deep psychological change is seen as a whole-person experience in which intellectual insight and emotional maturity are reflected in the body.

mind and spirit. At that time, that definition baffled me utterly. And even as I began to write this chapter, some twenty-five years later, I was still puzzled. From the awakened perspective, Spirit *is* Life, and it is not an energy or a force. Nor are there different bits called body, emotions, mind and spirit that need to be united. They are already One.

However, on reflection, I wonder whether the 'life energy or force' of Radix, rather than *underlying* 'spirit', actually *is* Spirit or Awareness. This would fit not only with my experience of Radix but also all that it eventually made possible in my life. Although I feel it is important to write here of my confusion because it is relevant to this story, I do wish to make the point that this in no way detracted from the realness, relevance and transformative power of Radix at that time.[5]

I walked into my first session panic-stricken, anxious and dissociated. Without a sense of my body and without any capacity to maintain bodily boundaries, my world and my interactions with people had become overwhelming and terrifying; I suffered from the debilitating panic attacks of agoraphobia, I was no longer able to work and I was increasingly isolated. I did not trust people, I did not trust food, I did not trust my environment, I did not trust my body and I did not trust myself. I was frequently suicidal and yet terrified that every bodily sensation was an indication that I was about to die. I also feared I would be poisoned by my food, through gases in shops, at the dentist, at the hairdressers or even that someone might come into my bedroom in the middle of the night and try to poison me. Added to this, I had gained a lot of weight (perhaps as an unconscious attempt to create a degree of bodily protection or boundary) and my health was deteriorating rapidly. In my journal of that time, I describe myself as "obsessive, perfectionistic, controlling, inappropriately angry, constantly nervous and unable to adequately articulate anything I think or feel." I was in deep trouble and very unwell.

I have no doubt that Mollie immediately intuited my distress and my inability to be in my body. After introductions, she asked permission to hold my head – to put her hands on either side of my head. I felt an initial spike of panic at the thought of having someone I hardly knew, touch me, but I also sensed that I was being offered the ultimate healing gesture and the most profound of invitations.

Mollie's gentle, intentional, aware, caring touch, was, in reality, all I had *ever* wanted. It spoke to a lifetime of bodily trauma and denial more than anything else ever could. Inside me a thousand heartbroken and fearful little girls

---

5. Perhaps Radix terminology was simply a product of its time.

clapped their hands and bawled their relief. I dared to venture momentarily into the forbidden territory that was my body and look at the woman in front of me. I saw the kindest of eyes looking back at me and knew without a doubt that I was in the right place. Of the session I wrote in my journal: "Going to Radix feels like the most natural and right thing to do. It feels as though the earth has cracked open. It feels as though my life has cracked open."

And so began the process of moving into my body. It was as though each step that had taken me away from my body, now had to be visited in reverse. As I felt Mollie's touch on my neck or on my back or on my hands, I brought into awareness the countless times I had felt my body imperiled. As I learnt to look into Mollie's eyes I remembered other eyes that had looked into mine with out-of-control anger or mal-intent. As I felt my joy gurgling from deep inside, I mourned the fact that I had never known this delight as my birthright. As I felt my anger surging through my arms, I had to break through the countless inner walls that had denied me such vital power and glorious strength. As I felt the wretched ache in my gut and in my heart I had to admit the validity of the small child I had been and her *aching* desire for unconditional holding and acceptance.

Five years later I walked from that room feeling safer in my body, stronger, more bounded, able to make meaningful contact with others, physically active, able to bear with and contain my feelings, less fearful, less anxious, healthier and much thinner. For probably the first time in my life, I was consciously *in the flesh* and able to function in the world from a reasonably solid sense of self or 'ego'.

I bought myself hiking boots and a backpack and began walking with my strong legs on this earth. I stretched out my arms and took it all in: wild beaches, remote bushland, desert tracks, red sand, rocky mountains. My skin was tanned and my eyes sparkled. I felt the joyous strength and fluidity of being in my body and being in the world. For a year or two, life was vibrant and vivid and I relished every moment.

But over time, with a gradually dawning dread I realized that something was missing.

Although prior to Radix, life in the world and in the body had been agonizingly difficult and confused, the quiet and gentle recesses of my soul had always remained as a place of consolation and respite.[6] But after Radix, without that need for refuge all the accustomed byways of my inner life no longer applied. I had

---

6. See chapter *Soul*.

lost the context but also motivation for connecting to the sensitivity and passion of my internal world. I no longer felt drawn to the beauty of music or art, the simplicity of nature was now tinged with boredom, and solitude and silence were now strangely unsettling. Added to that, when I tried to find a depth of embodied connection with the people around me, I realized that very few were actually *in* their bodies or even *in* their lives. They were somewhere else: in their heads, their dreams, their desires, their beliefs, their recriminations, their phones, their conversations. I tried to join them by taking an interest in new curtains and lounge suites, movies and shopping, but I felt like an empty body in an empty world.

I knew that the world of my body, feelings and everyday 'stuff' was not going to be enough.

The disappointment of having done so much work on myself and yet now returning to a life that felt pointless and barren, was too great. I tried to push myself forward, but I did not know what it was that I was pushing myself forward *to*. So I gave up. I could no longer dare to hope. I wanted to die.

My partner tried everything in her power to keep me alive. She bought a large four-wheel drive in the hope that travelling through the Australian outback, so vibrant with ancient spirits and Dreaming, would rekindle my desire to live. But when I looked at the rich red timeless earth, I saw nothing. When I walked down dry creek beds with white ghost gums silhouetted against red rock, my feet only dragged their boredom. When I sat with Aboriginal people on their Lands, I only felt irritation at the flies and the sand and the smells. I became crazed with the emptiness. I pounded on the earth, screaming for it to give me what I wanted. I wailed that I could no longer walk in an empty landscape. I ended up in Alice Springs Hospital. They looked at me with skeptical eyes and gave me a packet of pills.

I travelled home in despair, convinced now that I *had* to die. My body was my coffin and my mantra was "die".

My partner was deeply distressed at my death wish, so I decided to make a hollow attempt to appease her: I would act like I was making an effort to stay alive – I would get a job and pretend to live my life like everyone else – but secretly maintain my desire for death.

I found a counsellor, Paul, who I hoped would find me a suitable job. I described my life to him and all that had brought me to this point. Then in words for which I will forever be grateful, he said to me: "You don't want my help getting a job! Getting a job is complete and utter bullshit and you know it! *Spirit* is what you came to counselling for. Spirit!"

For many years Paul had been a friend and correspondent of British writer, independent philosophical thinker, and self-styled spiritual teacher, Peter Wilberg[7]. Paul introduced me to his writing – which at that time was primarily on soul, Spirit, depression, and the shortcomings of mainstream biological medicine – and we began a friendship based on discussion of that work. I later lost interest in Wilberg's writing as it moved into other arenas, but at that time I found it a glorious salvation: it was inspirational, thought-provoking and addressed my life in exactly the places where it had come undone. Virtually overnight my death-wish evaporated.

At the root of Wilberg's work was what he called 'The Awareness Principle'. As opposed to the work of Ken Wilber[8] whose Theory of Everything was based on a process of inclusion – including as many different viewpoints as possible in order to make up an integrated whole – Wilberg turned things the other way around: he started with that which was already whole.

Wilberg claimed that *everything* – every *thing*, every self, every being and every body – was an expression or embodiment of an infinite field of Awareness which we might also term 'God'. That infinite field of Awareness could never be explained by or reduced to anything *within* that field, whether our brain, our mind, our senses, matter or 'energy'. Wilberg understood the human body as a unique and individual expression of that field, distinct from its background but in no way separate.

For Wilberg our bodies are fleshly utterances of the Divine.

Wilberg went on to describe in great detail the felt inner space of the human body. He identified three distinct centers of awareness[9]: that of the head, the heart (chest) and the *hara* (abdomen). In the West, our culture is very much based on the head and the heart[10], with very little or no recognition of the lowest

---

7. I have also written about Wilberg's work in the chapter *Depression and Descent*.
8. See the section *Flatland* in the chapter *Flatland and the dilemma of 'normality'*.
9. Awareness is an extraordinarily fluid medium that has a capacity to be both of a field/non-local nature or be focussed/localized as a body, center or point. Here I use upper case 'Awareness' for the former and lower case for the latter.
10. The head and heart are, however, generally seen in quite superficial ways eg. the head is seen as the center of egoic consciousness and the heart as the center of emotionality or sentimentality. There is, however, an enormous deepening possible: we can allow Essential qualities such as Clarity, Joy, Sincerity, Courage, Compassion and Strength to increasingly speak through each of the three centers, until eventually our whole body opens.

center, the *hara*. The *hara*, just below the level of the navel, is the physical and the spiritual center of the body; it is from the *hara* that we feel grounded in our physical body but also expand into the enormity of the infinite field of Awareness that is our True Home or Ground.[11]

The first few times I read the word *hara*, I was skeptical: "I don't need to know about this *hara* stuff, do I? How can this be relevant to me?" And yet, even at that time, I knew from experience that anything I rejected without cause, would probably end up having some meaning for me. And so I started to experiment.

Over many months I used my morning walks as my testing ground. I tried to feel my awareness in my head, then in my heart and then lower it into the *hara*. Initially I didn't understand what it was to *move* my awareness – I had imagined that this somehow entailed moving my mind or my brain – but over time I came to realize that awareness was prior to the mind or the brain. For instance, my awareness did not need to be in my mind for me to carry out complex thought processes or calculations, and in fact I found I could probably do them with more ease and clarity if my awareness was in the *hara*.

As my awareness was increasingly in my belly, it was as though the *hara* became like the axle or hub of a wheel from which all else radiated; my legs and arms and life were like the spokes, moving freely and loosely around their center. I felt more stable, calmer, more certain of myself, more courageous. I felt a gentle solidity and groundedness in my body that I had never before experienced.

In Radix I had practiced physical 'grounding' exercises that focused on feeling my feet on the ground or my buttocks on a chair. These exercises had been an important step for me at that time, but I had only ever had limited success with them. Now I knew why: our true and deeper grounding is in the *hara*. A grounding in the feet or the buttocks could only ever be partial, because it considered only the body, without reference to Spirit.

As time passed, I realized that without in any way having intended or willed it, the eyes with which I was now looking out at the world were changing. They weren't the eyes of the mind and its judgements and beliefs, nor were they the eyes of a small scared child. They were eyes of a deeper seeing. Quiet

---

11. Although it was in Wilberg's writing that I initially read of the *hara*, the *hara* is important in many cultures and spiritual teachings. In Eastern spiritual traditions, martial arts and healing practices, hara is the seat of Life and the center of our vital spiritual energy. In Japanese culture *hara* is a rootedness in one's True Self that allows us to remain unaffected or swayed by the disturbances of the head or the heart. The *hara* 'state of mind' is anchored, composed, solid, stable, silent and effortless; this is reflected by the prominence given to the belly in statues of The Buddha.

eyes. Objective eyes. And yet open and compassionate eyes. It wasn't that my suffering was now magically done with, but rather that I felt myself increasingly open to Spirit. But that opening to Spirit did not in any way entail denying the body or the leaving the body behind; it was not the ungrounded 'spirit' of astral travelling, angels and bright points of light. Rather I was moving *into* the body and it was *from* the body that I was finding my connection into Spirit. *Hara* was both the path of Spirit into my body and from my body into Spirit.

Radix work had been vital in bringing me into my body, but, perhaps due to the vagueness of its definitions or perhaps simply due to the enormity of the healing work that had been necessary at that time, Spirit had been assumed; it was an afterthought, an added-on extra, with no clear context within which I was to connect with it. For a while I had certainly reveled in being 'just a body', but I had come to realize that a body without Spirit was ultimately a meaningless one.

However, the profound gift of Radix work, was that I now had the ever-deepening capacity to be fearlessly present and open to all the subtleties, nuances and feelings of the body – tension, rigidity, pain, contraction and also color, shading, meaning and fluidity – in a way that was prior to the mind's conceptual overlays, wording, judgements or interpretation. And it was this capacity to be with the raw experience of my body that enabled me, almost seamlessly, to expand from the felt inner space of the body, into the subtle realms of the soul and then eventually into the profound presence and openness of Spirit.

It was from the 'now-ness' and immediacy of the body that I deepened into the 'now-ness' and immediacy of Spirit.

Then in 2008, I spontaneously awoke.

Awakening is a profound shift of identity from the small 'me' or ego, to one's true identity in Spirit. After awakening I no longer felt myself to be a separate person with an extra bit tagged on the end called 'Spirit', I actually knew myself *as* Spirit.[12]

The sense after awakening was one of surprise, relief and of coming Home. Here was the vastness of my True Nature or Spirit that I had been seeking much of my life. All the words that I had ever heard or read about Spirit or about awakening suddenly made sense. I was what I had been seeking and it was

---

12. I describe awakening more fully in the preface.

closer than close, more obvious than obvious. For a time I lived from deep and vast Peace and Stillness.[13]

However, awakening had turned my life on its head: everything I had ever thought or believed about the world and existence had essentially collapsed and without the guidance or support from a teacher or teaching, I had no clue how to actually *live* that awakening in the everyday world. It was as though I was a child again, learning how to function from a completely new perspective.

In addition, although Wilberg's writing had been a catalyst in opening me to Spirit, it made no mention of 'awakening' or 'enlightenment', and so did little to provide me with any further direction or understanding. Frankly, although I had come across the words 'awakening' and 'enlightenment' many times before, I had assumed they were merely the preserve of sages sitting in loincloths in India or Western spiritual big-noters and definitely not 'ordinary people' like me. I knew I needed a teacher.

I found an enlightened Zen-based teacher. He confirmed my awakening and I set about meditating intensively with him for the next two years.

From the outset I had doubts and questions about his practice.

I had come to awakening by a journey that included therapy, personal and psychological work, deep listening, art, journaling, reading, intense suffering and its transformation, inquiry and contemplation. That breadth had been my teacher and had brought understanding, insight, inner strength, compassion and ultimately awakening.

In comparison, my teacher's practice of sitting on a zafu for hours on end, seemed to me to be very narrow. Although I did not doubt the sincerity, clarity and depth of his enlightenment and the simplicity and beauty of the space he created for meditation, I wasn't sure that 'zafu suffering' could replace the fierce suffering at the coalface of life. Added to this, I did not find the empty crystalline clarity of his gaze at all appealing. If this was how enlightenment manifested in the world, I wasn't sure I wanted this for my life. What was the point of being alive in this vibrant, joyous, crazy world, only to be unaffected by it in the detachment of impersonal transcendence?

---

13. Although profound, I realize now that this was a 'honeymoon' period. This 'honeymoon' period is frequently described by those who awaken. Without adequate guidance it is easy to think that this is an 'end' state. However, it is just the beginning. Infinite expansion is possible and it is also necessary for the awakening to come 'full circle' and back into life. Also, there can still be much internal work to do.

My teacher told me that I had done enough psychological work and that all talking was illusory and of the mind, and with no room for disagreement, I decided to keep my mouth shut, try to ignore my niggling doubts, become a good meditator, learn what I could and hope that in the course of time my questions about how to live my awakening would be answered.[14]

My teacher's practice of meditation was indeed a movement *into* the body, but after a time I came to realize that that movement, was a means by which the body was somehow to be overcome. And with my every wriggle, twitch and pain seen by him as an indication that my practice was weak and my desire for total liberation not earnest enough, without realizing it, I started to fight with my body and ignore its needs. I tried to convince myself that if only I could will myself through the meditation-induced pain and sit hour-after-hour as the embodiment of a serene spiritual person, then all that still lay unresolved and unseen within my body would eventually dissolve and I would be 'enlightened'.

But after two years, my seeing of the Truth was no more complete than when I had started, and my inquiry as to how to live from Truth in this world remained. I knew I continued to stay with my teacher simply because I had nowhere else to go; I felt lost and a little saddened but knew I had to leave.

But a legacy remained: without realizing it, I continued to ignore my body and push through its needs believing that Spirit would remain unwavering regardless: I could meet people's needs with no thought to my own, I could travel when I really didn't want to, I could be the infinitely compassionate friend, I could finally be a dutiful daughter, I could act calm and smiling even when I wasn't. I thought I had come upon a deep acceptance of sorts; a way of living in the world. But of course, my body would not be denied.

And so ensued a period of profound physical collapse. Even though now, as I sit to write this chapter, I still have within my body the aftermath of that collapse – I live with Disembarkment Syndrome – it was that collapse that brought about my gradual movement *back* into the body. It enabled me to revisit many difficult or contracted places but now from the perspective of awakening.[15]

ooo

Although this chapter, *The Body*, is not the last in the book, I did leave its writing till last. I knew it would be difficult to write.

---

14. Also see chapter *Therapists and Teachers*.
15. I write about this further in the remainder of the book

Although the body and my relationship to it, had been an integral part of my journey out of suffering, that relationship was very much a *lived* one and I was doubtful I could translate it into words. Moreover I wasn't even sure I knew what the body actually *is*. How could I write about the body, when my only qualification seemed to be that I had one?

I started to ask people around me, particularly those with a deeply-lived spirituality: "What is the body?" And strangely, without exception, there was a faint look of puzzlement and then a reply along the lines of, "Hmmm ... that's a good question. I've never really thought about it. I'll dwell on it and get back to you." Interestingly nobody got back to me.

So although in the meantime I wrote other chapters, I spent many many months in contemplation of this one: What is the body? What is the body? What is this 'thing' that I am in? And in asking that question I moved deeper and deeper into the body. What is the body? What is the body? My inquiry went deeper and deeper. And yet, the further into depth I went, the further I seemed to move away from any neat-and-tidy answer. The body, it seemed, was a complete mystery.

And then one day, sitting on my park bench, contemplating my question and feeling all of the body – its skin and bones, its felt interiority, it subtle fluidity, its depths-upon-depths – suddenly the body evaporated. And everything else evaporated too.

There was complete Absence. Infinity. Emptiness. Prior to everything. Prior to God, to Spirit, to Love. Prior to any notion, idea or concept. Prior. Prior. And I knew my True Identity in That.

But then almost immediately that Infinite woke itself up through everything. It poured itself straight back in ... into the grass, the trees, the sky, the people playing football. And also into this little focal point of a body sitting on a bench that I call 'me'. It all poured straight back in. And as it poured back in I knew it *all* as 'me'. It was *all* my 'body'. This. This. This. The sun, the moon, the stars, my arms, my mind, my feelings, my legs. Everything and everybody, was my 'body'. It was all just this One thing. It was not separate bits making up a whole in some sort of happy holistic way. No, it always was and always will be, One. There is nothing other than this One. And it was all 'me'.

When we go on a spiritual journey it is easy to assume that we leave the body behind. But we have been gifted this body as our starting point to know ourselves.

It is only by fully moving *into* the body, the *whole* body, and making conscious all that is happening in the right-here-and-right-now, that we can deepen *through* the body and know ourselves as the Truth itself …

***

homage to my body

I feel myself in my body.

There is oh-such-a gentleness now. Attentive. Caring. Listening.

There is sadness at all that this warrior-body has been through; sadness that for so long I pushed my body so very hard.

There is respect and admiration for this body's extraordinary creative aliveness that, despite so many voices telling me to the contrary, has allowed the cells, brain, muscles and nervous system, to heal, reorganize and regenerate as my desperate suffering transformed into lived Peace.

There is such gratitude that after so much suffering, I am still alive in this body.

There is now a very natural desire to take care of my body as best I can: to feed it fresh, organic, nutritious food, to exercise, to breathe, to rest and recuperate, to consult only with practitioners who are true healers, and to never again push my body.

There is an acceptance and compassion for the effects of ageing and the legacies of the past: the sore knee, the sore neck, the constant motion of Disembarkment Syndrome.

There is such delight and wonder in allowing the simple uncontrived wholeness of Spirit to speak *through* and *with* and *in* every living cell of my body in every moment.

There is such blessed peace, love and completion as this body knows itself as not separate from the Totality.

There is such a joy in walking, singing, crying, eating, gardening, writing, watching, smiling …

***

postscript

What follows is a beautiful little story that I think serves as a fitting end to this chapter.

A few years ago, my partner and I spent some considerable time with a traditional Aboriginal man. Whenever we travelled together on the land, he was always able to find his way, even if we were in unfamiliar surroundings.

As we rode in the car, he always sat quietly, grounded deeply in his body. With his body he listened to the spirits of the places where we were and then gently pointed out the directions: "Take that trail, go over that hill, drive past that bush." The land was not separate from him and his 'map' an internal one.

At one stage I met with him in the city. I asked him if he was also able to find his way amidst the buildings, signs, cars and roads. He grinned back at me, waving his hands in front of him and said, "Too many tracks here." He then sat back, pondering and quietly taking in the people around him. After a short while he looked at me, shook his head, and indicating his body with a wave of his hands and then pointing to the region of the *hara*, said, "Not connected. They can't feel where they're going."

***

the child and the fundamental abandonment

Here, within us, there is a child.

Over and over she calls to us. And yet over and over we abandon her.

And still she waits. Hoping, hoping. Hoping that one day we won't run from her suffering … hoping that one day we will take her hand. That is all she wants.

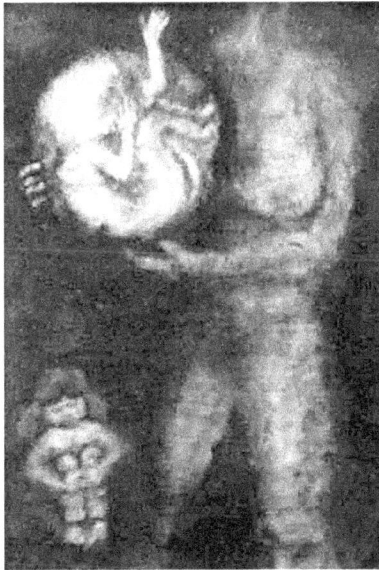

Firestorm, acrylic, detail.

***

the abandoned child – walking the path to freedom

Throughout my journey there were periods without suffering, when for days, weeks, months and even for years, I lived from a solid, peaceful and grounded adulthood.

And yet, as much as I always hoped otherwise, these periods didn't last. At some point, bewildered and exasperated, I inevitably returned to suffering.

> *Again! Again there is fear! There is pain! Why do I feel so fragile, so unable to cope? Where has the quiet joy of my yesterdays gone? My equanimity? I'm so tired of this crap. Why am I still suffering?*

However, on each occasion, I dutifully dusted myself off, took stock of the situation and of my resources, and then did whatever was necessary to find my way through: I rested, nurtured myself, questioned, contemplated, worked through ever-deeper layers of pain and incomprehension and if necessary, sought out help. And each time, there was indeed healing, understanding and growth. My life got back on track and things 'got better'.[1]

But it was never the last time. A family member's uncaring words, a health difficulty, a lost or difficult relationship, not enough sleep, too much busy-ness, pain in my body ... once more I would feel pushed to my limits, overwhelmed, vulnerable or uncertain.

> *Oh no! No! I don't want this. What's happening? What's gone wrong? I do all this work and things never seem to get better! Why? Go away. Please go away.*

But for all my pleas that my suffering go away, there was always just that little bit more.

Certainly, when I looked back over my life I could see that my suffering was much *less* than in previous years: I could engage with the world and people around me with reasonable ease and solidity, I had tremendous insight, capacity and courage as I moved within and shone a light into the shadows of my soul, I knew myself deeper and deeper as the love, compassion and peace of Spirit as it was lived through me – and yet regardless of this, it never seemed to be quite enough. There was always 'something' that propelled me back into difficulty.

---

1. Also see *The Spiralling Journey*, in the chapter *The Journey*. .

I am an intelligent insightful woman! I have done SO much work and yet here I am back with this stuff. What is it that still threatens to engulf and overwhelm me? What is it that still pulls me into self-doubt? I thought I was done with this wretchedness years ago!

Even after awakening, I was aware that there was something yet to be reclaimed and understood. In one sense my search for Truth was over, and yet in another it was incomplete. Although the vacillations of my everyday self were now like waves arising out of an ocean of stillness, there was still 'something' not quite right, 'something' on which over and over I got caught.

There were times I thought I might be able to get away with ignoring this 'something'; sweeping it under the proverbial rug. But I couldn't kid myself. Truth could never be a partial enterprise; Truth would always come back to claim *everything* as its own.

Early one morning, I was sitting at my computer replying to emails. I turned to look out the window at the trees and the pale blue morning sky, and I knew without a doubt that I could not live without completion. I *had* to find out what the 'something' actually was.

With no forethought and with total conviction, I pleaded with God: "Please God, give me the life circumstances that I might find completion. Give me *anything* whatsoever. Send me *any* task. I will be up to *any* task. I would much rather walk through hell itself, than not have completion."

Interestingly, some time later, when I recounted this episode to a friend, she said, "Oooo, you should have been *very* careful making such a plea to God." Yes. Hindsight.

ooo

Throughout much of my life there had been a part within that I termed 'The Pusher'.[2]

With awakening, The Pusher had at first relinquished control. But slowly and almost imperceptibly The Pusher had returned. But now it commandeered

---

2. I describe The Pusher in more detail in the section *The Death of 'The Pusher'* in the chapter *Holes and Emptiness*.

the stillness and peace of True Nature as its own. Although the sense that 'something' was missing remained, through The Pusher's determination to maintain an unwavering 'spiritual' gaze, I began to believe that it didn't really matter.

But in the space of only a few months, the world of which I believed I was so accepting, turned on its head.

During house renovations I suffered an electric shock in the shower. A little later I stepped on a rusty nail which penetrated through my foot. The injury became badly infected and I had to take multiple courses of antibiotics. I was on crutches for eight weeks but still forced myself through a beachside holiday. Shortly after, I came down with a serious chest infection, and was very sick; again I took antibiotics, but I continued to push forward. It felt as though something was strangely amiss in my body but I chose to ignore it.

By then I had long forgotten my early-morning plea to God, but God most definitely had not.

Then one Saturday, late in 2012, while eating lunch at a local café, I physically collapsed; my body could not continue. I was rushed by ambulance to hospital. Their tests found nothing of note, so a week later my partner and I left for an eight-week driving holiday as planned. I continued to push forward, meeting with family and friends, walking for hours in the bush, sitting on the beach, camping, going for long drives, sightseeing and doing my best to project a calm and cheery countenance into the world.

But as we travelled I felt increasingly unwell. Although to all appearances I looked perfectly normal, my body as I felt it from the inside, had begun to sway and rock.

At times I was unable to walk in a straight line. Invisible forces pushed me up and down, left to right. I frequently stumbled or walked into things. I felt a growing unease and alarm, but still I pushed forward trying to act as though nothing was wrong.

We stopped at hospitals and clinics along the way, but I was told that my symptoms were merely those of anxiety. So I braced myself harder and forced myself on. However, soon I struggled to walk.

We finished the holiday early and drove home. Before long I found myself in the stroke ward of a major hospital, but after a barrage of tests and scans, doctors could find nothing wrong and so I was sent home. It was only after a visit to my own doctor, that I found a diagnosis: Mal de Debarquement or Disembarkment Syndrome. Quite by chance, my doctor's grandmother had suffered from it.[3]

Despite the relief of a diagnosis, my health continued to worsen.

Without my balance and with the world in constant and unpredictable motion, every undertaking was difficult. To sit up in bed, swing my feet over the side and stand up took me ten minutes. I fell onto the floor when I tried to put on my shoes. On occasion I had difficulty speaking and even thinking. To lie in bed was like bobbing on a turbulent sea; I longed for even a few moments of peaceful rest. I couldn't venture beyond the backyard, then the back door. My body was in a state of constant tension as it struggled to find equilibrium. I could only exist moment to moment: get through this moment, get through the next. Unsurprisingly I stopped pushing, not because I had some major epiphany in this regard, but rather, because I simply had *no* option.

A terrible exhaustion set in and I knew I was living on dangerous ground. I was deeply traumatized by the daily struggle of living with the condition, but also drained from having relentlessly pushed myself over so many months. I felt my body deteriorating dramatically and I was terrified. At times I felt death very close. Many mornings I opened my eyes and was surprised I was still alive.

At some point during this ordeal, I did however remember my plea to God. I wondered if God had indeed taken me up on my willingness to walk through hell itself in order to find completion. But as much as I would have liked to believe that there was some overarching intelligence at play, in reality I believed I was already too far gone.

ooo

Prior to my descent into ill health, I had assumed that I would never again have therapy.

I had done a tremendous amount of personal work, and awakening had brought a powerful sense of coming Home. I had believed that any remaining obscurity or muddiness would eventually be transformed in the gaze of Truth.

But carefully sequestered off to one side, barely perceptible at that time,

---

3. See the preface for a more detailed description of Disembarkment Syndrome.

was another motive for never again wanting to enter into a therapeutic relationship: I never again wanted to feel the powerful and all-consuming attachment to a therapist, and I never again wanted to go through the wrenching pain of severance when therapy was over.

I knew that in the far reaches of my soul, in my most vulnerable heart, I had a very very young and indeed achingly primal longing for a 'mummy' and I knew that any relationship with a therapist would rekindle it and then set my heart afire. I had always believed that this need was simply too childish, too 'icky', too stupid but also too painfully raw and real to entertain or address in any way. And so, I had always kept it pushed to the side. Obscured. Buried. I had assumed that one day I would look within and find that it had magically vanished.

But as things were in my life, I knew that if I did not seek out help, I would probably die. So I decided that whatever therapy I pursued, would be brief and focus only on strategies for coping with my health issues; I decided I would get in, get help and then get out as quickly as possible. I would make sure *not* to get attached in any way and I would make clear to the therapist that all other issues were off-limits.

But of course, that's not what happened.

ooo

I hadn't expected to find someone able to help me, particularly not someone who might understand the contradictions and questions I was living.

Who would understand that I was spiritually awake and psychologically aware, but now also traumatized, incapacitated and in very serious trouble? Who would understand my lifelong quest for Truth, and also the fact that it had taken me to the point of not being able to tie my shoelaces? Who would understand a plea to God?

But I did find someone.

Both professionally and personally, Colette understood that terrain intimately.[4] From Colette's perspective we are both psychological and spiritual beings, with Spirit as the basis of who we are. Although the ego is generally not conscious

---

4. Collette's spiritual foundation was in the extensive work of the Diamond Approach of AH Almaas.

of its foundation in Spirit, we may however sense that we have become disconnected from our ground: we might intuit that something is missing in our lives, we might feel that we are never truly 'at Home', we might believe we are unworthy or somehow 'wrong'. I had long understood this in my own life, and it had been the drive behind my search for Truth.

But in addition, rather than seeing the ego as the fall guy (as many spiritual paths do), Colette saw that the ego, with very best intent, sets about trying to remedy this situation; it strives to emulate Spirit.

The ego makes its very best and most earnest attempt to bring the essential qualities of Spirit[5], which are our rightful inheritance, into our lives. However, within its limited perspective and without a clear or conscious connection to Spirit, these attempts are ineffective and almost inevitably doomed to failure and further suffering.[6]

However, every difficulty and every wounding within the psyche will have latent within it, the essential quality of Spirit to which it corresponds; this quality is both the healer and ultimately the Healed. The path that took us away from Spirit is actually the path by which we also find our way Home; the ego is a very necessary step on that journey. From the perspective of Essence, there is absolutely nothing wrong and nothing that needs to be excluded. We aren't flawed.

As Colette and I began to journey within, I was able to revisit many difficult places or issues from the perspective of awakening. It was as though in casting the eyes of awakening on them, holding them in that gaze of Consciousness, they could now transform into their corresponding Essential quality. Everything could be given its Ultimate Holding and as such, its freedom; it could all come Home.[7]

---

5. Essential qualities of Spirit are, for example, Perfection, Peace, Strength, Clarity, Joy, Aliveness, Will, Love, True Power and Compassion. Unlike the ego which strives for these qualities and attempts its best reproduction of them in the everyday world, True Nature actually *is* these. They are the qualitative expression of our True Nature as it is lived in this world.

6. We might go base-jumping to get a sense that we are truly alive, when as Spirit we already *are* this Aliveness even when we're sitting in a chair doing absolutely nothing. We might try to gain people's approval so that they will love us, whereas from the perspective of Spirit we already are Love. Militant extremists may wish to kill their enemy to create their perfect world, without realising that as Spirit they already *are* Perfection.

7. My deep wounding, when experienced (Truth) and accepted (Love), opened into Compassion. My anger, when experienced and accepted, opened into Strength. When I experienced and accepted the pushing, I opened into the profound softness of Peace and also Nourishment (and I stopped pushing). Even when I experienced and accepted how bits of my life had been turned to shit, I opened into immense Purity.

But in addition, we also walked the path ever further into the vast breadth of Spirit. As had been the case before awakening, life remained a process of ever-deepening and profoundly dynamic unfoldment.

It seemed that God had heeded my plea big time.

But ... but ...

... but spiritual paths don't always go along in such lovely straight storybook lines ... at least mine doesn't.

And sometimes the path isn't necessarily the one you *think* are on!

Aside from all the spiritual and personal explorations into which I willingly and hungrily delved, the very thing that I had resolved would never ever happen again, had of course, happened: I had become very attached to Colette. My get-in-and-get-out-quickly scheme had fallen in a very big heap.

On the one hand my attachment felt like everything I had ever wanted, but on the other I struggled against it with all my might. It was an internal push-pull, no-win, tormented impasse.

Despite all my years of work and transformation, the part of me that wanted a 'mummy' had not changed her mind or her heart *one* iota. She didn't care in the slightest about Truth, spiritual processes, egos, Perfection, Strength, Joy, Truth, God or True Nature. *All* she cared about, *all* she wanted, was a 'mummy'. And if this 'mummy' would just come and hold her then all would be well with the world forever and ever after. It was a fairy story that this part *absolutely* and *unequivocally* believed.

But as an intelligent, capable, 50-something-year-old, spiritually-awake woman, I truly *hated* that I was still carrying on with such childish attachment rubbish. It was the sort of stuff I assumed everyone else but me, had outgrown. And if they hadn't, they certainly would never admit to it. I found it embarrassingly, cringingly *awful*.

Frequently in the course of therapy or in general discussion, Colette had made gentle mention of my 'little one' or my 'child' or my 'wounded inner children'. Each time I heard the word 'child' issue from Colette's lips, I wanted to scream. It pissed me off. I didn't care about working on the child. This 'child' seemed totally beside the point in my spiritual process and in my attempt to regain my health. I wanted to shout at Colette, "There's no bloody child here, there's only *me*, the *adult!* And there's only Spirit! Stop going on about that stupid child!"

On occasion I thought of running as far away from Colette as I possibly could, but I knew that what I was learning was quite exceptional, and so I stayed and kept my internal stalemate just far enough out of reach so that I could continue believing it was irrelevant to the main arena of my life.

ooo

There came a time in our therapy, when due to the physical limitations of Disembarkment Syndrome I found it difficult to travel to Colette's office. We had a number of sessions by Skype but at a time in our therapy when the work was intense and powerful, I felt the lack of face-to-face contact immensely.

Then, one day, completely unprompted, Colette offered to come to *my* house for therapy.[8]

To Colette's face, I did my best to act nonchalant, calmly mature and casually grateful, but internally I felt her offer as a literal body blow. It came as a deep deep shock. The 'child' within me, the child who *so* wanted a mummy, the child who assumed that her clinging *clinging* need for attachment would always be rejected, had no internal context whatsoever from which to take in or comprehend Colette's kindness, understanding and generosity.

As I slowly allowed the implications of her offer to sink in, my body began to shake uncontrollably and I literally struggled for breath.

A lifetime of carefully-constructed containment lines had been breached, and as, creaking and groaning, they began to fall away, I realized that in their midst stood the small and achingly innocent child I had once been. Colette had tried to lovingly point her out to me over and over, but now, for the first time, I truly saw her for myself. That little girl for whom attachment was her whole world, felt at long last that she was going to get everything she had *ever ever* wanted:

---

8. According to the recognized ethics of psychotherapy, it is generally considered inappropriate for a therapist to visit or conduct therapy at a client's house. However, in this case, there were a number of extenuating circumstances, foremost of which was the fact that I was disabled by Disembarkment Syndrome. However, it is also worth noting that Colette's offer took place in a therapy that was committed and long-standing, there was a deep and adult trust between us, we were both acutely aware of the necessity of maintaining other therapeutic boundaries and there was an abiding recognition that the therapy was taking place within the overarching Intelligence of Spirit (there was "something bigger going on").

"Mummy is coming to my house! Mummy cares for me! Mummy thinks I am important!"

Despite feeling that it would necessitate the ultimate vulnerability, the absolute stripping away of all pretensions to adulthood, spiritual maturity or 'being in control', despite fearing that it might lead to abandonment, scorn or the dissolution of our relationship, I knew I *had* to confide my attachment to Colette.

And so I did.

And in response, Colette, with the greatest of wisdom, compassion and insight, invited me to feel, express and experiment with whatever form my feelings of attachment wanted to take. In essence she was saying, "Attach to me all you like". It was the ultimate gift. It was the gift that the child within had been waiting a lifetime for. And in my whole being, I felt ecstatic relief.

But it wasn't the end. It was just the beginning. That child still spoke to me from time to time of her grief or her insecurity or her pain, and it took a long time for me to *truly* feel those feelings as those of a child. It took a long time before I could take her by the hand, ask her what she wants and needs, embrace her and genuinely welcome her into my life. It took a long time before the love and generosity that Colette had shown me, became *mine* to give to that child.

And it took a long time before I fully understood that it was Spirit as it moved through me that was the Ultimate Mother and as such also the Ultimate Healer for that child.

But at least I now knew what the 'something' was that I had always been missing.

ooo

In each of us there are remnants of the child we once were. In different healing modalities she is given different names: The Inner Child, The Little One, The Exile, The Child Within, The Wounded Child ...

Countless times over the years, I had done my best to meet this child: I had felt and moved through her feelings, I had worked through her memories, I had read books about her, I had repeatedly tried to give her everything she had missed out on, I had shone a light on her profound resilience and also her desperate need for mothering, I had bought her soft fluffy toys, I had asked for her fragility to be cradled by others, I had modelled her pained little soul out of paper, I had carved her innocence out of wood, I had tried to cradle her to my inner bosom, I had painted her tearful face over and over and over ....

And although on one level all my efforts had led to much transformation, they had never brought about her ultimate healing. And I didn't know why.

But I realize now, that in all these endeavors and activities, despite their appearance of love and tenderness, my motive had always *always* been to get rid of her; to remove her from my life.

Whenever she had raised her voice to tell me of her pain, my immediate reaction had *always* been to want her to go away. Whenever I painted her or tried to nurture her, I was hoping that if I did so, she would finally leave me alone and I would be able to get on with my life.

I had seen that child within as an annoyance, an ogre, a problem-to-be-solved. With her furrowed brow, face streaming with tears, with her hard-and-held body, her anguish, her fear, her confusion and her need for mothering, she has always brought disruption to my life. She has brought chaos, grief and memories I would rather forget. Many times she has been so merged with my adult self, that I had taken her feelings to be my own; I saw her as the part of me that was seemingly never healed, the part over which I always despaired, the part that was ruining my life, the part that I was sick to death of dealing with.

And I see now that the crushing and brutal reality is that *this* is exactly how she was seen in her childhood. She was seen as a rotten child, a miserable child, a child that God had damned, a child borne of despair. Her tears were an affront, a difficulty, an abhorrence, an ingratitude. She was seen as a child who was trying to ruin other people's lives.

She was hit for her tears, for her confusion and for her grief. Her entire inner world, her emotions, her feelings, her thoughts, her soul, her bodily integrity and her Spirit, were denied. They did not exist. They were of no consequence or relevance. If anything, they were only seen as a deliberate attempt to cause aggravation and anger.

And in my adulthood, as over and over that child had continued to speak her tears into this world, speak the horrific schism that she was forced to live,

I had done exactly the same to her. I had done to that child, what was done to her in her childhood. I had denied her inner world. I had abandoned her. Over and over I had abandoned her. Even after awakening I had tried to escape that child in the peace of transcendence.

I was blind. I was blind. Not deliberately blind. Not knowingly blind. But blind all the same.

Whenever I was in the midst of difficulty, when tears streamed down my face or anguish clutched at my heart, when it once again seemed that my life was falling apart, and I screamed at the cosmos for my torment to go away, I have never, ever, thought to ask myself the question: "What *is* it that I wish would go away?"

But I see so clearly now … it is a child!

What I had believed to be disruption, wretchedness, misery … *It was only a child! Dear God … only a child!*

ooo

I had never dared to believe that I may have been abandoned as a child. I never felt I had a right to complain in any way. My physical needs were very well taken care of.

But in an inner way, I was completely abandoned. And it is *this* abandonment of our innerness that is **the most excruciatingly painful and primal wound** because it is the denial of our most fundamental Truth. All other injury or trauma – rejection, criticism, abuse, cruelty – can only be perpetrated if first and foremost there is the denial of the other's inner reality.

My tears, my complaints, were not an indication that I was a miserable child, a recalcitrant naughty child who wouldn't do what she was told, they were the very understandable and utterly valid response to living a life in which my fundamental innerness was consistently and sweepingly denied.

ooo

In the depths of our souls we all long for a mummy.

Abandonment is our core wound: the disconnection from Mother, from Oneness, from our True Nature.

And we can spend our entire lives trying to rectify that situation.

All around we look for the 'mummy' or 'perfect object' that will finally make us whole again: our teddy bear, our perfect partner, our child, a teacher, our therapist, our identity, the ideal holiday, lots of money, a new dress, the perfect life circumstances. We even look for it as we search for that 'thing' called enlightenment: "If I was enlightened I might at last feel whole."

If only 'mummy' would come, we would finally feel like the most important, most precious wonderful person in the whole wide world. If only 'mummy' would come we would be happy and complete forevermore. We know deep inside that a sense of delicious wholeness is our birthright, and we are terrified we will never get it. We feel dejected when people don't do what we want them to do, we cry when things don't go our way, we stomp our feet when we don't get what we want, we blame, we point fingers.

But it is not until we can open fully to the child we were, and then hold her in the loving embrace of the Ultimate Mother that is Spirit, that she is returned to the Wholeness of what she truly is, and as such can finally be healed. That healing happens when we surrender up all notion that there is a perfect 'object' or 'mummy' *out there* somewhere, separate from us, that will one day give us everything we want and make us whole.

The entire structure of duality and separation that underpins the 'ego' identity is based on wanting a 'mummy' or 'completing ourselves' through the 'perfect other.'

When that truly collapses and we see that there is no 'other', we are able to feel ourselves as All That Is. And it is as the Totality, that we are free.

I had thought that in my torment, I was back at the beginning of my journey; back at square one. I had cringed at my desire for a 'mummy'. I had thought my life was falling quite spectacularly apart. But the opposite was very much the case: my life was falling very much together.

It is only by accessing the truth of our fundamental abandonment and feeling that most heartrending vulnerability of our deepest longing, that it can be transformed.

Truth and Wholeness can never be attained by leaving something behind.

***

home

In each chapter I have written of Spirit. Little more needs to be said.

I am Home.

I am what I have always wanted.
I am what I have always been.

***

… and she lived happily ever after.

When we set out on a spiritual quest, whether that be for Truth, or for happiness, or for an end to our suffering, we imagine that one day we will lay down our swords, our wounded hearts, our flaws and our desires, and cross the finish line. We assume that from that point on we'll live happily ever after: we'll be bathed in peace or bliss or harmony, we'll have everything we ever wanted, we'll have perfect relationships, we'll have enough money and a job as a wise spiritual teacher. Perhaps in our most hidden of fancies we might even imagine some sort of enlightened superiority or specialness for ourselves … the ultimate prize for years of hard work.

But these are all the ego's stories, and the ego doesn't come along for this bit of the ride. The ego or mind knows nothing of Truth or Reality. Ever.

So what does life look like as I sit here typing these words for the final chapter of this book?

The best word I can come up with in this moment is Emptiness. Certainly I could still use God or True Nature or any of the others I have used throughout this book … but truly, this is Emptiness. I know myself as clear, clear, radiant

Emptiness. This Emptiness is what I directly and unequivocally know I *am*. It is what we all *are*. It is what the sky, and the sun, and the litter on the street, and all the politicians of this world, *are*.

I know that when the ego hears the word 'emptiness' it recoils. For the ego, 'emptiness' signifies lack or deficiency, destruction or nihilism. The ego wants something *real*, something tangible, something to hang onto, something from which it can claim a stance. What can the ego do with emptiness? Nothing. Emptiness spells doom for the ego.

But in lived reality, Emptiness is none of those things ... and in a way I could *never* explain and *never* find words for or articulate, Emptiness is the saving grace of everything. It *truly* is. But we can only ever find that out for ourselves ...

Emptiness knows itself intuitively as what it is. It recognizes itself *as* our True Home. *As* our deepest rest. *As* our deepest breath. *As* our Ground, our Source ...

Emptiness sees itself in and as everything and everyone without limitation. There is no center, no edge, no definition, no boundary, no bits and pieces all stuck together, nothing to grab onto, nothing to claim, nothing to jar or grate against ... only its infinite glorious enormity speaking through each speck of dust, each earthworm, each flower ...

In Emptiness the mind is seen, and its opinions and ideals, dreams and grasping can dissolve because there is nothing to fight and no-one to say that this moment is not the most extraordinary moment in all of Creation ...

This Emptiness, simply by virtue of what it is, has an intelligence far far beyond anything the mind could ever conceive of. It is an intelligence that Is forever opening into wordless insight upon insight, depth upon depth, mystery upon mystery. Here is the wisdom that *is* Reality, Humanity and Truth flowing through us in each moment. And there is no end to it ...

This Emptiness is a vivid and radiant aliveness ... my hand and fingers moving as I am typing these words, the sunlight shining through the leaves of a tree, the footsteps of my partner ...

And yes, there is a peace I never thought possible for my life, there is simple simple joy, there is a sense that all is deeply well ...

But I also know that there is no final and fantastic finish line here ... there is no over-and-done-with, no end of the story, no 'happily ever after'. I'm not off the hook. Ever.

The ego is still there from time to time, wanting to have its say about something, wanting to feel its own existence simply by virtue of the never-ending loop of its own storytelling. Today it was adamant that the neighbor's barking dogs should not be included in Reality. Last week in barely perceptible undertones it whispered to me its well-worn tale of self-doubt. And I know that if a particularly difficult life situation arose I would most probably feel the sharp sting of its contraction and separation once more.

But I also know that the ego doesn't have its own inbuilt on/off switch … egos do what egos do, and so I'm not as surprised or concerned by its meanderings as I once was.

I will continue to meet everything that arises with uncompromising honesty, love and compassion as I have always done. I will continue to allow the gaze of Truth to see through everything that still needs to be seen through. *Everything*. I will continue to allow *all* separation to surrender back into the infinite Emptiness that is my true essence … over and over and over if that is what's necessary. I will continue to let go of any notion or any belief that I know what's going on … because I don't. I will continue to be lived by life moment by moment by moment … knowing that the deepening into this glorious humanity and its extraordinary Mystery has no end.

I will continue to be humbled, awed, filled with wonder … and oh-so-very-grateful …

> Here now
> unbidden
> unannounced
> is clear clear water
> quenching every thirst
> every longing.
>
> Beyond colors
> or fanfare,
> beyond studied words
> or embellishment,
> beyond thrill
> or beauty.
> Beyond.

Here is indescribable transparency.
Clarity.
A quiet
and unadorned simplicity.
Absolute purity.

Clear clear water.
No separation.

I abide as that.

***

just this

I have nothing more to say, nothing more to write. In the end what do I have that will point you to the Truth?

Nothing. Just this. It seems so very simple: just this.

Computer screen. Fingers. Chair. Window. Trees. Birds. Dog barking. Movement. Pain. Hunger. Dinner smells. Silence. Love.

Can you give yourself completely to 'just this'?

In the end it is all very simple.

***

bibliography

Adyashanti, *Emptiness Dancing*. Boulder, CO: Sounds True, 2006.

Adyashanti, *The End of your World*. Boulder, CO: Sounds True, 2008.

Almaas, A. H. *The Inner Journey Home: Soul's Realization of the Unity of Reality*. Boston: Shambhala, 2004.

Almaas, A. H. *The Pearl beyond Price: Integration of Personality into Being, an Object Relations Approach*. Berkeley, CA: Diamond Books, 1988.

Broug, Marianne. *Flute with a Twist: Volume One*. Templestowe, Vic.: Bushfire Press, 2003.

Broug, Marianne. *www.meaningofdepression.com*. Adelaide, South Australia, 2004-2017.

Broug, Marianne. *Seventeen Voices: Life and Wisdom from inside 'mental Illness'* Kent Town, S. Aust.: Wakefield Press, 2008.

David-Néel, Alexandra. *Magic and Mystery in Tibet*. New York: Dover Publications, 1971.

David-Néel, Alexandra. *My Journey to Lhasa*. Boston: Beacon Press, 1986.

Davidson, Robyn. *Tracks*. New York: Pantheon Books, 1980.

Hay, Louise L. *You Can Heal Your Life*. Santa Monica, CA: Hay House, 1987.

MacLaine, Shirley. *Out On a Limb*. Toronto: Bantam Books, 1983.

McKenzie, Narelle, and Jacqui Showell. *Living Fully: An Introduction to Radix Body-Centred Personal Growth Work*. Daw Park: N. McKenzie and J. Showell, 1998.

Matthiessen, Peter. *The Snow Leopard*. New York: Viking Press, 1978.

Metzger, Deena. *Writing for Your Life: A Guide and Companion to the Inner Worlds*. San Francisco: Harper San Francisco, 1992.

Miller, Alice. *For your own good: Hidden cruelty in child-rearing and the roots of violence*. New York: Farrar, Straus, Giroux, 1983

Ratushinskaîa, Irina. *Grey Is the Colour of Hope*. London: Hodder and Stoughton, 1988.

Trungpa, Chögyam, and John Baker. *Cutting Through Spiritual Materialism*. Berkeley: Shambhala, 1973.

Wilber, Ken. *Grace and Grit: Spirituality and Healing in the Life and Death of Treya Killam Wilber*. Boston: Shambhala, 1991.

Wilber, Ken. *One Taste: Daily Reflections on Integral Spirituality*. Boston: Shambhala, 2000.

Wilberg, Peter. *Head, Heart and Hara: The Soul-Centres of East and West*. London: New Gnosis Publications, 2003.

Wilberg, Peter. *The Qualia Revolution*. London: New Gnosis Publications, 2008.

Wilby, Sorrel. *Across the Top: The World's First Complete Traverse of the Himalaya*. Sydney: Pan Macmillan, 1992.

***

www.ingramcontent.com/pod-product-compliance
Lightning Source LLC
Chambersburg PA
CBHW020150090426
42734CB00008B/773